COMPETITIVE BUSINESS

For CCEA AS Unit 1

Eddie McKee

Colourpoint
Educational

ISBN: 978 1 906578 01 5

First Edition
Third Impression, 2014

Layout and design: April Sky Design, Newtownards
Printed by: W&G Baird Ltd, Antrim

Colourpoint Educational
An imprint of Colourpoint Creative Ltd
Colourpoint House
Jubilee Business Park
21 Jubilee Road
Newtownards
County Down
Northern Ireland
BT23 4YH

Tel: 028 9182 6339
Fax: 028 9182 1900
E-mail: info@colourpoint.co.uk
Web site: www.colourpoint.co.uk

The Author

Eddie McKee is coordinator of Applied Business and e-learning at St Louise's Comprehensive College, Belfast. He is also an experienced examiner having acted as assistant examiner for GCE Applied Business and currently acting as principal examiner for GCE Economics.

Eddie is also the author of the popular text for GCE Applied Business entitled *External Influences on the Business Enterprise*, also published by Colourpoint.

Acknowledgements

Thanks must go to a number of people without whose help this book would not have been completed.

Firstly, to my wife Natasha for her unending patience and support; to my parents, Eamon and Kathleen, for their guidance and kindness throughout the years and to Amanda Swann at CCEA, and Sheila Johnston at Colourpoint, for their words of advice and encouragement.

Go raibh míle maith agaibh.

For Jack

Is páiste fíor speisialta e

Picture credits

IStockphoto: 4, 6, 8, 10, 15, 24, 33, 37, 42, 47, 68, 76, 92, 109, 111, 119, 123, 146, 152, 182, 186, 190, 201

Malcolm Johnston: 50, 82, 98, 102, 138

Sheila Johnston: 25, 32, 40, 55, 70, 79, 83, 90, 94, 95, 114, 142, 148, 150

Wesley Johnston: 35, 78, 87, 137

Montupet: 44

Slieve Russell Hotel, Golf and Country Club: 87

CONTENTS

This text covers AS Unit 1 (Competitive Business) of the CCEA Specification for GCE Business Studies.

CHAPTER 1	**FORMS OF BUSINESS ORGANISATION**	**4**
CHAPTER 2	**CENTRAL PURPOSE OF BUSINESS ACTIVITY**	**30**
CHAPTER 3	**MARKETS**	**42**
CHAPTER 4	**MARKET FORCES AND THE THEORY OF DEMAND AND SUPPLY**	**53**
CHAPTER 5	**MARKET STRUCTURE AND THE DEGREE OF COMPETITION**	**72**
CHAPTER 6	**COMPETITION AND GOVERNMENT POLICY**	**86**
CHAPTER 7	**MARKETING AND MARKET RESEARCH**	**107**
CHAPTER 8	**THE MARKETING MIX: PRODUCT AND PRICE**	**129**
CHAPTER 9	**THE MARKETING MIX: PROMOTION AND PLACE**	**145**
CHAPTER 10	**MARKET PLANNING AND STRATEGY**	**159**
CHAPTER 11	**INVESTMENT AND PRODUCTIVITY**	**172**
CHAPTER 12	**QUALITY MANAGEMENT**	**193**
COPYRIGHT INFORMATION		**207**
ALSO AVAILABLE ...		**208**

Chapter 1: FORMS OF BUSINESS ORGANISATION

1

WHAT IS A BUSINESS?

A business is typically defined as any activity carried out by one or more people with the intention of producing goods or services that can then be sold on to others.

The aim of most businesses, although not all, is to carry out this production in such a way as to maximise the return for the owners of the business. In other words, the main objective of most business enterprises is to maximise profits.

There are many different types of business operating in the UK that produce a wide range of goods and services to sell in a variety of different markets. These businesses vary from very small local enterprises, which are owned and run by one person, to very large multinational businesses which employ thousands of people and operate across a number of different countries.

In this chapter we will examine the different forms of business organisation in the UK and we will consider the advantages and disadvantages associated with each business type.

SOLE TRADER

A sole trader is a business that is fully owned by one person who has complete control over how the firm is run.

A sole trader is the most common form of business ownership in the UK with approximately 63% of all UK enterprises classified as sole proprietors (source: Department for Business, Enterprise and Regulatory Reform).

A sole-trading business is usually small in size, with a low turnover and few, if any employees; indeed, data from the Department for Business, Enterprise and Regulatory Reform (formerly known as the Department of Trade and Industry) suggest that of the 2.5 million sole proprietors in the UK, 86.3% have no employees.

The majority of sole-trading businesses in the UK operate in the services sector and include businesses such as hairdressers, shops, plumbers and electricians.

The popularity of sole trading as a form of business enterprise reflects the ease with which a sole proprietor can set up and begin trading. Statistics suggest that over 80% of sole traders take less than six months to get the business up and running.

Setting up as a sole trader is relatively straightforward and does not require the completion of numerous documents and forms, as is the case with other business types. Essentially, all a sole trader has to do to begin trading is to register him or herself as self-employed with Revenue and Customs within three months of starting up (where the three month limit starts from the last day of the first month of trading). Failure to do this will result in a fine of £100.

In some cases the sole trader may also need to apply for a special trading licence. For example, trade licences are required for the operation of nightclubs, restaurants, nursing homes and pet kennels. In addition, if the sole trader's yearly income is above a certain level (currently £64,000, although this may be subject to changes announced in the government's budget), then they will also have to apply for VAT registration.

The vast majority of sole-trading businesses are started using the owner's own capital. However, some sole traders borrow money from a bank or relatives in order to get the business up and running. Data from the Annual Survey of Small Businesses suggest that 87% of sole traders rely on their own funds during the first twelve months of business.

Many sole traders will trade under their own name, but the majority will register a trade name or register as "trading as". This allows the owner to carry on business under a name other than his or her legal name and also allows them to open a separate business account with a bank.

If a sole trader wishes to trade under a name different to their own, they are legally obliged to display clearly on all business stationery and premises the legal name of the proprietor and an address where documents can be served.

ADVANTAGES OF OPERATING AS A SOLE TRADER

Low start-up costs

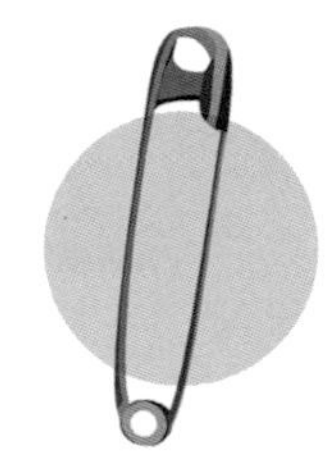

As we have already seen, setting up as a sole trader is a relatively straightforward, low cost process when compared to other forms of business ownership. There are very few legal formalities involved in the creation or dissolution of a sole-trading business and therefore starting or winding up the business is a relatively simple and inexpensive procedure.

All profits are retained

Since a sole-trading business is fully owned by one person, that person gets to keep all of the profits that are made by the business. There is no legal obligation to share the profits with anyone, as is the case in other business types.

Better control

Running a business as a sole trader means that the proprietor is able to make all decisions without the need to consult others or call meetings. This means that decisions can be made promptly and so the firm may be better able to react to sudden changes in market conditions.

Financial privacy

Sole traders are under no obligation to publish their financial affairs and therefore their business dealings can be kept private. The only obligation on a sole trader is that they fully complete their tax returns twice a year under Schedule D for Revenue and Customs.

Increased flexibility

Sole traders have more freedom from government regulation than any other business type. While every form of business faces government regulation, sole traders generally face the least. This means the business can be more flexible and better able to adapt and change in line with shifting market conditions.

DISADVANTAGES OF OPERATING AS A SOLE TRADER

Unlimited liability

Under UK law a sole-trading business, even one that trades under a distinct trading name, has no separate legal existence from that of its owner. As a result the proprietor or sole trader will be personally liable for all of the debts of the business. This means that if the business does not have enough money to cover its debts the owner will have to use their own money to ensure the debts are paid. In extreme cases the owner may have to sell their house, car or other possessions in order to raise enough money to cover the business's debts.

Difficulty raising capital

It is often very difficult for sole traders to find the money to start or grow their business. The amount of start-up capital is limited to the amount the sole proprietor can raise through their own savings or borrowing. In addition, banks are often reluctant to lend to sole traders as they present a much higher level of risk than larger incorporated businesses.

Long hours

Many sole traders end up working extremely long hours as they are often the only one who works for the business. If the owner becomes ill or goes on holiday the business may suffer as a result. These problems may be overcome by hiring a manager or other employees in order to take some of the strain off the owner.

Lack of expertise

The success of a sole-trading business is very dependent on the skills of the owner. As the sole owner, and often sole employee, the proprietor needs to be skilled in marketing, accounts, purchasing and all other aspects of business. Failure to fulfil these roles effectively may lead to the failure of the business.

Lack of competitiveness

Sole traders tend to be smaller than other forms of business enterprise and as a result they are unable to avail of economies of scale such as bulk-buying. Therefore, their prices tend to be higher than those of larger businesses. Sole traders can however, minimise this disadvantage through either clubbing together with other sole traders to buy their raw materials in bulk (see case study) or by offering a more personal service to their customers as a way of justifying the higher price.

CASE STUDY

SPAR: SOLE TRADERS ACTING COOPERATIVELY

SPAR is the world's largest international food retail chain with nearly 16,000 stores in 34 countries. They are also the UK's leading convenience store group with over 2,700 stores throughout the country, the vast majority of which are sole traders.

SPAR was founded in Holland in 1932 by Adriaan Van Well, who believed that independent wholesalers and retailers should work in collaboration and use their collective purchasing power to offer the best deal to consumers.

In 1932 Van Well called his new concept 'De Spar': 'Door Eendrachtig Samenwerken Profiteren Allen Regelmatig' which translates into 'We all benefit from joint co-operation'.

SPAR is classified as a symbol group, which simply means that each individual SPAR member remains independent, but enjoys access to collective buying and marketing power.

SPAR members benefit from a range of services which include:

- the ability to purchase stock at lower prices as a result of SPAR's increased purchasing power;
- a totally integrated advertising package consisting of television, national and local radio and national magazines;
- promotions support including key seasonal and themed events, designed to maximize footfall year round;

CASE STUDY...

eye-catching Point of Purchase materials, direct mail and advertising support, and preferential rates for services such as:

- Telephone calls
- Waste disposal
- Washroom roller towels
- Weighing scales
- Insurance
- Pest-control
- SPAR logo floor mats
- Alarm systems
- Store safes
- EPOS equipment

(Source: www.spar.co.uk)

ACTIVITY 1.1

TINY TERRORS CLOTHING

Nicola McAllister is a wife and mother to three lively boys. The boys, aged 6, 9 and 13, are very active and love skateboarding and mountain biking. When the youngest of her sons started school last year Nicola began making clothes for young boys.

The designs and materials are inspired by her three sons who, because of their active lifestyle, go through clothes very quickly.

She currently operates as a sole trader, trading under the name Tiny Terrors Clothing. However, recently, someone suggested to her she that should either take on a partner or convert the business to a limited company.

Nicola designs and makes the products by hand in her spare bedroom and sells them over the internet and to two local stores. She always had high hopes that she could make a successful business selling her products, but even she has been surprised to find that she now sells £35,000 worth of goods a year.

1. Explain what is meant by the term 'sole trader'.
2. Explain why, currently, Nicola does not have to apply for VAT registration.
3. Analyse three advantages Nicola enjoys through operating as a sole trader.
4. Analyse three disadvantages Nicola might experience through operating as a sole trader.

PARTNERSHIP

A partnership occurs when two or more people combine to form a business enterprise. The partners share the responsibility of running the business and therefore any decisions relating to the business should be taken with the agreement of all partners.

Partnerships are the second most popular type of business and are commonly found in professional enterprises such as architects, solicitors and accountants. However, they are also frequently found in the retail trade and in small service-sector firms.

In many partnerships, individual partners will specialise in specific areas of the business. For example, in a solicitors' partnership one partner may specialise in tax law while another may specialise in marital law.

As is the case with sole traders, partnerships are generally small in size and employ few workers. Data from the Department for Business, Enterprise and Regulatory Reform suggests that there are approximately 540,000 partnerships in the UK of which 60% have no employees and are therefore regarded as 'class size zero' firms.

There are three main types of partnership: a general or full partnership, a limited partnership, and limited liability partnership (LLP).

GENERAL PARTNERSHIP

(PARTNERSHIP ACT 1890)

This is the most common form of partnership and occurs when partners take on equal responsibility for decision-making and running of the firm. Under UK law a general partnership must have a minimum of two and a maximum of 20 partners, with each partner having unlimited liability for the debts of the company. Partners who invest capital into a business and take a share of the profits but who choose not to take any part in the running of the business, are often referred to as **sleeping partners.**

LIMITED PARTNERSHIP

(LIMITED PARTNERSHIP ACT 1907)

A limited partnership is formed under different legal arrangements to a general partnership. It is chosen when one or more partners wish to invest capital in a business but do not want to take part in its management, and want protection from the risks of unlimited liability. These limited partners have limited liability and can therefore only lose the money they have invested in the business. However, the general partner(s) remain fully liable for the debts of the business, but have total control of the management of the firm. The law governing limited partnerships in the UK states that at least one partner must have unlimited liability (general partner) and at least one must have limited liability.
The law also allows limited partnerships to have more than 20 partners in some cases.

NOTE: Confusion often exists as to the distinction between a **sleeping partner** and a **limited partner.** As we have seen, a sleeping partner is a partner in a *general partnership* who **CHOOSES** not to become involved in the running of the business. However, this does not confer on them any legal advantage. They are still fully liable, with the other partner(s), for the full debts of the business. In contrast however, by law, a limited partner in a **limited partnership MUST NOT** take part in the running of the business, but in return enjoys the protection of limited liability status.

LIMITED LIABILITY PARTNERSHIP (LLP)

(LIMITED LIABILITY PARTNERSHIP ACT 2000)

A limited liability partnership, or LLP, is an alternative form of business model which allows a business to organise its internal structures as a traditional partnership, while at the same time also giving all members the benefit of limited liability.

Limited liability partnerships are different to limited partnerships in that in an LLP, limited liability is granted to all members and not just to a small group of non-managing partners, as is the case with limited partnerships.

A limited liability partnership is a corporate body – that is to say, it has a continuing legal existence independent of its members and in this sense is much like a limited company. However, LLPs are different to limited companies in that they do not themselves pay any tax; the tax liability falls on the individual members, not the LLP itself.

All profits earned by an LLP are distributed to the partners who must then declare this income for tax purposes. In most cases the partners will be self-employed and therefore will pay income tax through the self-assessment mechanism. However, if the LLP member is another company then they will also be liable for corporation tax on any income they receive from the LLP.

LLPs are a relatively new form of business organisation in the UK, having only been introduced in 2000 as a result of the Limited Liability Partnership Act, and as such are relatively rare. However, their popularity is increasing, particularly among financial institutions. Well known examples include PricewaterhouseCoopers and KPMG.

SETTING UP A PARTNERSHIP

Setting up a partnership is relatively simple and whilst there are no specific legal requirements involved, it is recommended that a legally drafted partnership agreement or deed of partnership be drawn up to clarify and provide written evidence of what the partners have agreed. Such a document will help to avoid or clear up any disputes which may arise with regard to, for example, distribution of profits, liabilities or each partner's role or responsibilities and can help in keeping the resolution of such disputes out of the courts.

It is recommended that a solicitor should be used when drawing up this agreement and that it includes the following points:

- *The trading name and function of the business*
- *The amount of capital each partner will invest*
- *Profit ratio (normally dependent on the amount invested)*
- *Seniority and control over the business*
- *The rules on admitting new partners*
- *Rules on ending the partnership*

Should a dispute arise and there is no written partnership agreement, then it would be settled by a court using the provisions set out in the Partnership Act 1890 for a general partnership, the Limited Partnership Act 1907, or the Limited Liability Partnership Act 2000 for those types of partnerships.

ADVANTAGES OF OPERATING AS A PARTNERSHIP

Low start up costs

As with a sole trader, setting up as a partnership is a relatively straightforward, low cost process when compared to other forms of business ownership. There are very few legal formalities to complete when creating a partnership and it is a fairly simple process.

Shared workload

When compared to a sole trader, partnerships should have a lower workload since the burden of work can be shared between the partners. Unlike a sole trader, a partnership should be able to cope more easily with illness or an individual partner taking a holiday. In addition, each partner can specialise in a particular aspect of the business's operations where they may have a comparative skills advantage. This will allow for much higher levels of productivity.

Raising capital

Partnerships can typically raise more capital than most sole traders since there will be more owners to contribute capital to the business. In addition, partnerships are generally larger than sole traders and are therefore regarded as being less risky. For this reason they typically find it easier to acquire loans and other forms of finance from banks.

Financial privacy

Like sole traders, partnerships are under no obligation to publish their financial affairs and in this way their business dealings can be kept private. The only obligation on a partnership is that they fully complete a partnership self-assessment return, which includes the profit allocation in force for the accounting period.

More effective decision-making

Having a partner or a number of partners allows for more effective decision-making since each partner will bring a different perspective to any particular problem. Being able to look at a problem from a number of different viewpoints should help the firm achieve more creative and innovative solutions.

DISADVANTAGES OF OPERATING AS A PARTNERSHIP

Loss of autonomy

Running a business as a partnership means that no single partner is able to make all the big decisions without first consulting the other partners. This means that decisions cannot be made as swiftly as is the case with a sole trader and therefore the firm may be less able to react to a sudden crisis or changing market conditions.

Conflict between partners

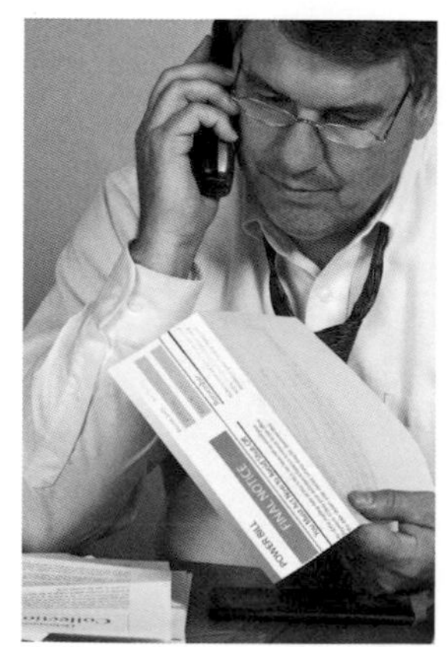

Running a business with a partner or partners can be very stressful particularly if the partners have different views on how the business should be run. If these views are incompatible then the partnership may have to be dissolved. Evidence suggests that approximately 40% of all enterprises which are started collaboratively end up dissolving, leaving only one of the original co-owners running the business (see case study opposite).

Unlimited liability

As in the case of the sole trader, a huge disadvantage of a general partnership is that all partners have unlimited liability. This means that if the business does not have enough money to cover its debts, each partner will be personally liable for the total amount of those debts. Even where one partner has been dishonest, all partners are liable for that partner's actions and therefore their private property may have to be sold to cover that particular partner's malpractice.

Clearly this does not apply to limited partners in the two versions of the limited partnership, who benefit from the protection of limited liability status, but it does apply to the general partners in a limited partnership under the 1907 Act.

Lack of continuity

Problems arise in partnerships upon the death and even divorce of one of the partners. If one partner dies then the partnership normally dissolves unless the other partners buy that particular partner out. In some cases partnership businesses have to be dissolved upon the divorce of one partner from their spouse. This is because under British law a spouse is typically entitled to half of the value of the other's business. The partnership often has to be dissolved to allow the divorcing partner to pay the cost of the final settlement.

Lack of capital

Even though partnerships can typically raise more capital than sole traders, the amount of capital they can raise is still limited since the number of partners is limited. When compared to other forms of business enterprise, such as private or public limited companies, the amount of capital in a typical partnership is relatively small. Furthermore, banks often regard partnerships as more risky propositions than larger companies and therefore when lending them money they will often require a higher rate of interest to compensate for this risk.

CASE STUDY

SECURITY FIRM BOSS SHOOTS FORMER PARTNER

A security firm boss who shot his former business partner in the stomach has been jailed for seven years. Partner A was left "within an inch of his life" after being shot by Partner B in February last year.

The two men had been partners in two security firms **SAS Security Action Services,** which provided door staff for pubs and clubs in the north-east of England, and **Team Security,** which provided day-time security staff.

Partner B, 39, had bought Partner A's share of the business for £10,000, but later discovered a £60,000 tax bill.

The jury was told the two men agreed to meet in Preston Park to have a fist fight and settle their differences. The court heard that partner B came to the park on 27 February 2001, equipped with a sawn-off shotgun and shot his former partner. Eighty pellets were removed from Partner A's stomach and he later suffered a heart attack while recovering in hospital.

(Adapted from BBC News, 22 July 2002)

ACTIVITY 1.2

TINY TERROR CLOTHING (CONTINUED)

Tiny Terror clothing has been operating for the past 18 months as a sole-trading operation under the ownership of Nicola McAllister. Nicola currently performs all the management functions of the business including design, manufacture, sales and marketing.

The business continues to grow from strength to strength and currently Nicola is finding it difficult to complete all the work she has to do.

Nicola regards herself as a talented designer but by her own admission she feels she could

ACTIVITY 1.2

improve her business knowledge and recently one of her close friends suggested that she should either take on a partner or change the business to a limited company. Indeed, one of her closest friends, Wendy, has suggested that she would be willing to become a sleeping partner in the business and contribute £10,000 of capital.

Currently orders are outstripping her ability to supply and Nicola would like to grow the business in some way.

1. Explain why forming a partnership might be a good idea for Nicola.
2. Explain to Wendy the implications of becoming a sleeping partner.
3. Analyse two difficulties Nicola might face as a result of taking on a partner other than Wendy.
4. Nicola has been advised that if she does form a partnership she should draw up a partnership agreement. Explain what areas should be covered in this partnership agreement.

KNOWLEDGE REVIEW

- A **SOLE TRADER** is a business which is fully owned by one person who has complete control over how the firm is run.
- **UNLIMITED LIABILITY** means that if the business does not have enough money to cover its debts the owner will have to use their own money to ensure the debts are paid.
- A **PARTNERSHIP** occurs when two or more people combine to form a business enterprise. Under UK law a General Partnership must have a minimum of two and a maximum of 20 partners with each partner having unlimited liability for the debts of the company.
- A **SLEEPING PARTNER** is someone who invests capital in a General Partnership, takes a share of the profits but chooses not to take any part in the running of the business. A sleeping partner is still a general partner and as such shares the risks of unlimited liability with the other active partners.
- A **LIMITED PARTNER** in a **LIMITED PARTNERSHIP (1907 ACT)** is someone who invests capital in a Limited Partnership, enjoys the protection of limited liability, takes a share of the profits, but who, by law, must not take any part in the running of the business. If they do take part, they lose their limited liability protection.
- A **LIMITED PARTNER** in a **LIMITED LIABILITY PARTNERSHIP (LLP – 2000 ACT)** is someone who invests capital in a limited liability partnership, and can take a full part in the running of the business while still enjoying the protection of limited liability.

LIMITED COMPANIES

A limited company is a very different form of business enterprise compared to a sole trader or a partnership in that a limited company is a separate legal entity from its members. This means that the company can raise finance in its own right and any debt incurred belongs to the company, not its owners.

Limited companies are owned by shareholders who have the protection of **limited liability** under law. This means that individual shareholders are not personally liable for the debts of the company; they are liable only up to the value of their investment in the company. Therefore, if the company becomes insolvent, the individual shareholders will not have to sell their private possessions to cover the debts, but they will lose the money they have invested in the business.

A limited company must be registered. In Britain they are registered with Companies House. In Northern Ireland they are registered with the Companies Registry. Setting up a company can be a time-consuming process and can involve a large amount of administrative work to ensure that the company complies with UK company law. Currently, there are approximately 960,000 limited companies registered in the UK.

To form a limited company in the UK, a number of important documents, along with the correct registration fee, must be sent to the appropriate registering authority. These documents include:

THE MEMORANDUM OF ASSOCIATION

The memorandum of association is the document which sets out the relationship between a company and the outside world. It includes details such as the official name of the company, the type of company (public limited or private limited), the objectives of the company, the amount of initial share capital and the names of the original subscribers or shareholders.

THE ARTICLES OF ASSOCIATION

The articles of association contain the regulations which relate to the internal relationships between the shareholders and the directors of a company. Typically, they cover areas such as the different voting rights associated with different types of shares, the rules of board meetings, how profits will be divided and the duties of directors.

Companies House publishes a set of model articles known as 'Table A' and it is these model articles that many small firms use when incorporating.

Changes to these two documents come into force in 2008 as a result of The Companies Act 2006. A new set of model articles will be introduced, which will be incorporated into one legal document that will also subsume the function currently carried out by the memorandum of association.

Form 10

Form 10 is a document which records details such as the name, address, date of birth and occupation of the first directors of the firm, as well as details of any other directorships held by those directors in the previous five years.

Form 12

This is a form where one or all directors legally declare their compliance with all legal requirements relating to the formation of the limited company. A solicitor or a justice of the peace must witness the signing of this document.

Once these forms and documents have been completed, the company will be issued with a trading certificate and the company will be free to begin trading.

There are three main types of limited company in the UK: a **private limited company** (LTD or Ltd), **a public limited company** (PLC or plc), and a **company limited by guarantee** (also LTD or Ltd).

PRIVATE LIMITED COMPANY (LTD)

A private limited company (or more accurately a private company limited by shares) is a business which is incorporated and therefore is a separate legal entity from its owners.

Ownership of the company is established through the division of shares, and so the owners are known as shareholders. Each shareholder's liability is limited to the amount of capital they have invested in the business.

Private limited companies are required by law to carry the suffix 'Limited', or more commonly 'Ltd', as part of their company name. This is to ensure that all relevant stakeholders are aware of the company's limited liability status.

Members of the general public cannot buy shares in a private limited company. Those who hold shares in a private limited company can sell these shares only privately and with the express consent of the other shareholders. This inability to sell shares publicly is the key difference between a private limited company and a public limited company.

ADVANTAGES OF OPERATING AS A PRIVATE LIMITED COMPANY

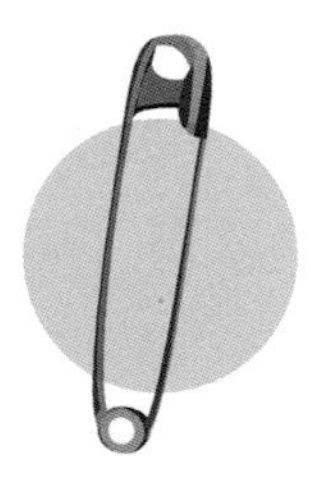

Raising capital

Due to the fact that there is no limit to the number of members a private limited company can have, it will be able to raise more capital than a partnership or a sole trader. Private limited companies are generally larger than sole traders or partnerships and are therefore normally regarded as being less risky. For this reason they typically find it easier to acquire finance from banks and other financial institutions.

Limited liability

A private limited company is an incorporated business and so is a separate legal entity from its owners. This means that the company can raise finance in its own right, and take action on its own behalf. It also means that any debts incurred by the business belong to the company and are not the responsibility of the individual shareholders. Therefore, if the company becomes insolvent, the individual shareholders will not have to sell their private possessions to cover the debts, as would be the case with partnerships and sole traders. In a private limited company the shareholders will only lose the money they have invested in the business.

Continuity

Because a private limited company has a legal existence separate from that of its owners it will not be affected if one particular shareholder leaves, retires or indeed dies. A private limited company has an ongoing life, which can only be ended through an official wind-up or liquidation.

Specialisation

A private limited company will typically have more members than a sole trader or partnership. Having a greater number of directors or managers means that the workload can be shared amongst them, and each manager can specialise in the area where they have a comparative skills advantage. This, in turn, should lead to greater efficiency and productivity.

Control

Because private limited companies cannot sell their shares publicly, they tend to have fewer shareholders than public limited companies. In this way, each individual shareholder retains a greater degree of control over the operation of the business than would be the case in a public limited company.

In addition, because shares in a private limited company can be sold only with the consent of the other shareholders, the company cannot become a target for a hostile takeover bid (see page 19).

DISADVANTAGES OF OPERATING AS A PRIVATE LIMITED COMPANY

Lack of privacy

All private companies are required under UK law to make certain aspects of their affairs available to the public for general inspection. For example, every private limited company must publish its accounts annually with the appropriate registrar of companies. Although these accounts are not published publicly they are available to members of the public for inspection. This may give competitors, or indeed any interested party, valuable insights into the running of the company.

Set-up costs

Compared to a sole trader or partnership, setting up a private limited company can be a time-consuming and indeed costly process as there are official procedures to complete to ensure that the business complies fully with UK company law.

We learned earlier how all limited companies must draw up a memorandum and articles of association and send these, along with the correct registration fee, to the appropriate registering authority. Completing these documents properly can take time and often requires the assistance of a solicitor.

In recent years Companies House has attempted to make this process much more expedient and straightforward through the introduction of model articles and an on-line registration process. This has significantly reduced the time taken to form a company; indeed Companies House's record for the fastest electronic company formation is five minutes!

Taxation

Many sole traders and partnerships are reluctant to incorporate their businesses as they believe they will end up paying more tax. The point is often made that the owners of private limited companies pay tax twice, once on their earnings and once on their profits. The belief is based on the fact that private limited companies are legal entities in their own right and are therefore liable for corporation tax. This is coupled with the fact that the salaries of the directors and the dividends of the shareholders are also liable for tax.

However, careful tax planning should ensure that the tax liability of a business is reduced after incorporation, rather than increased. This is the case because firstly, UK corporation tax rates are much lower than income tax rates, and secondly, company owners can pay themselves dividends, which are taxed much less heavily than other forms of income.

Therefore, incorporation should actually reduce the tax bill rather than increase it (see case study on page 16).

Limit on capital

Private limited companies are not able to issue or sell their shares publicly as is the case with public limited companies. This means that it is more difficult for a private limited company to raise the capital required to finance expansion and growth. In fact, it is sometimes argued that private limited companies find securing finance from banks quite difficult as banks are put off by their limited liability status. Indeed, banks often require personal guarantees from shareholders before they lend money to private limited companies, begging the question: Just how limited are private limited companies?

CASE STUDY

MILKMEN CHOOSE COMPANY STATUS

Milkmen who work for a food group are being encouraged to turn themselves into one-person companies.

At the moment each milk round is run as a franchise, which individuals take on from the group and operate for a profit. Until now it has been the norm to work as a self-employed sole trader, paying personal tax in the usual way.

But the group's panel of accountants has been informing milkmen that they can take advantage of 'opportunities' introduced in Gordon Brown's Budget last year.

All they have to do, they have been told, is to conduct their business through a new limited company.

The company pays the milkman a salary roughly equivalent to the annual personal allowance of £4,615, which is tax free.

The first £10,000 of profit which the milk round company makes on top of that is also free of tax, under Gordon Brown's new rules. The milkman can take that money as a dividend.

However even though the gains sound impressive, many are worried about hidden costs such as accountant's fees, which can add up to £800 in the first year. In addition, many fear that some business costs, such as phone calls, will not be tax deductible and will therefore add to the cost of doing business.

Freelance contractors in the information technology industry have also poured cold water on the idea. They pointed out that they were prevented from exploiting a similar opportunity three years ago when the Inland Revenue introduced a new rule, called IR35, which allowed the taxman to bypass one-person limited companies and tax the worker in the normal way.

(Adapted from BBC News, 1 April 2003)

ACTIVITY 1.3

LIMITED COMPANIES ON THE INCREASE

Recent reports suggest that small business owners and the self-employed are taking advantage of tax breaks and are converting their businesses to limited companies.

In the UK last year, new company incorporations increased by 42%, a much higher figure than in previous years.

The self-employed, existing businesses and partnerships trying to take advantage of new tax concessions for limited companies are thought to be responsible for most or even all of the growth.

However, the rise in incorporated firms has raised concerns that thousands of small businesses could fall foul of the law because they don't understand the legal requirements involved.

Economists are worried that many of those who have set up companies don't understand the legal obligations of a limited company and the potential fines and prosecution they face for not complying with them.

Companies House, which has seen a significant increase in workload because of the flood of new formation applications, has also voiced concerns about those applicants who have rushed to set up a limited company without fully understanding the legal duties involved.

"There are civil and criminal penalties for failure to act upon the responsibilities," said a spokesman.

"Failure to file accounts on time, for example, can lead to fines of up to £5,000 and in some cases to the winding up of the company. Directors can also be prosecuted, and in 2001/02 Companies House took more than 900 directors to court for failing to file accounts and 149,200 companies were dissolved because they had failed to file any documents at all. When companies are dissolved in these circumstances, their assets are frozen and become the property of the Crown."

(Adapted from www.scotsman.com 11 May 2003)

1. Explain the difference between a sole trader, a partnership and a private limited company.
2. Analyse some of the advantages that a small business, such as a self-employed taxi driver, might gain from converting his business into a private limited company.
3. Explain why some small business owners might be reluctant to incorporate their businesses.

PUBLIC LIMITED COMPANY

Like a private limited company, a public limited company is an incorporated business and is therefore a separate legal entity from its owners. The owners of a public limited company are its shareholders and each shareholder enjoys the benefit of limited liability.

Public limited companies are required by law to carry the suffix 'PLC' or 'plc' as part of their company name. Again this is to ensure that all relevant stakeholders are aware that the liability of the owners is limited.

The key difference between a public limited company and a private company is that the former can offer its shares for sale to the general through a recognized stock exchange.

Public limited companies do not have to 'float' their shares on a stock exchange, though most choose to do so. In the UK the shares of public limited companies are traded on the London Stock Exchange (LSE) in either the Main Market or the Alternative Investments Market (AIM), which is a market that specialises in the trading of shares in smaller, growing businesses.

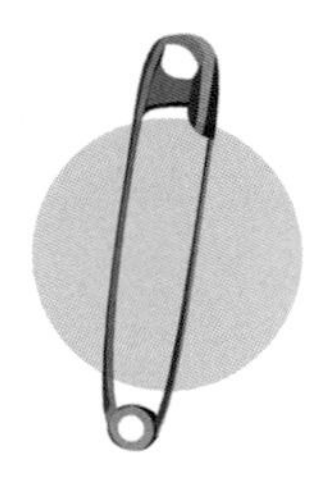

ADVANTAGES OF OPERATING AS A PUBLIC LIMITED COMPANY

Raising capital

A public limited company can issue shares for sale to the general public and so it should be able to raise more capital than any other form of business enterprise. Furthermore, public limited companies are generally larger than other forms of business enterprise and are normally regarded as being less risky. For this reason they typically find it easier to acquire finance from banks and other financial institutions.

Limited liability

A public limited company is an incorporated business and so is a separate legal entity from its owners. This means that the company can take legal action without the direct involvement of its owners. It also means that any debts or losses accrued by the business are not the responsibility of the individual shareholders. Therefore, if the company becomes insolvent, the individual shareholders will lose only the money they have invested in the business.

Continuity

Because a public limited company has a legal existence separate from that of its owners, it will not be affected if one particular shareholder decides to sell his shares. Shares in public limited companies change hands regularly with very limited impact on the operation of the business.

Specialisation

Public limited companies are generally large companies who typically have a greater number of directors or managers than would be the case in other forms of business enterprise. This, therefore, means that each manager can specialise in the area where they have a comparative skills advantage. This specialisation and division of labour should in turn lead to greater efficiency and productivity.

DISADVANTAGES OF OPERATING AS A PUBLIC LIMITED COMPANY

Set-up costs

Setting up a public limited company can be a time-consuming and costly process as there are official procedures to complete to ensure that the business complies fully with UK company law.

In order to set up a public limited company a business must have allotted shares to the value of at least £50,000, with each allotted share being paid up to at least one quarter of its nominal value. In other words, £12,500 worth of shares must be paid up before a public limited company can begin trading.

There are a number of other restrictions that apply to the creation of a public limited company and which do not apply to a private limited company. For example, there are restrictions with regard to the role and office of the company directors and the company secretary, and it is these restrictions that make creating a public limited company a more complicated process than that of creating a private limited company.

Less privacy

All public companies are required under UK law to make certain aspects of their affairs available to the public for general inspection. For example, every public limited company has to comply with the rules of the specific exchange on which the company is listed; these rules are likely to include an obligation to make public all company results. This obligation usually applies to annual and mid-year results and, in some instances, quarterly results.

In addition, the market will need to be informed of any specific details that are likely to have an impact on the company's share price. The company will also be expected to provide explanations of any key decisions taken by the company and its officers.

This information will be available to the financial media and city analysts to scrutinise and may help competitors gain valuable insights into the operation and management of the company.

Divorce of ownership and control

In a public limited company the shareholders are the owners of the company but it is the directors and managers who make the day-to-day decisions and therefore it is they who control the company.

This situation, which is also known as the principal-agent problem, can cause difficulties if the objectives of those who control the company (the agents) differ from the objectives of those who own it (the principals).

In theory this problem should not arise since it is the shareholders who have the power to appoint and fire directors and therefore the directors should always act in the best interests of the shareholders. However, in reality, the incentives of the directors may differ from those of the owners and it is very difficult for the shareholders to closely monitor all the decisions of the directors.

In recent years public limited companies have tried to reduce the extent of the principal-agent problem through introducing share option and share ownership schemes, which are designed to ensure that the incentives and objectives of the directors match those of the owners.

Threat of takeover

The value of a public limited company is determined by the financial markets through trading of the company's shares. This means that the value of the company will be determined by the market's view of the company's performance over a given period of time. However, it also means that the value of the company depends upon the general condition of the market. If the value that the market places on a company falls below a certain level, then the company may become an attractive target to competitors, who may then launch a takeover bid. If the bidding company can acquire enough shares on the open market then it can force the remaining shareholders to release their shareholdings.

In recent times some of the UK's best known companies, such as Birds Eye and Alliance Boots, have been taken over by **private equity** groups. Private equity groups borrow the money required to purchase underperforming companies, with the aim of improving them and selling them on at a profit. These private equity buy-outs have come in for a lot of criticism, with some economists arguing that they are nothing more than asset-strippers, who finance these buy-outs with huge amounts of borrowed money (sometimes referred to as 'leveraged buy-outs'), and to enable them to finance this debt, they are forced to lay off workers and sell valuable property.

Some economists are also concerned about the ability of private equity firms to meet the pension obligations of the acquired firms. However, veteran Chancellor of the Exchequer and Labour Prime Minister at the time of writing, Gordon Brown, is a fan of private equity and has praised its ability to create jobs and contribute to the economy.

CASE STUDY

SHAREHOLDERS FORCE DIRECTORS TO ACCEPT RIVAL BID

Shareholders at Dutch bank ABN Amro have insisted that the bank's managers sell the business to the highest bidder.

ABN Amro's managers are in favour of a proposed £45bn takeover bid by British rival Barclays. However, shareholders are in favour of a rival offer from a consortium of banks, led by UK bank RBS, which values the bank at £49bn.

ABN Amro shareholders sent a strong message to the Dutch firm's management by approving a motion which states that the management should "actively pursue any possibility to sell some or all of the major businesses of the company to maximise shareholder value".

The vote came during an unruly meeting in The Hague, where the head of the Netherland's shareholders' rights association, Peter de Vries, had to be escorted from the stage by security guards.

Mr de Vries threatened to take the company's management to court if plans to sell ABN's US operations, LaSalle, to Bank of America went ahead.

The proposed sale, which was made without seeking the consent of ABN's investors, was seen by many as a deliberate attempt to halt a bid from the RBS-led group. But chief executive Rijkman Groenink defended the $21bn sale of LaSalle as a strategic move ahead of a US economic downturn.

CASE STUDY...

He insisted that the deal with Barclays was in the best interests of both investors and the company.

"Price isn't the only thing that counts," Mr Groenink said. "As human beings and responsible citizens ... we have the obligation to look farther than the last quarter."

However as a result of shareholder pressure, ABN said it would allow the Royal Bank of Scotland group to examine its books ahead of the meeting, setting the stage for a hostile takeover battle for the Dutch bank.

(Adapted from BBC News, 26 April 2007)

ACTIVITY 1.4

PRIVATE EQUITY GROUP CARLYLE BID FOR VIRGIN MEDIA PLC

Virgin Media has become the latest subject of a takeover bid by US private equity firm Carlyle.

It is the most recent in a long line of bid approaches, which have resulted in private equity firms taking control of top UK companies.

Carlyle Group has offered to buy Virgin Media – formed by the merger of cable TV operator NTL and Virgin Mobile last year – for about £5.6bn or $11.5bn including debt.

If the bid is successful, it would be the second largest private equity takeover of a British firm after high street chemists Alliance Boots, bought by Kohlberg Kravis Roberts.

Analysts say Virgin Media, whose shares are listed in the US rather than the UK, is undervalued compared with similar US businesses.

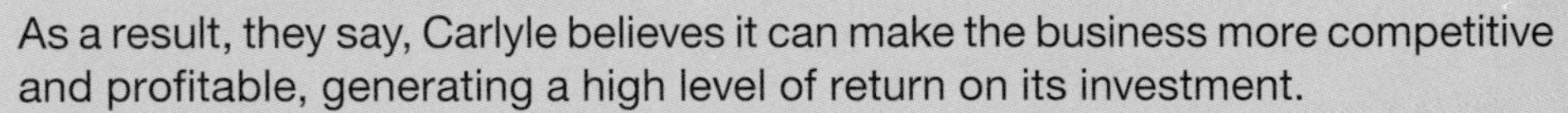

As a result, they say, Carlyle believes it can make the business more competitive and profitable, generating a high level of return on its investment.

Virgin Media has had a difficult time since the merger, becoming embroiled in a bitter legal dispute with chief rival BSkyB over the cost of carrying Sky TV channels on its platform.

The dispute is currently unresolved and is costing both companies a lot of money.

Business analysts argue that by making the business private, it will be easier for Carlyle to invest in growing the company and its various services – TV, broadband, fixed-line phone and mobile phone.

Virgin has confirmed that it has received a proposal to buy the company, which it said it will consider as part of a review of the business.

The group did not name the bidder or give any further details about the offer, saying that the proposal would be withdrawn if its terms were publicly disclosed.

It insisted no negotiations had been entered into with the bidder, and gave no guarantee that any transaction would result and, if so, at what price.

ACTIVITY 1.4

But the company did confirm it had appointed investment bank Goldman Sachs to advise on its options, which could include a sale.

It is thought the bank will take about six weeks to compile a shortlist of serious bidders. This could include other private equity firms and maybe, other media and technology firms.

(Adapted from BBC News, 2 July 2007)

1. Explain how a public limited company differs from a private limited company.
2. Explain how private equity groups such as Carlyle operate.
3. Analyse some of the reasons why Virgin Media might be an attractive target for private equity firms.
4. Explain why some city analysts are opposed to private equity takeovers.

KNOWLEDGE REVIEW

KEY TERMS

- A **PRIVATE LIMITED COMPANY** (or more accurately a private company limited by shares) is a business which is incorporated and is therefore a separate legal entity from its owners. Shares in a private limited company cannot be bought by members of the general public.

- A **PUBLIC LIMITED COMPANY** is also a business which is incorporated and is therefore a separate legal entity from its owners. However a public limited company can offer its shares for sale to the general public through a recognized stock exchange.

- **LIMITED LIABILITY** means that individual shareholders are not personally liable for the debts of the company; they are liable only up to the value of their investment in the company.

- **DIVORCE OF OWNERSHIP AND CONTROL** is the term used to describe the problem faced by PLCs where there is a distinction between the owners of the firm (the shareholders) and the people who run the firm (the managers).

- The **MEMORANDUM OF ASSOCIATION** is the document which sets out the relationship between a company and the outside world.

- The **ARTICLES OF ASSOCIATION** are the regulations which govern the internal relationships between the shareholders and the directors of a company.

COMPANY LIMITED BY GUARANTEE

A company limited by guarantee is an alternative type of corporation, which does not have share capital or shareholders but rather has guarantors or trustees. These guarantors enjoy limited liability status and undertake to contribute a nominal sum (normally £1) in the event of the company being wound up.

A company limited by guarantee is similar in many ways to a private limited company and indeed must carry the suffix LTD after its name. However, a company limited by guarantee cannot distribute its profits to members and is therefore eligible to apply for charitable status.

Limited by guarantee companies are often formed to manage sports clubs, non governmental organisations or charities. Well known examples include OXFAM, the PGA (Professional Golfers' Association) and the Institute for Fiscal Studies (IFS) (see case study below).

CASE STUDY

COMPANY INFORMATION

THE INSTITUTE FOR FISCAL STUDIES

(A Company Limited by Guarantee not having a Share Capital)

CONSTITUTION

The Institute of Fiscal Studies is incorporated as a company limited by guarantee not having a share capital guarantee (No. 954616) and a registered charity (No. 258815). The governing document of the company is the memorandum and articles of association.

OBJECTS OF THE INSTITUTE

To advance education for the benefit of the public by promoting on a non-political basis the study and discussion of and the exchange and dissemination of information and knowledge concerning national economic and social effects and influences of existing taxes and proposed changes in fiscal systems.

HOW IS THE INSTITUTE ORGANISED?

The Institute directly employs some forty staff based at its offices in London. Research staff are divided into sectors and a small core of administrative and secretarial staff provide support facilities. The Institute employs a small number of senior academic staff on joint contracts with UK universities on a part-time basis. In addition, a number of other academics from both UK and overseas institutions work with the staff as Research Fellows and Research Associates on an ad-hoc collaborative basis. A regional grouping of IFS members in NW England meet regularly to discuss matters of mutual interest and occasionally sponsor related activities in that area.

FINANCIAL POLICY

The financial policy laid down by the Executive Committee in 2002 was that the Institute should aim to break even at the operating level after any contributions to reserves.

The Institute attempts to raise its research funds from a range of organisations so that it is not dependent upon a single source of funding although 37% was provided by the Economic and Social Research Council.

CASE STUDY...

With regard to its publishing and mainstream conference activities, the Institute aims to break even, whilst keeping prices as low as possible to maximise public access to its findings. Conferences run by our Centre for Microdata Methods and Practice (cemmap) aim to make a moderate surplus which contributes to the overhead recovery of the Centre.

(Adapted from IFS executive committee report 2002)

FRANCHISE

A franchise is an agreement between two parties, which gives one party (the franchisee) the rights to market a product or service using the trademark of another business (the franchisor). In return the franchisee normally agrees to pay the franchisor certain fees and royalties.

The term 'franchising' has been used to describe many different forms of business relationships, from licensing agreements to distributor and agency arrangements. However, when the term 'franchising' is used it normally refers to one of the two main types of franchise agreement: Business Format Franchising and Product and Trade-name Franchising.

BUSINESS FORMAT FRANCHISING

Business Format Franchising is the most common form of franchise agreement and is a scheme whereby the franchisor offers a wide variety of services to the franchisees, which include the use of trademarks and logos, as well as a complete system of doing business.

In business format franchising the franchisor will normally assist the franchisee with site selection, interior layout and design, hiring and training staff, advertising and marketing, and product supply. In return for these services the franchisee will pay an upfront franchise fee and ongoing royalties to the franchisor. These payments are used by the franchisor to provide research, development and marketing support for the entire franchise organisation.

Business format franchising is most commonly found in industries such as fast-food restaurants, estate agents and recruitment agencies. Well known business format franchises include Burger King and Subway.

PRODUCT AND TRADE-NAME FRANCHISING

Product and Trade-name Franchising is a less involved form of franchising whereby the franchisor provides trademarks and logos, national advertising campaigns and products but does not provide a complete business system. In return for these services the franchisee pays the franchisor an upfront fee but is not obliged to pay any additional royalties.

This type of franchise agreement is common in soft drink and car sales industries. For example, the Charles Hurst motor group has product and trade-name franchise agreements with a wide range of car manufacturers including BMW, Land Rover, Volvo and Mazda.

Franchising has proven to be an increasingly popular way of doing business in the UK, with the number of franchises growing by over 44% in the last ten years.
(source: British Franchise Association)

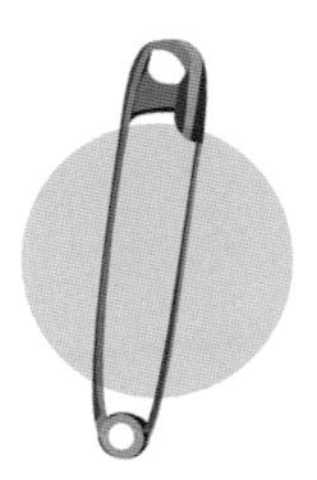

ADVANTAGES OF OPERATING A FRANCHISE

Operating a franchise brings benefits to both the franchisee and the franchisor. For the franchisee the benefits include:

WELL KNOWN BRAND

Working under a well-known brand name, such as Burger King or Subway, has obvious benefits for franchisees. There is increased security for the franchisee since they are using a tried and tested format and selling a well known brand.

They will also not have to worry about generating publicity to raise the profile of their business since customers will already know what to expect from a big chain.

DEFINED TERRITORY

An integral part of any franchise agreement is the sole right to sell the product in a defined geographical area. This means franchisees will not have to worry about other franchisees eating into their market share.

TRAINING AND SUPPORT

Although the level of assistance varies between franchises, most business format franchises offer an extensive programme of training and support which is designed to turn untrained franchisees into competent managers capable of operating a successful business. This support typically includes financial assistance, help in finding and retaining customers and organising large scale advertising and marketing campaigns.

ACCESS TO FUNDS

Compared to starting your own business, the financial burden of opening a franchise is quite light since the franchisor will generally assist the franchisee with the costs of starting up. In addition, because franchising is regarded as a relatively low-risk option, banks are generally willing to lend substantial amounts of money to franchisees safe in the knowledge that they are likely to get their money back.

BENEFITS FOR THE FRANCHISOR

Increased opportunities for growth

Franchising the business out to others allows the company to grow much more rapidly than would be the case if the firm tried to grow organically. This rapid growth should enable the company to benefit from economies of scale.

Increased profits

The profits of the franchisor should increase with each franchise agreement since the franchisor typically receives an upfront fee plus royalties based on the profits or sales of the franchisee.

Less administration

Having a large franchised operation will reduce the management and administrative duties of the original firm since each individual franchise will be owned and managed by the franchisee.

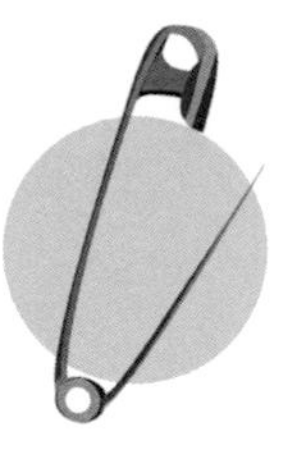

DISADVANTAGES OF OPERATING A FRANCHISE

Initial and ongoing fees

In most franchise agreements the franchisors normally charge new franchisees a lump sum to start up a business using their brand name. These charges vary, depending on the franchise, with the average fee being approximately £45,000 (source: British Franchise Association). However, the fee for large organisations, such as McDonald's, can vary between £150,000 and £1,000,000.

Most business format franchisors also take a regular slice of the franchisee's income as royalty payments. These payments are typically based on turnover rather than profit and therefore have a huge impact on firms which are operating on tight profit margins.

Loss of autonomy

Most franchisors insist that franchisees organise their business in a particular way, and each franchisee is given detailed training and guidelines on how the business should be run. In the most popular franchises these guidelines cover everything from store layout to employment policy. Some franchisees may find these guidelines restricting and may feel more like a manager than an entrepreneur.

Interdependency

One major problem with operating a franchise is that the actions and decisions of other people can adversely affect your business. For instance, a particular franchisee who operates a highly successful outlet may find that his business suffers because of the poor business decisions of the original franchisor or other franchisees. The actions of one bad franchisee could drag down the name of the whole business and therefore affect the profits of all franchisees.

POTENTIAL PROBLEMS FOR FRANCHISOR

Loss of control

When a business franchises its operations it hands over control of the day-to-day running of each separate unit to the franchisee. This reduces the amount of control the original owner has over the business name and reputation. If one franchisee acts in an unbefitting manner, the good name and reputation of the business could suffer, resulting in a decline in profits.

Diseconomies of scale

Diseconomies of scale is the term used to describe the problems that large firms face as a result of their size, which result in an increase in average costs.

When firms grow quickly they can experience problems which result in a loss of efficiency and therefore competitiveness. These problems, which typically arise as a result of trying to manage a too-large organisation, are known as diseconomies of scale.

If a franchise grows too large too quickly it may experience these diseconomies of scale, which may in turn lead to the business becoming less competitive.

CASE STUDY

MOLLY MAID

Molly Maid, founded in 1979, can today be found in the USA, Puerto Rico, Canada, Japan and the UK. It is one of the world's largest professional domestic maid cleaning services, carrying out two million home cleans every year worldwide.

Over the last ten years residential housecleaning has been one of the fastest growing industries in the UK with over 12 million households using paid cleaning services.

As a member of Service Brands International (SBI), Molly Maid provides a variety of house-keeping services for the busy consumer, which can be tailored to meet each individual customer's needs.

The Molly Maid franchise, where the franchisee manages a team of maids, has a £7,800 franchise fee. The fee includes £3,500 for logos, business knowledge and format details and £4,300 for a local market survey, accommodation while training, advertising, stationery and uniforms. The franchisee also needs to provide £10,000 working capital for staff recruitment and training, ongoing advertising, and £1,000 each for the leasing deposit on three vans, cleaning materials and equipment.

Therefore, the total initial outlay is approximately £20,800.

The franchise agreement also requires every franchisee to pay yearly royalty fees which begin at 6.5% of sales revenue for new franchises and fall to 3.5% for the larger more established businesses.

(Adapted from www.mollymaid.com)

DREAM DOORS

John and Elaine Ryan purchased a franchise for kitchen facelift company Dream Doors after visiting an International Franchise Exhibition in their local exhibition centre.

Mr Ryan, who had been in the printing industry for 27 years, said "I was fed up with the unsocial hours and tremendous pressure, but was nervous about starting on my own, so franchising, with a proven system and support, appealed to me."

ACTIVITY 1.5

"Then we saw the Dream Doors' exhibit, and my wife said 'I'd definitely have those in my kitchen', so I thought I would give it a go."

Dream Doors had been operating a franchise network for six years. The first franchises were sold for £5,000 but the charge has now increased to £15,000.

The Ryans took two months to mull over the idea, and then decided to purchase the franchise with their savings and a one-third loan from the bank.

"The arrangement is that we order all the doors from Dream Doors who take eight per cent of the sale, and appliances are also ordered through them. Some franchisees resent paying the percentage, but it goes partly towards the support we receive. We were given a lot of advice on advertising, how to conduct appointments and sales interviews, and went through a four-day training programme."

They started trading in September 2005. "The first month was scary and we just made one sale, then in the second month it came good."

The first customers came through advertising in free newspapers and leaflets and also from national advertising by the parent company, mainly through Saga magazine.

The Ryans opened a showroom in March, which has already made a huge difference to sales.

"Business for the first two months has already doubled. We now sub-contract two teams of fitters and plan to recruit our own driver to do deliveries."

Having support from head office is invaluable claims Mr Ryan. "I was given a mentor and I trusted his advice. After all, the company has done it all before and it's in their interests as much as mine that the business grows and succeeds."

(Adapted from The Telegraph, 19 June 2007)

1. Explain the relationship between a franchisee and a franchisor.
2. Analyse why franchising might be an attractive option to someone like Mr Ryan.
3. Analyse why some entrepreneurs might be reluctant to franchise an established business such as Dream Doors.
4. Evaluate the pros and cons for Dream Doors of using franchising as a method of growth.
5. Discuss some of the personal qualities you feel Dream Doors might look for in a potential franchisee.

KNOWLEDGE REVIEW

KEY TERMS

- A **COMPANY LIMITED BY GUARANTEE** is a type of corporation that is usually formed to manage sports clubs, non governmental organisations or charities. It does not have shareholders but rather has trustees who enjoy limited liability status and who undertake to contribute a nominal sum in the event of the company being wound up.

- A **FRANCHISE** is an agreement between two parties, which gives one party (the franchisee) the rights to market a product or service using the trademark of another business (the franchisor). In return the franchisee normally agrees to pay the franchisor certain fees and royalties.

- **DISECONOMIES OF SCALE** are the problems that large firms face as a result of their size, which cause an increase in average costs.

Chapter 2:

CENTRAL PURPOSE OF BUSINESS ACTIVITY

CENTRAL PURPOSE OF BUSINESS ACTIVITY

Many people think that running a business is a very easy proposition; all you have to do is produce a product or service that people are willing to pay you more for than it costs you to make. However, running a successful business is very difficult. Every day in the UK hundreds of firms are forced to close down because they are unable to make enough money to stay in business.

In the previous chapter, we looked at the different legal forms of business organisation in the UK and we considered the benefits and drawbacks of each structure. We learned that the term 'business' refers to any activity carried out by one or more people with the intention of producing goods or services that can then be sold on to others.

In this chapter, and indeed the rest of this book, we will look at the wide range of strategies that firms can use to ensure that they are able to survive and be profitable in a competitive market place.

PRODUCTION PROCESS

The process of producing these goods or services generally involves taking a range of resources or inputs such as labour and raw materials and processing them in a particular way to produce an output, which a consumer in their particular market would be willing to pay for.

The production process can be illustrated on the simple diagram below.

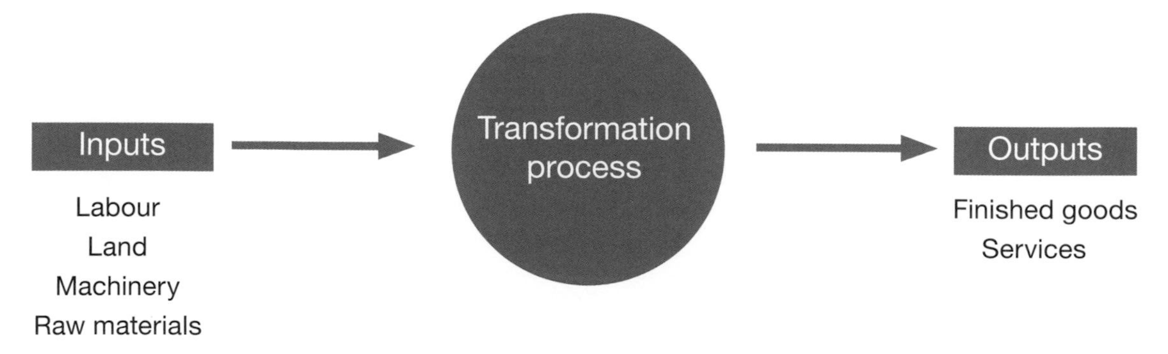

The production process

If we consider the production of a bar of chocolate, the **inputs** would include the raw materials (such as cocoa beans, sugar, milk); the workers; the electricity; and the machinery. The **process** would include mixing and cooking the ingredients, and the **output** would be the final bar of chocolate that is ready to be sold to the consumer.

In the production of a service such as hairdressing, the **inputs** would include scissors, shampoo, dyes and the hairdressers. The **process** would be the washing, drying, cutting and styling of the hair, with the **output** being the final haircut.

PRODUCTION AND ADDED VALUE

The aim of any production process is to add value to the inputs to create an output that can be sold at a profit.

Adding value to a product simply means making the product more desirable to consumers. For example, by taking all the raw materials and mixing them in a particular way, the chocolate manufacturer is adding value since consumers are willing to pay substantially more for a finished bar of chocolate than they would for the unprepared raw materials that go into it.

Added value can be defined as the difference between a particular product's final selling price and the cost of the direct and indirect inputs used in making that product.

Value added is calculated as sales revenue less the cost of bought-in goods and services and measures the wealth created by a company.

VALUE ADDED *= SALES REVENUE LESS THE COST OF BOUGHT-IN GOODS AND SERVICES*

The definition of value added shows that there are two main ways in which a company can increase its value added. These are:

1. By introducing new or improved products and services that provide even greater value to its customers. If firms can do this they should be able to increase the revenue they get from selling their products.

   For instance, a potato producer could add value to his products by washing the potatoes before selling them. He could add further value by peeling the potatoes, slicing the potatoes, and cooking them. This is because consumers will normally pay more for cooked potatoes than for uncooked potatoes.

   A car manufacturer on the other hand, would add value to a car by offering alloy wheels, a stereo system, and leather seats.

2. By reducing the cost of bought-in items through more effective procurement and more efficient use of all inputs.

   If a firm can source its raw materials at a lower cost, or if it can increase labour or capital productivity, then it will be able to increase the value added dimension of its business.

Clearly, one of the best ways for UK companies to compete in a global economy, where developing countries have lower labour costs and can therefore offer lower prices, is to take the first option and supply products and services which provide real value that customers are prepared to pay high prices for.

Many of the most successful UK companies have built their success on offering products and services with a value added that is substantially higher than the costs of the labour and equipment used to make the final product or service.

This source of sustainable value added lies with customers who readily pay much more for the company's products and services than the company itself paid for the materials, components and services it used to create them.

The different ways in which value can be added by these companies varies substantially between companies and sectors. Examples include:

- The creation of a respected brand. Examples include luxury brands such as Aston Martin and Bang and Olufsen where the value of the brand (and company reputation) is carefully maintained.
- The production of an effective product, which has a clear and lasting performance advantage over its rivals. Examples include patented pharmaceuticals such as Disprin and Lemsip.
- The production of an original product or service, for example, a film, book, electronic game or piece of music.

CASE STUDY

VALUE ADDED STRATEGY WORKS FOR TATE & LYLE

Shares in Tate & Lyle, Europe's leading cane sugar refiner, have risen sharply as strong demand for sweeteners and other products boosted sales.

The British firm reported a 10% jump in sales to £3.72bn ($6.95bn) over the past year and said it was confident about its future trading prospects.

Tate said it was encouraged by growing sales of "high value" products, such as its sweetener Splenda, which are making a greater contribution to profits.

"This has been another strong financial performance," said chairman Sir David Lees.

"This time last year we said that we viewed the future with confidence. The success of our value added strategy makes it entirely appropriate to repeat that message."

Tate & Lyle shares were up more than 4% in morning trading.

(Source: BBC News, 25 May 2006)

ACTIVITY 2.1

JOHNSON MATTHEY PLC

Johnson Matthey is a specialist chemicals company, which focuses on catalysts, precious metals and fine chemicals.

Its principal activities are the manufacture of emission control catalysts for motor vehicles, process catalysts, catalysts and components for fuel cells, pharmaceutical compounds and fine chemicals and the refining, fabrication and marketing of precious metals. Founded in 1817, the company has continued to develop its technology for almost 200 years, demonstrating an ability to maintain world leadership by adapting constantly to rapidly changing customer needs. Today Johnson Matthey holds market leading positions in all of its major areas of activity; for example, it makes around a third of all the emission control catalysts that are fitted to cars each year around the world.

A strategy of adding value

Johnson Matthey's strategy is to achieve consistent growth in earnings by concentrating on the development of high added value products and services in areas where its expertise provides a competitive edge, particularly in catalysis, precious metals, fine chemicals and materials technology.

Investment in technology

Technology is the key driver for all of Johnson Matthey's businesses and it invests heavily in research and development (R&D) and manufacturing technology in order to develop the new products and world class manufacturing processes that differentiates it from its global competitors. For example, it reinvested over 10% of its total VA in R&D to ensure that new products and processes were developed sufficiently rapidly to maintain their competitive edge.

Johnson Matthey's company literature states that "adding value at Johnson Matthey is all about the process of investing in R&D, in the areas where we have a core competence, to continuously improve the performance of our products to better serve our customers".

(Source: DTI value added scoreboard)

1. Explain what is meant by the term 'added value'.
2. Explain how Johnson Matthey adds value to its products.
3. Analyse why it might be better for companies like Johnson Matthey to compete on the basis of quality and design rather than on the basis of price.

ADDED VALUE AND COMPETITIVE ADVANTAGE

The table below shows the ten top-performing UK companies in terms of value added in 2007.

What is clear from the table is that the companies which topped the list in 2007 are the same companies which topped the list in 2002.

Only one company from outside the top ten in 2002 made the 2007 list – the mining company BHP Billiton.

Rank in UK 800				
2007	2002	Company	Sector	Value Added £bn
1	1	Royal Dutch Shell	Oil and gas	34.1
2	2	BP	Oil and gas	26.6
3	3	HSBC	Banks	19.7
4	7	Royal Bank of Scotland	Banks	15.8
5	4	GlaxoSmithKline	Pharmaceuticals	13.2
6	6	Vodaphone	Mobile Telecomms	12.1
7	9	Barclays	Banks	12
8	5	BT	Fixed Line Telecomms	10.4
9	14	BHP Billiton	Mining	10
10	8	Unilever	Food Producers	8.4

(Source: DTI value added scoreboard)

When firms, such as BP or HSBC (which have held their positions in the top three since 2002), are able to sustain profits or value added at a level that exceeds the average in an industry, they are said to possess a competitive advantage.

The term **competitive advantage** refers to the advantage that a firm has over its competitors, which allows it to attract and retain more customers than its rivals and therefore generate greater sales and profits.

There are two main types of competitive advantage that a firm might have over its competitors: a cost advantage and a differentiation advantage.

COST ADVANTAGE

The term 'cost advantage' refers to the ability of a particular firm to produce a good or service at a lower cost than its rivals. If a firm has a cost advantage then it will be able to sell its output at a lower price than its main competitors and so be able to gain a larger share of the market.

Alternatively, a firm with a cost advantage can keep its prices at a level that are similar to its main competitors and so make a larger profit margin on each sale.

It should be noted at this point that a competitive advantage which is based on cost does not necessarily mean that the firm will produce an output which is of inferior quality, nor does it mean that the firm will adopt a competitive stance based on price.

Having a cost advantage simply means that the firm has the ability to produce the goods and services that consumers require, at a cost which is consistently below that of its main rivals.

The basis of a competitive cost advantage will vary in different industries. Nonetheless, typical examples include:

ECONOMIES OF SCALE

One reason why some firms are able to produce goods and services much more cheaply than their main rivals is that the firm may be large enough to enable it to avail of economies of scale.

Economies of scale are defined as those advantages of increased size that lead to falling average costs. Essentially, economies of scale are the cost advantages that a firm receives from operating on a larger scale. (For more detail on economies of scale see page 187.)

As firms grow in size they often find that their average costs of production fall as they are able to buy their raw materials and components in bulk or they find it easier to secure credit at competitive rates of interest.

The larger the firm becomes, the greater the economies it can take advantage of and the lower its average costs will be. Clearly, if a firm can avail of economies of scale it will be able to lower its average cost of production and therefore gain a competitive cost advantage over its smaller rivals. Oil companies such as BP and Royal Dutch Shell are able to maintain a competitive cost advantage over their smaller rivals because they operate on this basis.

ECONOMIES OF EXPERIENCE

Another reason why one firm may have lower costs than many of its competitors is that the firm has accumulated significant experience of operating in the industry and as a result it is better able to produce high quality goods and services in an efficient manner.

Consider the experience that would be gained by a company such as Royal Bank of Scotland, which has been operating in the UK since 1727 or HSBC which has been operating in the financial services industry since 1865.

These economies of experience or learning curve effects are very difficult to quantify and measure. Therefore, it is very difficult for competing firms to discover what it is the firm actually does that gives it this cost advantage.

SUPERIOR TECHNOLOGY

One further source of a competitive cost advantage relates to the effective use of technology. If a firm is able to source the most up-to-date capital equipment and is able to use it effectively, then it should be able to produce goods and services more efficiently than firms which are using dated or inferior technology.

CASE STUDY

LOW COST AIRLINES

Budget airlines, such as easyJet and Ryanair, have built their success on a business model that enables them to strip away costs and overheads and therefore offer their customers flights at very competitive prices.

The concept of the low cost, no frills airlines originated in the United States with Pacific Southwest Airlines before spreading to Europe in the early 1990s and subsequently to much of the rest of the world.

EasyJet, the Luton-based airline, was established by Stelios Haji-Ioannou in 1998, and is one of the pioneers of low-cost travel in the UK. The orange coloured airline flies 289 routes across 74 airports around the UK and in Ireland, France, Spain, Portugal, Switzerland, The Netherlands, Denmark, Italy, Greece and Germany. Since the accession of ten new states to the EU in 2004, easyJet has expanded into Eastern and Central Europe with flights to the Czech Republic, Poland, Hungary, Croatia, Slovenia, Slovakia, Latvia and Estonia. Flights to Istanbul and Marrakesh commenced in 2006.

EasyJet is the clear market leader in the UK flying almost 30 million customers each year and making an operating profit of £68m in 2005.

The key to easyJet's success is its low cost approach, which is based on the following strategies:

- To fly to smaller regional airports where landing fees are much lower. These regional airports also tend to be less congested and therefore there is less risk of costly delays.
- Using only one type of plane: EasyJet use only modern Boeing 737 planes, which despite costing more than the older planes used by some of their rivals, have very low operating costs. Using only one type of plane also reduces the cost of staff training, since staff do not need to be trained to operate a number of different planes, and reduces the costs associated with repairs and spare parts.
- Removing business class seats: easyJet do not have business class seats, which enables the number of seats on each plane to be increased from 109 to 149. EasyJet have also removed one toilet from each plane, which allows them to fit one extra seat.
- No free food: EasyJet, and many of the other low cost carriers, do not provide a free meal, which again helps to reduce cost and crew overheads.
- No Tickets: EasyJet is a ticketless airline, which reduces costs and speeds up turnaround times.
- Unreserved seating: This encourages passengers to board early and quickly.
- On-line booking: EasyJet do not use agents to sell their tickets; instead they are sold via their website, which again helps to reduce overheads.

Each of these strategies helps easyJet to keep costs low and therefore gives them a competitive advantage over their main rivals.

DIFFERENTIATION ADVANTAGE

Having a competitive cost position is a very effective tool in helping a firm compete but the problem with pursuing a cost advantage as a basis for your competitive advantage is that there is normally only enough room in an industry for one or two cost leaders, who are normally the largest firms in the industry.

The key for new or small firms therefore, is to choose differentiation as a source of their competitive advantage.

Differentiation refers to a firm's ability to separate itself and its products from that of its main competitors and therefore make its offering more attractive to a particular target market. Successful product differentiation helps to create a competitive advantage for the seller, since customers will view their products as unique or superior.

There are a number of different ways through which firms can differentiate themselves and their products from those of their rivals. However, the two most common methods used are:

1. Create a unique selling proposition (USP)

The most obvious way a firm can differentiate itself from its main rivals is to change the actual product in some way so as to give the firm a unique selling proposition. Also known as a unique selling point, a USP is something that sets one firm's product or service apart from that of its competitors in the eyes and minds of potential customers.

A firm can create a USP by adding new features or by improving the quality or reliability of the product.

A good USP is one that sets the firm's product apart from its rivals and offers an experience which is strong enough to attract customers to the product. Ideally, a USP should also offer customers an experience that is not offered by any other firm.

Consider the USP for a product like Head & Shoulders; while there may be many products which help get rid of dandruff, only Head & Shoulders would be widely recognized as fulfilling that function.

If a firm can create a USP then it will find that it is able to attract more customers than its main rivals.

CASE STUDY

MOBILE PHONE TARGETS THE 50+ GENERATION

A mobile phone with a built-in emergency button has been produced for elderly and older people.

The Life phone is aimed at those aged 50+ who do not want a handset crammed with every possible feature.

Instead of a camera or music player it has a loudspeaker (tuned for those who are either partially sighted or use a hearing aid), a big screen and buttons.

Created by Austrian firm Emporia, the phone has been specifically developed for the older generation who find existing handsets too fiddly and complicated to use.

The Life phone has only the most basic functions on board and lets its owners make and take calls only, send and receive text messages and manage their directory of numbers.

CASE STUDY...

The dualband Life phone can be programmed with up to five emergency numbers.

On the rear of the phone is a big red button that can be pressed in the event of an emergency and which will call one of the stored emergency numbers to summon aid.

Text messages that should be sent in the event of an emergency can also be created and stored on the handset.

The orange backlight for the 2.7 inch (6.8 cm) mono-colour screen has been chosen because it is easy to read for those with failing sight.

Volume on ringing tones and loudspeaker can also be set to be very loud to help the hard of hearing.

It also has an extra-strong vibration function to alert its owner that someone is calling.

It is hoped that these special features will create the unique selling point required to attract sufficient numbers of older customers.

(Adapted from BBC News, 17 March 2007)

2. *Create a strong brand*

A brand can be a name, term, symbol or design or a combination of these, which aims to make the product easily recognizable and distinguishable from the products of other firms.

Branding a product or service is one of the most common means of differentiating a company's product or service from those of its competitors.

When branding is used as the basis for differentiation the actual differences in the product or service may be very minor, as the key to the differentiation is simply to convince consumers that the product is different. This perception can be achieved through marketing and advertising.

Branding a product will reduce its price elasticity of demand (more on this in chapter 4) and therefore makes it less sensitive to changes in price. Indeed, numerous studies have shown that consumers will pay a substantial price premium for a good brand and will also remain loyal to that brand.

Having a strong brand is also very useful when the firm is introducing a new product onto the market and can allow the firm to extend its product range without having to spend huge sums of money in an attempt to raise consumer awareness.

Consider, for example, the range of products produced by the main fashion houses such as Gucci and Calvin Klein, both of whom have extended their brand into perfume, glasses, furniture and home décor.

Differentiating a product or service through a strong brand will benefit the firm as it reduces the amount of direct competition the firm faces. This is because in the eyes of consumers the products sold by competitors do not represent direct substitutes for the firm's product, and therefore the firm gains a clear competitive advantage.

ACTIVITY 2.2

THE POWER OF BRANDS

1. Draw the logos for the following five brands: Apple, Toyota, Nestlé, Translink and Mazda.

2. Which products have used the following strap lines in their advertising?
   - Just do it
   - Va Va Voom
   - Every little helps
   - I'm lovin' it
   - Water you wear
   - Probably the best lager in the world
   - Because I'm worth it

An artist's impression of Custom House Square, Belfast.

CASE STUDY

RE-BRANDING BELFAST

Marketing gurus working on re-branding Belfast have asked residents and visitors how the city could be sold on the international stage.

Belfast City Council has employed consultants Lloyd Northover to come up with a makeover for the city's image.

A questionnaire has been put up on a new website, yourviewsonbelfast.com.

Councillor Diane Dodds said 11 years had passed since the last re-branding exercise, and a new approach was needed "to reflect the transformed city".

During the Troubles, Belfast used to be a tough sell to tourists, but it has transformed its image in recent years.

The consultants have been looking at how cities like Glasgow and New York have succeeded in building strong brands and are hoping to replicate some of that success here.

The question however of what image should be projected to the wider world remains a difficult one, and the branding experts have come up with three different themes.

CASE STUDY...

- "We're Belfast, just a bit larger than life." A city where straight talk, easy banter and gritty wit permeate the scene. From stylish restaurants and smart hotels, via festivals, gigs and bars, right onto the street.
- "Here is a city of welcome surprises." Here, between the mountains and the sea, is a city buzzing with confidence and zest for life. Energy and optimism fill the air, inspiring enterprise, creativity and change, opening up new opportunities and new things to discover every time you return.
- "Belfast is easy and open, vibrant without the hustle and hassle." Easy-going and self-assured, Belfast buzzes with lively conversation, a relaxed style and a warm and welcoming atmosphere.

(Adapted from BBC News Northern Ireland, 12 October 2007)

SUSTAINABLE COMPETITIVE ADVANTAGE

As stated earlier, a competitive advantage refers to the advantage that a firm has over its competitors, which allows it to attract and retain more customers than its rivals and so generate greater sales and profits. If a firm can sustain this position over a long period of time then it is described as having a sustainable competitive advantage.

A **sustainable competitive advantage** (SCA) is a long-term advantage possessed by an organisation, which is not easily copied or eroded by its competitors.

A SCA is usually the consequence of distinctive skills and competencies possessed by employees and/or the owners of a company. These core competencies include good leadership, constant innovation, a culture of teamwork and superior knowledge.

For example, the car maker, Honda, could be described as having a sustainable competitive advantage in the production of engines. As a company, Honda is able to produce high quality engines, which can be applied to a range of products, including motorbikes, lawnmowers, jet engines, generators and motorcars.

Honda's core competency lies in its ability to produce high-quality, innovative engines for a wide range of uses. It is this ability that has allowed Honda to survive against intense competition over a long period of time and remain the world's largest engine manufacturer selling over 14 million engines per year.

ACTIVITY 2.3

THE FALLING PRICE OF ELECTRONICS

Tesco is offering what it claims is the UK's cheapest digital set-top box. With a price tag of just £10, the Freeview box will certainly sound like a bargain to anyone who forked out over £100 to be in the first wave of the digital switch-over.

Sitting next to it on the shelf could be Tesco's newly-launched £9 DVD player, while other supermarkets and the internet are offering equally knock-down prices for a range of electronic goods.

Consumer electronics have been falling inexorably in price as gadgets are added to the shopping trolley alongside the bread and milk. It is great news for customers but it begs the question – how did they get to be so cheap?

ACTIVITY 2.3

Tesco wouldn't discuss the margins on the £10 set-top box, saying simply that "we are able to sell it for £10 because we have a competitive cost advantage and can buy in bulk".

However, others argue that the low price comes at the expense of poorer quality. Chris Price, publisher of consumer electronics website TechDigest says, "I guess if you pay £69 for something that a couple of years ago would have cost £400 then the quality isn't going to be the same.

"Goods like this are made cheaply, often in Chinese factories where the quality control is not what it should be."

However, Tesco maintains that there has been no compromise on quality.

"Corners are definitely not being cut on quality to get these cheap goods on the shelves; there is no way we would jeopardise our brand by knowingly selling poor quality products," said a Tesco spokeswoman.

(Adapted from BBC News, 30 August 2007)

1. Explain what is meant by a competitive cost advantage.
2. Explain what is meant by the term 'branding'.
3. Evaluate whether pursuing a cost-based strategy is the best way for Tesco to achieve a competitive advantage.

KNOWLEDGE REVIEW

KEY TERMS

- **ADDED VALUE** can be defined as the difference between a particular product's final selling price and the cost of the direct and indirect inputs used in making that particular product.
- **A COMPETITIVE ADVANTAGE** refers to the advantage that a firm has over its competitors, which allows it to attract and retain more customers.
- **COST ADVANTAGE** refers to the ability of a particular firm to produce a good or service at a lower cost than its rivals.
- **ECONOMIES OF SCALE** are the cost advantages a firm receives from operating on a larger scale.
- **DIFFERENTIATION** refers to a firm's ability to separate itself and its products from that of its main competitors and therefore make its product more attractive to a particular target market.
- A **UNIQUE SELLING POINT** is something that sets one firm's product or service apart from that of its competitors in the eyes and minds of potential customers.
- A **SUSTAINABLE COMPETITIVE ADVANTAGE** (SCA) is a long-term advantage possessed by an organisation, which is not easily copied or eroded by its competitors.

Chapter 3: MARKETS

WHAT IS A MARKET?

A market is any place where buyers and sellers come together to exchange goods and services.

There are millions of markets all over the world selling everything from oil to computers to financial assets like Bonds and Shares. There is even a market for footballers!

Traditionally, a market was a physical space where producers and consumers came together to engage in trade. Many of the larger towns in Northern Ireland developed as a result of the fact that they had a popular market. These towns are still often referred to as market towns, eg Cookstown in County Tyrone and Draperstown in County Derry.

Within Belfast some of the most famous areas are named after the market which was held there, eg Cornmarket in the heart of Belfast city centre.

Today however, many markets involve trade that does not take place in a particular physical space. The term 'market' is simply used metaphorically to describe the trade which occurs in that industry.

With advances in technology and the development of e-commerce, producers and consumers no longer have to meet to engage in trade. Consider the trade which takes place on the internet auction site eBay and you will get some idea of just how successful a virtual market can be.

ACTIVITY 3.1

E-COMMERCE ON THE INCREASE

According to the latest figures from the Office for National Statistics, consumers spent a record £21.4bn on internet shopping during 2005. This was a rise of almost 30% on the figure for 2004.
Two factors helping to fuel this increased on-line business have been the increased availability of broadband internet access, and an improved confidence in internet security.

The survey showed that e-commerce generated an overall total of £103.3bn for the UK economy, a significant rise on the 2004 figure of £66.2bn.

The results of the 2005 survey, which was based on businesses with ten or more employees, show growth in the use of Information and Communication Technologies (ICT) and large increases in the value of trade over the Internet.

ACTIVITY 3.1

Other key findings of the survey include:

- 14.6% of businesses sold over the internet in 2005 (12% in 2004) while 56.3% made purchases over the internet in 2005 (50.3% in 2004).
- Internet purchases by businesses rose 50.4%, from £48.4bn in 2004 to £72.8bn in 2005.
- 69.8% of businesses had a website in 2005, compared to 66.9% of businesses in 2004.
- 50.5% of businesses used the internet to interact with public authorities, such as government departments, and local and regional authorities in 2005.
- 24.8% of businesses reported having electronic systems for placing or receiving orders in 2005.

1. Explain what is meant by the term 'e-commerce'.
2. Analyse some of the benefits that a business would gain from engaging in e-commerce.
3. Analyse some of the costs a firm might face as it attempts to sell its goods or services on-line.
4. *Consumer spending on internet shopping increased significantly in 2005. However, as a proportion of total consumer spending the figure is still very small.*

   Explain some of the reasons why on-line shopping still makes up a small fraction of total consumer spending.

TYPES OF MARKET

Markets can be classified under a number of different headings:

A **COMMODITY MARKET** is a market that involves trade in raw materials, which will later be transformed into finished products. Commodities include industrial metals such as copper and tin, precious metals such as gold and silver, raw food products such as coffee beans, sugar and wheat as well as oil and other raw materials.
Commodities are traded in specialised markets called exchanges. For example, the London Metal Exchange (LME) is the arena for the trading of industrial metals such as copper, lead and zinc.
Because of price volatility, special contracts known as futures are often used when purchasing commodities. A futures contract is simply an agreement to purchase or sell a fixed quantity of a commodity at a future date at a pre-determined price.
Purchasing commodities on a futures contract allows a firm to plan ahead without having to worry about large changes to the price of its raw materials.

A **CONSUMER MARKET** is a market for finished consumer goods, which are purchased by the end consumer. Consumer goods include items such as a jar of coffee, a loaf of bread, a kilogram of cheese etc (often referred to as consumables or non-durable goods) and products such as cars, televisions, computers etc (which are generally referred to as consumer durables).

The consumer market also includes trade in intangibles (products which cannot be seen and touched). These are services such as personal banking, insurance and hairdressing.

A **CAPITAL GOODS MARKET** is a market which involves the trade of capital goods. Capital goods are goods that can be used in the production of other products but are not incorporated into the product, ie they are not a part of the final product, eg equipment, machinery and tools.

Capital goods are purchased by firms to assist them in the production of other goods.

The Larne-based company FG Wilson operates in the capital goods market since it produces gas and diesel-powered generator sets, which are used by other businesses.

An **INDUSTRIAL MARKET** is also a market for goods that are used by industry in the production of other goods and services. However, in this case, the goods are actually incorporated into the final product. Examples of items which are traded in an industrial market include sand and gravel.

An example of a Northern Ireland firm that operates in the industrial market is RLC Langford Lodge which produces seats and other cabin components for the airline industry.

ACTIVITY 3.2

Using the internet, identify which markets the following companies operate in:

1. The Body Shop
2. CAT
3. HSBC
4. Montupet
5. Audi
6. Toni & Guy
7. Readymix PLC

THE LABOUR MARKET

The labour market is the market that brings together the buyers of labour, the employers, and the sellers of labour, the workers.

The labour market is different from most other markets in that here individuals and households are the suppliers, and business organisations are the purchasers.

In the labour market individuals will supply firms with their labour as long as the reward for doing so, ie the payment they receive, is greater than the cost to them of giving up their free time.

On the other hand, firms will employ workers so long as the cost of doing so is lower than the value of the output produced by those workers.

The **LABOUR FORCE** is generally defined as those in employment plus those who are unemployed but actively seeking work. People not counted in the labour force include full time students, retired people and people in prisons.

In May 2007 the Office of National Statistics (ONS) estimated the UK labour force to be 30,735,000. Of this total, 29,075,000 were in employment with 1,660,000 (or 5.4%) considered to be unemployed.

LABOUR MARKET STATISTICS

The ONS collects a wide range of data on the UK labour market, which allows the government and businesses to analyse trends in the structure of both employment and unemployment.

EMPLOYMENT STRUCTURE BY SECTOR

The table below shows the structure of employment by sector for Northern Ireland in June 2007.

Industrial sector	No. of employee jobs	% change on previous year
Primary	12,250	-5.8
Secondary : (a) Construction	40,200	4.6%
(b) Manufacturing	85,560	-1.2%
Tertiary	570,480	1.9%
Total	708,490	1.5%

(Source: First Trust economic outlook and business review)

THE PRIMARY SECTOR The primary sector of the economy typically involves employment in the extraction of natural resources from the earth and the conversion of these natural resources into raw materials. Examples of primary production include agriculture, forestry and fishing, and mining and quarrying. *An example of a Northern Ireland company which employs workers in the primary sector would be Irish Salt Mining & Exploration Ltd, who operate in Kilroot, just outside Carrickfergus.*

THE SECONDARY SECTOR

The secondary sector of the economy typically involves employees taking the raw materials produced by the primary sector and converting them into finished or semi-finished goods to be sold to the final consumer or to other businesses. Examples of secondary activity include manufacturing (for example of clothing and electronics), and construction.

An example of a Northern Ireland company employing workers in the secondary sector would be FG Wilson who have bases in Belfast and Larne and are one of the world's largest manufacturers of electricity generators.

THE TERTIARY SECTOR

The tertiary sector is often referred to as the service sector of the economy and typically involves employees being engaged in the provision of services to business and the final consumer. Examples of tertiary sector activity include transport and distribution, insurance and banking and leisure and tourism. *An example of a Northern Ireland business whose employees operate in the Tertiary sector is 'Translink', the brand name under which Ulsterbus Ltd, Citybus Ltd (Metro), and Northern Ireland Railways Ltd trade.*

THE QUATERNARY SECTOR

Some people now refer to a fourth sector of the economy as the quaternary sector. This sector involves intellectual services such as research and development and information management.

However, for many economists, the quaternary sector is simply a sub-section of the tertiary sector. Indeed, official government classifications still consider this sector to be a subset of the tertiary sector. Examples of quaternary activity include education, consulting, and information and communication technology. *An example of a company operating in the quaternary sector in Northern Ireland is PricewaterhouseCoopers whose employees provide tax advisory and consultancy services to both public and private enterprises.*

OVERLAP BETWEEN SECTORS

It should be noted that there is considerable overlap between each of these sectors. We have already noted that for some the quaternary sector is simply a subset of the tertiary sector. In addition, in official classification, the packaging and processing of raw materials, which takes place close to the primary producers, is often considered to constitute primary activity even though processing and packaging would normally constitute secondary activity. This is especially true if the raw materials need some processing before they can be sold on to manufacturers.

An additional problem occurs when trying to classify an employee as operating mainly in the primary, secondary or tertiary sectors, since many firms operate across more than one sector. Employees who work for these firms may engage in the activities of two or more sectors.

CASE STUDY

MANUFACTURING IN DECLINE

Executives from all areas of manufacturing are becoming increasingly concerned about the erosion of industry's importance in Britain's economy. Trade figures recently revealed that manufacturing now accounts for less than 15% of the economy, while over the past decade the numbers employed are down by a million.

The increasing foreign ownership of the country's manufacturing base has also raised concerns that the new owners will make decisions in their own national interest rather than Britain's. Vital decisions on British jobs are often no longer being taken in offices in Broughton or London but instead in Toulouse or Fairfield, Connecticut.

Allan Cook, the chief executive of Cobham and a driver behind the establishment last month of the country's first National Skills Academy for Manufacturing said:

"There is no question that the UK manufacturing industry is suffering from skills shortages and this is hampering our ability to compete in the world marketplace."

His comments echo those of Sir John Rose, the chief executive of Rolls-Royce, who recently warned the UK was becoming a "monochrome" economy, reliant almost entirely on the services sector.

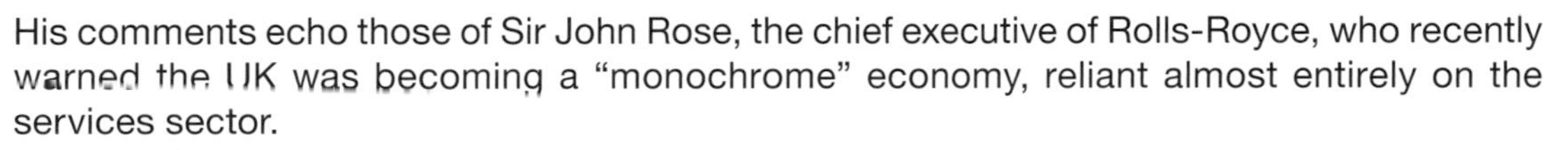

However, the government has attempted to respond to the challenge, by introducing a variety of initiatives, such as a Manufacturing Forum, and more recently setting up the National Skills Academies.

"This area has grown in political importance and we have done a huge amount of work developing the policy and the practice to be able to make that skills policy a reality," says Phil Hope, the government's skills minister.

But although the National Skills Academy for Manufacturing has been welcomed by industry and has the support of some of Britain's largest employers, such as Cobham, Toyota and BAE Systems, scepticism remains that government initiatives alone will solve the problem and manufacturing will continue to decline in the face of increased competition from China and India.

(Adapted from The Telegraph, 17 February 2007)

ACTIVITY 3.3

The table below shows the percentage of the labour force employed in the three industrial sectors in the UK between 1985 and 2006.

Industrial sector	1985	1995	2007
Primary	7	4	3
Secondary	37	32	19
Tertiary	56	64	78

Using the information in the table:

1. Draw a chart showing the trends in industrial sector employment from 1985 to 2006.
2. Describe the trends as shown in the chart.
3. Explain why you think these trends may be occurring.

UNEMPLOYMENT

Unemployment can be defined as those registered able, available and willing to work at the going wage rate in any suitable job, and who cannot find employment.

There are two main measures of unemployment in the UK: the **claimant count;** and the International Labour Organisation (ILO) measure – the **labour force survey**.

THE CLAIMANT COUNT

This measure of unemployment only counts those people out of work and claiming unemployment benefits, ie those claiming Job Seeker's Allowance.

The claimant count figures do not include:

- Married women whose husbands work
- Those on sickness and incapacity benefit
- Those under 18 (was previously 16)
- People on training schemes

For this reason some people do not consider the claimant count to be an accurate measure of unemployment and therefore they prefer to use the ILO measure.

THE ILO MEASURE

Since 1998 the government has published an alternative measure of unemployment based on the **labour force survey**. This measure, which is calculated by the International Labour Organisation (ILO), covers those aged 16 or over, without a job, who have looked for work in the past month and are able to start work in the next two weeks.

The advantage of the ILO measure is that it is an international standard and it therefore makes comparisons between countries much easier.

The ILO measure of unemployment is usually much larger (approximately 400,000 more in the UK) than the claimant count measure.

TRENDS IN CLAIMANT COUNT UNEMPLOYMENT

The graph below shows the trend in claimant count unemployment in Northern Ireland between 2001 and 2006. We can see from the graph that unemployment has fallen from over 6% in 2001 to about 4.7% at the end of 2006.

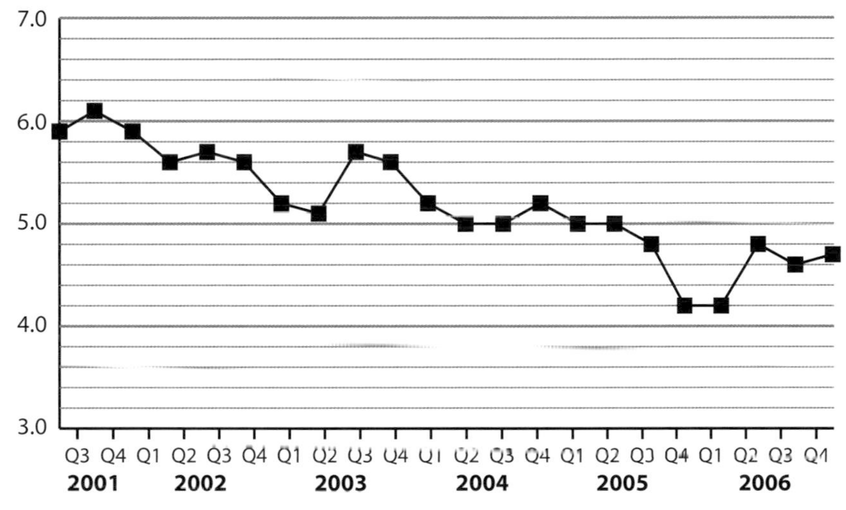

BUSINESS IS BOOMING

Business is booming in Northern Ireland, according to the latest economic survey from the Ulster Bank.

The report said that the economy was experiencing higher levels of customer spending and that firms are creating new jobs as a result.

Last month, local companies reported the strongest rise in new business for more than two years.

The report also stated that unemployment fell sharply during the past year giving Northern Ireland an unemployment rate of 4.7%, well below the UK average of 5%.

(Adapted from Ulster Bank economic survey 2006)

1. Explain the difference between the ILO and the claimant count measure of unemployment.
2. Explain why higher levels of consumer spending would lead to higher levels of employment.
3. Explain one advantage and one disadvantage that firms encounter as a result of lower levels of unemployment.

MASS AND NICHE MARKETS

A **mass market** is the term used to describe a broad, non-targeted, non-segmented market. Firms which produce for the mass market will generally produce large quantities of goods and services for consumption by a large number of consumers.

Examples of mass-market products include many of the widely available popular brands, from Ariel to Mars to the Ford Mondeo.

Many firms aim to produce for the mass market as they believe it is the most effective route to profitability and success.

Clearly, selling to such a market is advantageous in that it significantly increases the number of possible customers a firm can access and therefore potentially leads to greater levels of sales and turnover for the firm.

In addition, producing a standardised product for a mass market allows the firm to gain economies of scale (see page 187) and therefore reduces the firm's unit costs.

This reduction in unit costs coupled with higher levels of potential turnover should in turn lead to higher levels of profitability.

A **niche market,** on the other hand, is the term used to describe a narrow, or focused subset of a larger market sector.

When a business focuses on a niche market it is essentially trying to produce a product that meets the particular demands of a specific group of consumers, which are not currently being addressed by mainstream providers.

Examples of niche market products include lactose-free milk, custom-built cars and High and Mighty clothing.

Many firms choose to ignore niche markets, believing them to be small and therefore not very profitable. However, niche markets can be very lucrative for a number of reasons.

Firstly, one of the main advantages that a firm gains from operating in a niche market is that it is unlikely to face high levels of competition. This is because niche markets are often ignored by the larger mainstream providers.

Secondly, since the firm is meeting the specific demands of a particular group of consumers it should be able to charge a premium price for its services.

Finally, operating in a niche market allows the firm to focus its marketing budget much more closely on its potential customers. For instance, consider the firm that produces a product which meets the demands of a particular ethnic group. It will be able to advertise in ethnic magazines or on ethnic radio stations, which will generally be cheaper and allow the marketing budget to stretch to accommodate more frequent advertising.

ACTIVITY 3.5

NICHE FOOD MANUFACTURERS URGED TO GO MASS MARKET

Food manufacturers are being urged to cash in on the growing consumer demand for specialised food-intolerance products and to steer the trend more towards the mass market. According to Euromonitor International, the food industry is struggling to keep up with the rise in food allergies or 'sensitivities' in the UK, and as a result many sufferers have to seek out premium-priced food products in specialist outlets.

ACTIVITY 3.5

"For mainstream manufacturers and retailers, it is important to realise that foods for intolerances are no longer niche", comments Simone Baroke, health and wellness products analyst at Euromonitor International.

According to Allergy UK, 45% of the UK population battle food sensitivities at some point in their lives, and 2% suffer from a food allergy. This leaves a massive gap in the market for mainstream retailers to embrace the trend, said Euromonitor.

Indeed, supermarkets have already started to wake up to the new opportunity and are increasingly challenging the small health food shops and pharmacies by creating popular own brand product lines, such as Sainsbury's 'Free From' range.

According to the market researcher, the UK is the third-biggest market for gluten-free foods (after the US and Italy), amounting to £47m (€70m) in 2006. Sales of lactose-free products (dairy products, ice cream, baby foods) have increased by 29% since 2002, reaching £23m (€34m) in 2006.

Euromonitor stated that consumer awareness of allergies is on the rise, and people are therefore becoming more intuitive in creating a stable diet. As a result they are now seeking cheaper food alternatives with which to do so.

According to an interview with a food and drinks advisor at Coeliac UK, a gluten-intolerance network, allergy sufferers want to see more 'normal' foods adjusted to cater for their needs, such as gluten-free jaffa cakes, pitta breads, pizzas, sausage rolls or maybe even a pork pie. Such items are currently available, but remain limited to large stores.

The biggest problem posed in the food market for celiac sufferers remains breakfast cereals, with most large manufacturers, such as Kelloggs and Weetabix, creating ranges that contain ingredients such as barley malt extract and wheat gluten – all off-limits to the consumers who mainly have to limit themselves to cornflakes and puffed rice.

Euromonitor claims that larger manufacturers either completely ignore the growing food-sensitive consumer base or are unwilling to tackle the problem of cross-contamination.

The market researcher says the food-intolerance market in the UK holds **"massive growth potential"**. It is now encouraging manufacturers to further investments in products that can be labelled as free from wheat, gluten, cows' milk, lactose, egg, soya, nuts and ominous additives, such as sulphites.

Likewise, now is a good time for large industry players to acquire smaller, specialist companies who have the potential to prosper if they are given the proper resources.

The larger companies would benefit from their custom-built production facilities – providing uncontaminated products.

(Adapted from a report by Louise Prance in www.foodnavigator.com)

1. Explain the difference between a mass market and a niche market.
2. Explain why the producers of specific food-intolerance products are able to charge premium prices for their products.
3. Explain why mainstream manufacturers have been slow to enter the food-intolerance market.
4. How might food-intolerance sufferers benefit from the entry of mainstream suppliers into this market?

KNOWLEDGE REVIEW

- A **MARKET** is any place where buyers and sellers come together to exchange goods and services.
- A **COMMODITY MARKET** is a market which involves trade in raw materials, which will later be transformed into finished products.
- A **CONSUMER MARKET** is a market for finished consumer goods, which are purchased by the end consumer.
- A **CAPITAL GOODS MARKET** is a market that involves the trade of goods which can be used in the production of other products but are not incorporated into the product, eg machinery and equipment.
- The **LABOUR FORCE** is generally defined as those in employment plus those who are unemployed but actively seeking work.
- **UNEMPLOYMENT** refers to those registered able, available and willing to work at the going wage rate in any suitable job who cannot find employment. Unemployment is measured by the Claimant Count or the Labour Force Survey.
- A **MASS MARKET** is the term used to describe a broad, non-targeted, non-segmented market.
- A **NICHE MARKET** is the term used to describe a narrow, or focused subset of a larger market sector.

Chapter 4: MARKET FORCES AND THE THEORY OF DEMAND AND SUPPLY

4

As we saw in the previous chapter, a market is a place where buyers and sellers come together to exchange goods and services. In this exchange of goods and services, buyers **demand** goods from the market and sellers **supply** goods to the market.

The theory of demand and supply then, is an attempt to explain how the **price** of these goods and services would be determined in a competitive market.

DEMAND

The theory of demand deals with how consumers behave when they are faced with a change in the price of a good. If the price of a good changes, will consumers be likely to purchase more of the product or less of the product?

Economists define demand as 'the quantity of a good or service that a consumer is willing and able to buy at a given price in a given time period'.

The term 'willing and able' is very important in this definition as it is only when a consumer is both willing to purchase a product and able to purchase the product that the demand becomes effective.

I may be very willing to purchase a new BMW but if I do not have the funds to support this desire then I am not able to go to the market and demand the car.

HOW DOES THE QUANTITY DEMANDED OF A GOOD CHANGE WHEN PRICE CHANGES?

For most goods we would expect the quantity demanded (Qd) to increase when price decreases. If the price of a new BMW fell from £30,000 to £10,000 I might well be able to back up my desire to purchase the car with the funds to do so and therefore the quantity demanded of BMWs would increase.

Therefore, we can say that there is an inverse relationship between the price of a good and the quantity demanded of that good.

If we were to plot the price of a good on the vertical axis and the quantity demanded on the horizontal axis we could show this relationship as a graph or diagram.

The demand curve (D) for a good or service is downward sloping from left to right. As price increases people will buy less of the good and vice versa.

This is shown on the diagram.

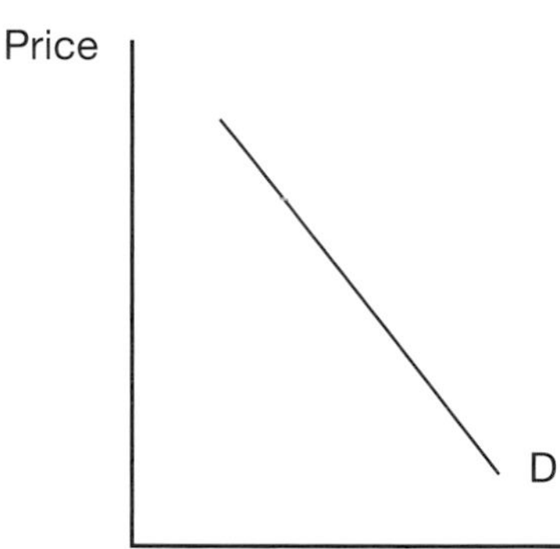

ACTIVITY 4.1

The table below shows the estimated daily sales of a local newspaper at five different prices.

Price	Daily sales (est)
55p	191,000
50p	234,000
45p	295,000
40p	325,000
30p	350,000

1. Using the information in the table above plot a daily demand curve for the newspaper.
2. Using the graph, estimate the likely daily sales if the selling price was:
   (a) 35p
   (b) 48p
3. Calculate the sales revenue that the publishers would be likely to receive if they sold the newspaper at 50p.

SUPPLY

The theory of supply deals with how producers behave when they are faced with a change in the price of a good. If the price of a product changes, will producers be likely to supply more of the product or less of the product?

Economists define supply as 'the quantity of a good or service that producers are willing and able to supply onto a market at a given price in a given time period'.

HOW DOES THE QUANTITY SUPPLIED OF A GOOD CHANGE WHEN PRICE CHANGES?

For most goods we would expect the quantity supplied to increase when price increases. As the price of a particular good increases, producers will shift resources to the production of that good as it represents a better return on their investment and therefore the quantity of the good supplied will increase.

Therefore, we can say that there is a positive relationship between the price of a good or service and the quantity supplied of that good or service.

If we were to plot the price of a good on the vertical axis and the quantity supplied on the horizontal axis we could show this relationship as a graph or diagram.

The supply curve (S) for a good or service is upward sloping from left to right. As price increases, the quantity that firms are willing to supply onto the market increases and vice versa.

This is shown on the diagram below.

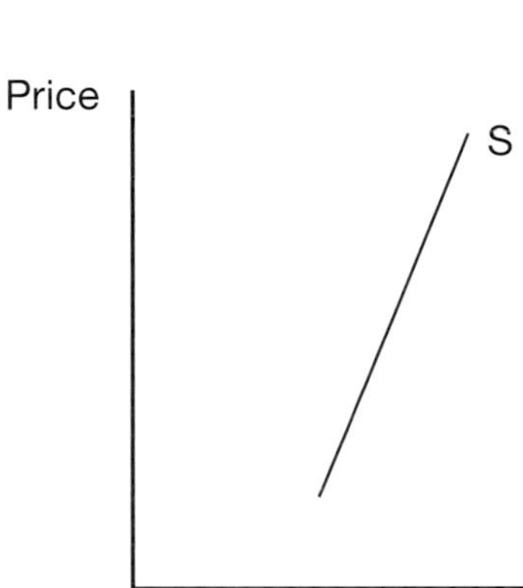

ACTIVITY 4.2

The table below shows the quantity of a local newspaper that the publishers would be willing to supply at five different prices.

Price	Daily production
55p	375,000
50p	334,000
45p	295,000
40p	225,000
30p	190,000

1. Using the information in the table above plot a daily supply curve for the newspaper.
2. Using the graph, estimate the likely daily print run if the selling price was:
   (a) 35p
   (b) 48p

PRICE DETERMINATION

The price at which the good or service is sold is determined by the interaction of demand for the good or service and the supply of the good or service. When buyers and sellers come together they create a market where demand and supply interact to determine what economists call the **market clearing** or **equilibrium price.**

The equilibrium or market clearing price is that price where quantity demanded is equal to quantity supplied.

This is shown on the diagram below:

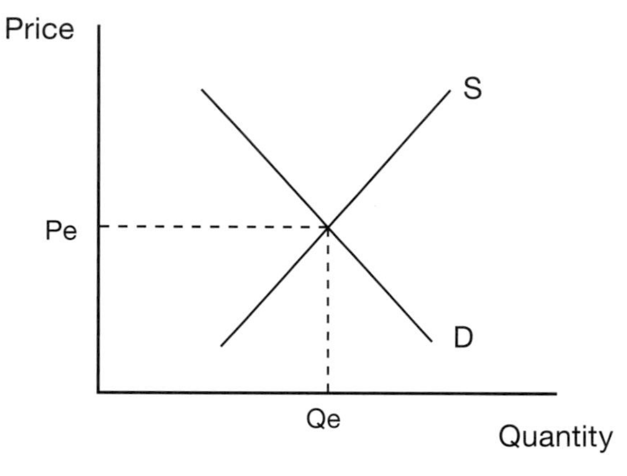

At price Pe, the amount producers are willing to supply is exactly equal to the amount consumers are willing to buy and therefore there is no tendency for the price to change.

DISEQUILIBRIUM

Disequilibrium occurs when there is a situation of excess demand, where quantity demanded is greater than the quantity supplied.

Disequilibrium also occurs when there is a situation of excess supply – quantity supplied is greater than quantity demanded.

1. EXCESS DEMAND

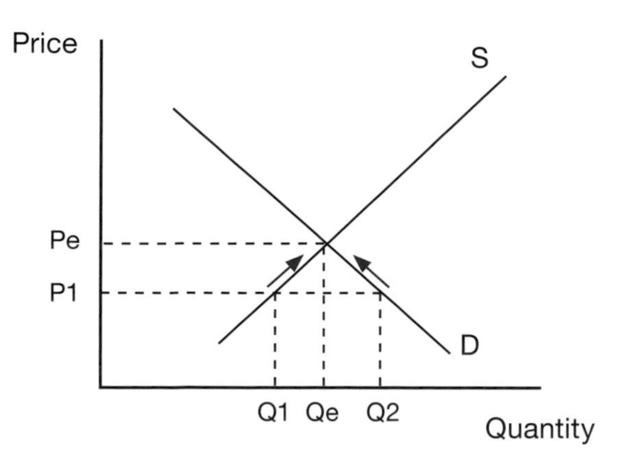

If a firm sets its price at P1 then the quantity that consumers are willing and able to buy would equal Q2, which is greater than the amount that producers are willing and able to supply Q1.

Therefore, there is a shortage of the good. When a shortage occurs, the price of the good would then be bid-up until the equilibrium price (Pe) is restored.

2. EXCESS SUPPLY

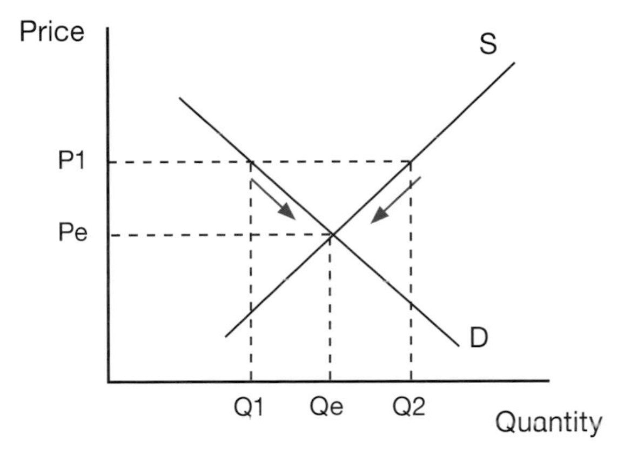

If a firm sets its price at P1 then the amount that producers are willing and able to supply increases to Q2, but the amount that consumers are willing and able to buy falls to Q1. Therefore, we have excess supply. In order to sell this excess supply the producer must reduce the price until the equilibrium price (Pe) is restored.

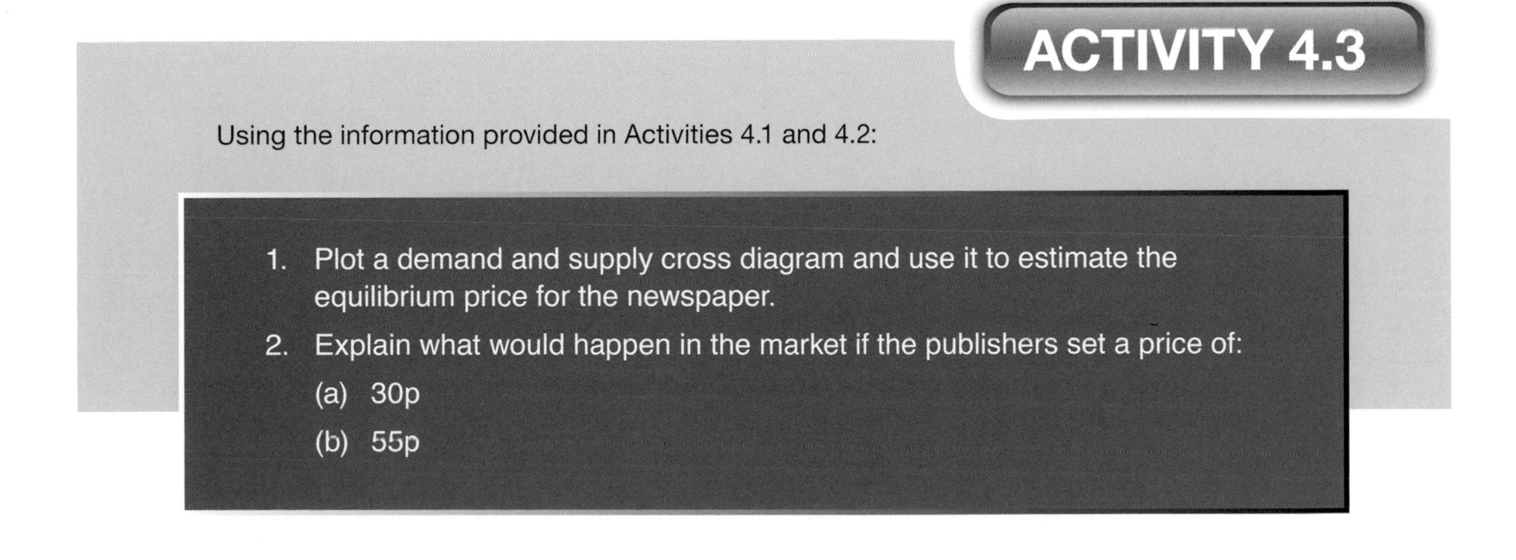

ACTIVITY 4.3

Using the information provided in Activities 4.1 and 4.2:

1. Plot a demand and supply cross diagram and use it to estimate the equilibrium price for the newspaper.
2. Explain what would happen in the market if the publishers set a price of:
   (a) 30p
   (b) 55p

THE CONDITIONS OF DEMAND

We have already seen how a change in the price of a good will cause a change in the quantity demanded of that good. As price increases, quantity demanded will fall and vice versa.

However, demand also depends on many factors other than price. These other factors are known as the **conditions of demand**.

A change in any one of the conditions of demand will cause the demand curve to shift.

If the demand curve shifts to the right this represents an increase in demand and if the demand curve shifts to the left this represents a decrease in demand.

1. INCOME

Income is a very important factor in determining the level of demand for a particular product or service.

For most goods, or what economists call **normal goods**, demand will increase as income increases. Consider the example of new cars; an increase in incomes will increase the demand for new cars and the demand curve will shift to the right as shown below. Therefore, more new cars will be demanded at every price level.

However, for some goods, or what economists call **inferior goods**, demand will fall when income rises. Consider the market for second-hand clothes; as incomes increase the demand for second hand clothes will fall and the demand curve will shift to the left.

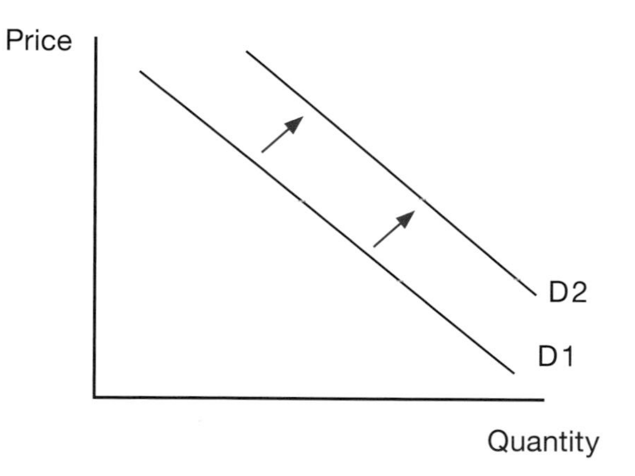

2. THE PRICE OF RELATED GOODS

Another important factor in determining the level of demand for a good or service is the price of other closely related goods and services.

(a) Complements

Sometimes two goods are demanded jointly, eg camera and film; economists refer to these goods as complements. When the price of **one** of these goods increases the demand for the other will fall.

(b) Substitutes

Sometimes goods are in competitive demand and can be used as substitutes for each other, eg Ariel and Persil. When the price of **one** of these goods increases the demand for the other is likely to increase. For example, an increase in the price of Persil will lead to an increase in the demand for Ariel as it now represents greater value for money relative to Persil.

3. TASTES AND FASHIONS

   Changes in tastes and fashions can have a huge impact on the demand for certain goods and services. When products become fashionable demand will increase; however, demand will fall if tastes change and the good becomes unfashionable. For example, the demand for flares has fluctuated greatly as tastes and fashions changed over the years.

4. ADVERTISING

   An effective advertising campaign can cause demand for a product to increase at every price level. This explains why firms spend such huge amounts of money in advertising and marketing their products.

5. GOVERNMENT POLICY

   Government policy is another important factor which influences the demand for a good or service. Changes to legislation can have huge effects on the demand for a good. Consider the likely impact of the introduction of the smoking ban in public places on the market for cigarettes (see case study overleaf).

   Changes to income tax and interest rates will also impact upon the demand for certain products. For example, if the Monetary Policy Committee (MPC) cut interest rates, the demand for housing and other goods bought on credit would be likely to increase.

6. POPULATION

   Another important factor influencing demand is population. As the population increases, the demand for most goods would increase. In addition, changes to the structure of the population can affect demand. For instance, an increase in the birth rate would lead to an increase in the demand for baby clothes.

7. EXPECTED PRICE CHANGES OR CHANGES IN EXPECTATIONS ABOUT FUTURE EVENTS

   If people believe that the price of oil, for example, is going to increase in the future they will increase their demand today.

   If you believe that the new coat that you want is going to be cheaper tomorrow when the sales start you may well wait until tomorrow before purchasing the coat.

   Similarly, businesses which use large quantities of a particular raw material may stockpile that raw material if they are worried that there might be a shortage in the future.

SHIFTS OF THE DEMAND CURVE

A change in any one of the conditions of demand will cause the demand curve to shift and will lead to a new equilibrium price and quantity. The diagram below shows an increase in demand.

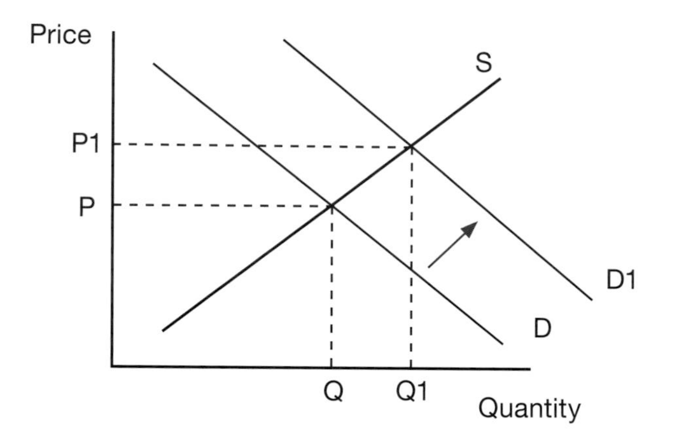

On the diagram above, an increase in demand has shifted the demand curve to the right and led to an increase in price and quantity demanded and supplied.

The increase in demand has caused an extension of supply, ie an increase in quantity supplied.

Similarly, a fall in demand will lead to a fall in the equilibrium price and a fall in quantity demanded and supplied.

CASE STUDY

TOBACCO FIRMS UNCONCERNED ABOUT IMPACT OF SMOKING BAN

The UK's main tobacco firms are remaining calm, in the face of the recent ban on smoking in public places, amid claims that all previous smoking bans have only caused a temporary fall in sales.

Tobacco industry analyst Andrew Darke of Evolution Securities points to the Republic of Ireland, which in March 2004 became the world's first country to ban smoking in all enclosed public places.

"The experience in places like Ireland is that immediately after the ban you see a 5 to 6% dip in sales, but then this soon wears off, and sales return to the normal 2 to 3% annual fall," says Mr Darke.

Official figures from the Republic of Ireland's Office of Tobacco Control seem to bear this out.

Its statistics show that the proportion of people in Ireland who smoked before the Irish ban started in March 2004 was about 26.5%, falling to just above 24% a year later, but then rising again to 25.5% in December 2005.

CASE STUDY...

The figures for the Republic of Ireland suggest that while many smokers initially quit, or at least cut down in order to avoid having to go outside for a cigarette, some soon learn to put up with this inconvenience.

"Smokers will continue to choose to smoke," says Simon Evans, spokesman for Imperial Tobacco, the best-selling tobacco company within the UK.

UK best selling cigarette brands:

1. Lambert & Butler (Imperial)
2. Benson & Hedges (Gallagher)
3. Marlboro Gold (Philip Morris)
4. Mayfair (Gallagher)
5. Richmond (Imperial)

(Figures for 2003. Source: Ash)

Perhaps unsurprisingly, anti-smoking group Ash – or Action on Smoking and Health – disagrees.

While it acknowledges that the Republic of Ireland has seen a partial rebound in smoking numbers, it says that a ban combined with health campaigns and other measures can lead to a real and lasting decline in cigarette consumption.

(Adapted from BBC News, 29 June 2007)

ACTIVITY 4.4

Explain, with the aid of a diagram, how the market would be affected in the following situations:

1. A rise in the demand for potato bread on the market for potatoes
2. A rise in train fares on bus and taxi services
3. A fall in interest rates on the market for housing
4. A fall in the price of tea on the market for coffee
5. A rise in the price of computers on the market for computers

THE CONDITIONS OF SUPPLY

We have already seen how a change in the price of a good will cause a change in the quantity supplied of that good, ie there will be a movement along the supply curve.

However, just like demand, supply also depends on factors other than price. These are known as the **conditions of supply.** A change in one of the conditions of supply will cause the supply curve to shift as shown below.

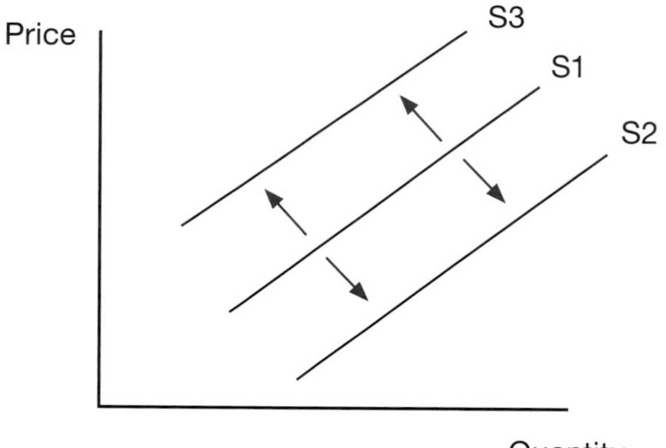

An increase in supply will shift the supply curve to the right from **S1** to **S2**. A decrease in supply on the other hand will shift the supply curve to the left from **S1** to **S3**.

Anything which increases the cost of production will reduce supply and therefore shift the supply curve to the left (S1 to S3).

Anything which decreases the cost of production will increase supply and shift the supply curve to the right (S1 to S2).

1. PRICE OF FACTORS OF PRODUCTION

One factor influencing the supply of a product is the price of the factors of production used in making that product. For example, an increase in the cost of raw materials or wages will cause the firm's costs to increase and will in turn cause the supply curve to shift to the left. In other words, an increase in the cost of raw materials and wages will cause a reduction in the supply.

2. PRODUCTIVITY OF FACTORS OF PRODUCTION

Changes in productivity rates will also have an influence on supply. If the firm is able to increase labour productivity it will shift the supply curve to the right. Similarly, a reduction in productivity rates caused by industrial action on behalf of the employees will reduce productivity and so the supply curve will shift to the left.

3. INDIRECT TAXES AND SUBSIDIES

Changes in government policy impact upon supply as well as demand. For example, if the government places an indirect tax such as VAT on a product it will shift the supply curve to the left. A subsidy, on the other hand, will reduce the cost of producing the good and would therefore shift the supply curve to the right.

4. TECHNOLOGICAL ADVANCES

Changes in the level of technology will also have an impact on the ability of a firm to supply goods onto a market. Technological advances such as the development of the internet and e-commerce will reduce the costs of supplying a good and the supply curve will shift to the right.

5. NATURAL FACTORS

The weather can play a very important role in the production of agricultural products in particular. For example, bad weather conditions and the resulting poor crop can cause the supply curve to shift to the left, which in turn will cause an increase in the price of the product (see case study below).

SHIFTS OF THE SUPPLY CURVE

A change in any one of the conditions of supply will cause the supply curve to shift and will lead to a new equilibrium price and quantity. The diagram below shows an increase in supply. An increase in supply will shift the supply curve to the right and lead to a reduction in the equilibrium price and an increase in the equilibrium quantity demanded and supplied as shown below:

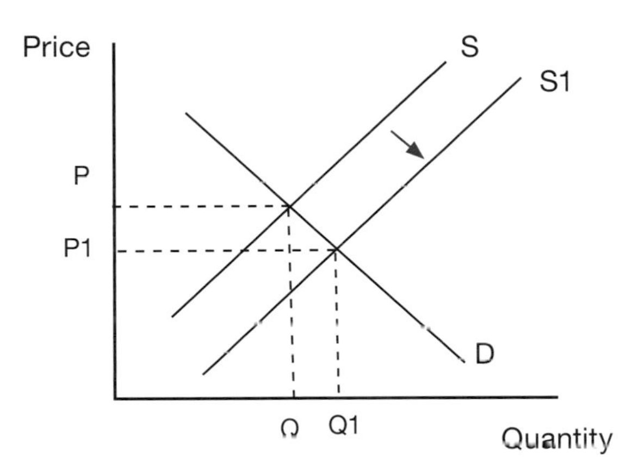

CASE STUDY

MILK COSTS HIT STILTON PRODUCERS

Cheese makers in the UK are struggling to keep prices down as a shortage of milk affects the dairy industry.

According to the Milk Development Council, the price of mild cheddar increased by £350 per tonne compared to June last year, unsalted butter prices were up £600 per tonne and bulk cream prices rose £390 per tonne.

These increases in price have all been caused by increases in the price of milk.

Milk prices at the farm gate in May were more than 4% higher than last year, according to the council.

The milk price increase is caused by a combination of factors, not least cost increases in the UK related to the recent spell of bad weather, a National Farmers' Union spokeswoman said.

The spokeswoman stated that "poor weather conditions force farmers to bring cattle inside which can increase feed costs and also results in lower yields".

However not everyone is upset by the higher prices, indeed the increase in milk prices has been welcomed by dairy farmers who hope to plough back some of the money into their businesses.

Dairy farmer Paul Egglestone of Long Clawson said: "These price rises are encouraging and hopefully they will allow reinvestment in dairying and encourage younger farmers into dairying in the UK."

(Adapted from BBC News, 18 July 2007)

ACTIVITY 4.5

Explain with the aid of a diagram how the market would be affected in the following situations:

1. A rise in the cost of steel on the market for new cars
2. An increase in subsidy given to Translink on the cost of train fares
3. A fall in the cost of timber on the market for new houses
4. A fall in the price of chocolate on the market for chocolate
5. An increase in VAT on the market for MP3 players

CHANGES TO DEMAND OR SUPPLY

When economists talk about an **increase in demand or supply** they mean that the demand curve or supply curve has shifted. If they talk about an **increase in quantity demanded or supplied** they mean there has been a movement along the demand or supply curve.

In the diagram on the previous page, there has been an increase in supply (the supply curve has shifted) and this has led to an increase in quantity demanded (a movement along the demand curve).

When explaining a diagram or a change in market conditions be careful not to confuse changes in demand with changes in quantity demanded, or changes in supply with changes in quantity supplied as they are very different things.

ACTIVITY 4.6

Using a diagram, explain how the following would affect the market for sugar:

1. Bad weather conditions
2. A fall in the price of fertiliser and sugar being seen as unhealthy
3. An increase in farm workers wages and an increase in income tax paid by consumers
4. A reduction in the subsidies paid to farmers through the common agricultural policy

ELASTICITY

As we have previously seen in this chapter, changes in price will cause changes in both quantity demanded and quantity supplied. For example, when the price increases we know that quantity demanded will fall and quantity supplied will rise.

However, firms would also be keen to know by exactly how much quantity demanded or supplied would be affected if the price changed. They can discover this information through using the concept of elasticity.

In an economic context, elasticity means **responsiveness**; it measures the responsiveness of one economic variable to a change in some other variable.

PRICE ELASTICITY OF DEMAND

Price elasticity of demand (PED) measures how responsive the quantity demanded is to a change in price. In other words, it tells us how important price is in determining whether or not consumers buy a product.

If demand is sensitive to price (ie when price increases, quantity demanded decreases by a large amount) then the demand is said to be price **elastic.**

If demand is not sensitive to price changes then the demand is said to be price **inelastic.**

PED is measured by using the following formula:

$$\frac{\textbf{\% CHANGE IN QUANTITY DEMANDED}}{\textbf{\% CHANGE IN PRICE}}$$

For example, if price increased from £20 to £25 and demand fell from 100 to 90 as a result, then the PED would be calculated as follows:

$$\textbf{\% change in Qd} = \frac{10}{100} \textbf{ multiplied by 100} = 10\%$$

$$\textbf{\% change in price} = \frac{5}{20} \textbf{ multiplied by 100} = 25\%$$

$$\textbf{PED} = \frac{10\%}{25\%} = 0.4$$

(Strictly speaking the answer should be –0.4 as quantity demanded fell as price rose. However, it is acceptable to omit the minus sign when calculating PED as the figure will always be negative.)

1. RELATIVELY INELASTIC

When demand is relatively inelastic it takes a large percentage change in price to cause a relatively small percentage change in quantity demanded. The numerical value will be between zero and one and the demand curve will be steeply sloping as shown below.

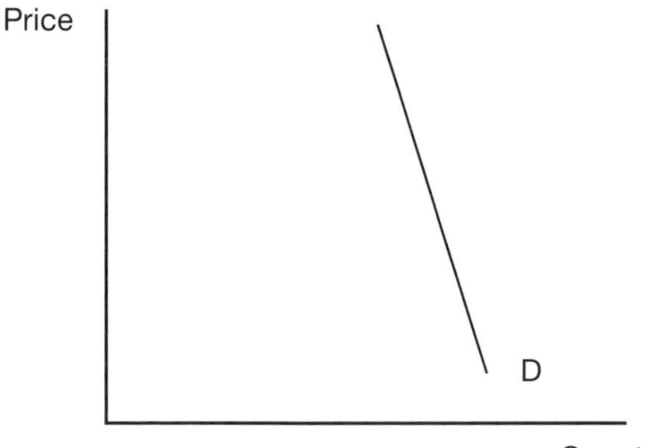

Relatively inelastic goods are normally addictive or have few substitutes, for example cigarettes. Therefore, when the price increases consumers continue to purchase these products.

2. RELATIVELY ELASTIC

In this case a small percentage change in price will lead to a relatively large percentage change in quantity demanded.

Relatively elastic goods normally have a large number of substitutes, and so when price increases consumers switch to the consumption of the substitute good.

The numerical value will be greater than one and the demand curve will be relatively flat as shown below.

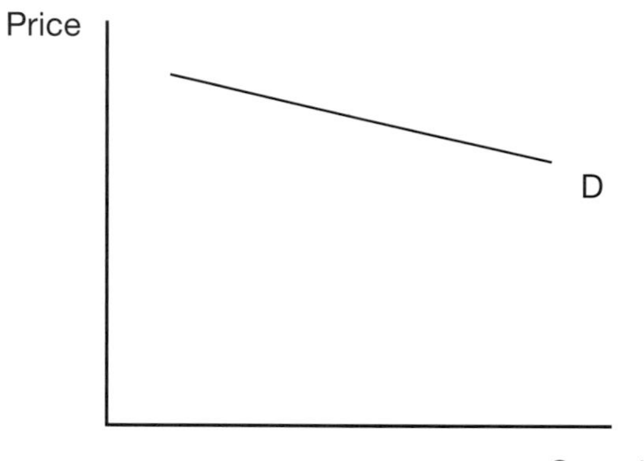

CALCULATING PRICE ELASTICITY OF DEMAND

Using the data in the table below calculate the price elasticity of demand for each example. The first one is done for you.

Good	Initial quantity	New quantity	% change in Qd	Initial price	New price	% change in P	PED	Elastic or Inelastic?
	800	600	25%	£4.00	£4.50	12.5%	2	Elastic
A	285	200		£1.50	£1.80			
B	674	890		£10.00	£8.00			
C	330	660		£12.00	£6.00			
D	870	450		£276	£345			

WHAT DETERMINES ELASTICITY OF DEMAND?

There are a number of factors which will influence whether the demand for a good is price elastic or price inelastic.

1. The degree of **necessity.** If a good is regarded as a necessity then people will continue to buy it even when price increases, and so demand will be price inelastic. For example, in modern developed societies such as the UK, electricity is regarded as being a necessity. If the price of electricity was to increase significantly, the quantity of electricity demanded would be likely to fall by a much lower proportion since individuals need electricity to run appliances such as televisions, fridges, microwaves, and computers.

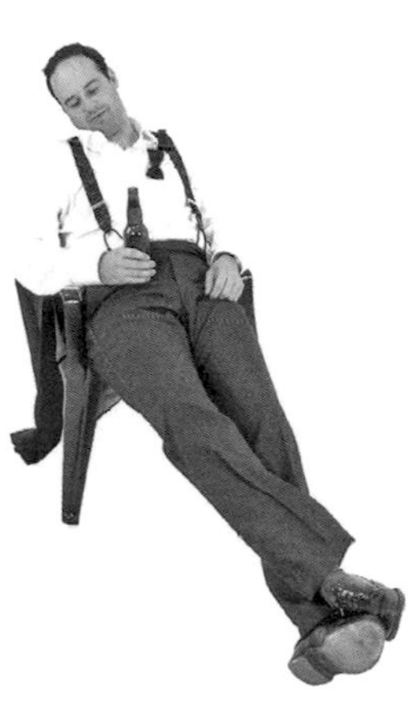

2. The **addictive** nature of the product. If goods are addictive or habit-forming then a large change in price will cause a very small change in quantity demanded and therefore the demand for goods will be price inelastic. For example, the demand for alcohol and drugs is likely to be inelastic since they are habit-forming and in some cases highly addictive.

3. The **availability of substitutes.** The greater the number of substitutes there are for a good, the more responsive demand will be to a change in price. Therefore, demand will be price elastic. For instance, the demand for package holidays is likely to be price elastic since there is a wide range of alternative package holidays on offer.

4. The **percentage of income which is spent on the good.**
If you spend a low percentage of your income on a good then you are unlikely to notice a large percentage change in price. For example, if a box of matches increased in price from 5p to 10p it is likely to have very little impact on sales even though price has increased by 100%.

5. The **time period** over which elasticity is measured. Demand tends to be more elastic over the long period. We can illustrate this point by looking at the market for oil. If oil prices increase, people who have oil central heating will still buy oil in the short term, as they need it, and so in the short run, demand is inelastic. However, if oil prices stay high then, over the longer term, these consumers may decide to switch their central heating systems to gas, and so in the long run, demand becomes more elastic.

WHY DO FIRMS CALCULATE PRICE ELASTICITY OF DEMAND?

If a firm is contemplating raising its price it would be useful to know whether this increase in price would lead to an increase in total revenue or a decrease.

If a firm has calculated its PED and knows that the demand for its product is price inelastic (PED<1) then the firm will be aware that an increase in price will lead to a smaller percentage change in quantity demanded and therefore total revenue will increase.

For example, if a firm has calculated its PED to be 0.5 then the firm will know that a 10% increase in its price would lead to a 5% decrease in quantity demanded and therefore total revenue would be higher after the price increase.

However, if the firm knows that the demand for its product is price elastic (PED>1) then it will know that an increase in price would lead to a larger percentage decrease in quantity demanded and therefore total revenue would decrease.

For instance, if the firm has calculated its PED to be 3 then it will know that if it increases price by 10% this increase would lead to a 30% decrease in quantity demanded and therefore total revenue would be lower after the price increase.

However, when PED is equal to 3 then the firm will also be aware that a 10% **reduction** in price would lead to a 30% **increase** in quantity demanded, which would in turn lead to an increase in total revenue.

SUMMARY

If a firm calculates that the demand for its product is price **inelastic**, then the firm should **increase** price to **increase** total revenue.

On the other hand, if the firm calculates that the demand for its product is price elastic then the firm should decrease price to increase total revenue.

Firms will find it useful to have knowledge of price elasticity of demand. However, its usefulness should not be overstated. There are a number of potential problems with the values calculated.

Often the estimated values for PED are calculated using past data. But just because a 10% fall in price brought about a 20% increase in quantity demanded in the past does not mean that a further 10% decrease in price will bring about a further 20% increase in quantity demanded. It must always be remembered that past performance can be a very poor indicator of future performance.

In addition, not all goods have a set price. Some goods, for example tea and sugar, are sold to consumers at different prices from different outlets, so when measuring PED how do we measure the change in price? Do we take an average price? If so, then this will surely affect the accuracy of the figure.

Finally, when calculating PED we use an assumption known as 'ceteris paribus', which means *'all other things remain unchanged'*. Therefore, if we calculate PED = 4, we make the claim that a 10% increase in price brought about a 40% decrease in quantity demanded.

However, in reality, the 40% decrease in quantity demanded may have occurred for reasons other than the increase in price, for example bad publicity about the product, a decrease in the income of consumers or a range of other factors.

For this reason, using PED estimates to make predictions about what might happen in the future is fraught with difficulties.

Despite these problems however, if used with caution and in conjunction with a range of other data, estimates of elasticity can prove to be very useful to firms.

THE NORTHERN IRELAND HOUSING MARKET

There has been a massive increase in house prices in the UK and Northern Ireland in recent years. Prices have grown on average by about 15% per year and the average house price in Northern Ireland is now over £200,000.

This increase in the price of houses is a result of both demand and supply-side factors.

DEMAND-SIDE FACTORS

1. There has been an increase in the population of house-buying age. This is the result of a number of factors, including high levels of immigration, and an unusually high birth rate in the 1970s and 1980s.

CASE STUDY...

2. There has also been an increase in the divorce rate, resulting in families needing more than one house.
3. There has been a significant increase in average incomes in Northern Ireland. Average earnings and incomes have grown quite rapidly in Northern Ireland in recent years. This increase in incomes has led to a large increase in the demand for housing as houses are an income-elastic good.
4. Societal changes have led to an increased independence of both the young and the old.
5. Although interest rates have been increasing over the last 18 months they are still very low in historical terms. This affects the demand for housing as houses are bought with credit.
6. The peace process has also led to an increase in demand for houses from speculators, particularly from the Republic of Ireland.

   Household incomes in the Republic of Ireland have increased substantially in recent years and this has led to citizens of the Republic of Ireland looking for investment opportunities in the North.

All of the above have shifted the demand curve for housing to the right.

At the same time the supply of housing for sale has not increased by the same quantity.

Housing supply is relatively **inelastic,** even in the long run, because of a lack of available building land and planning restrictions, which limit the number of houses that can be built.

This is especially true in and around Belfast, which has experienced some of the largest increases in prices.

The combination of these two factors has led to the huge increase in house prices as illustrated below:

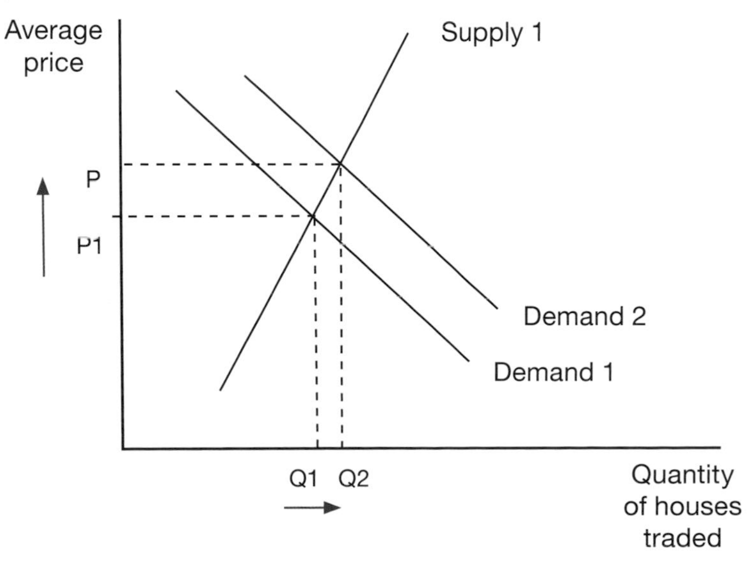

The diagram above shows the effect of an increase in demand on the price of housing. Because the supply of housing is relatively inelastic, any increase in demand is likely to lead to a large increase in price.

ACTIVITY 4.8

CADBURY WANTS TO BLITZ WRIGLEY WITH A NEW GUM CALLED TRIDENT

Cadbury Schweppes, the world's largest confectionery group, is to challenge the dominance of Wrigley's in the UK chewing gum market with the launch next year of its American brand, Trident.

The move, announced yesterday by Todd Stitzer, its chief executive, at an investor seminar, is part of Cadbury's wider efforts to focus its marketing activities on a smaller number of the group's stronger brands. The Cadbury's boss also told investors that the group, which is under pressure from rising production costs, was to abandon its long-standing targets for annual margin growth of between 0.5 and 0.75 of a percentage point.

Mr Stitzer also said that the group would adopt a dividend payment policy more in line with earnings. For the current year, the final dividend is likely to be increased by 10%, taking the total to 9.9p and leaving the annual rate of increase at 8%.

The British gum market has been shrinking over the last two years, but Wrigley's, the dominant firm in the market with a 98% share, insists it is confident it can fend off a competitor such as Cadbury without having to resort to a price war. "We believe Cadbury will be a solid competitor, but we know how to hold on to our market position," said Gharry Eccles, UK managing director of Wrigley's. The company is also market leader in the US market, where it sells twice as much gum as Cadbury brands.

Four years ago Cadbury had tried to take on Wrigley's dominance of the UK, its home market, with the launch of Trebor 24/7, a gum variant of the mint-flavoured sweet brand. The product flopped and was ditched within 18 months. Since then, however, Cadbury has acquired US gum specialist Adams, which brought with it the fast-growing Trident brand, the number two gum in the world behind Wrigley's Orbit. The Cadbury's gum stable also includes Dentyne, Bubblicious and Clorets.

Mr Stitzer noted that the UK gum market had shrunk by 6% last year and 5% in 2004. "The British chewing gum market is going backwards and needs competition to drive the market," he said. Cadbury's hopes its strong UK distribution network will help it mount a more serious challenge to Wrigley's this time.

Simon Baldry, Cadbury Trebor Bassett's managing director, said: "We see massive potential in the UK for Trident. [The UK] is one of the top 10 gum markets in the world."

Last week Cadbury blamed the hot summer for a weaker-than-expected confectionery market. Sales since the beginning of July fell by 5% compared with the same period in 2005.

Asked whether trends toward healthier eating were having an impact on sales, Mr Stitzer said: "Despite obesity scares, the global confectionery market still grows at 4% to 5% a year, while less than 2% of a British person's diet is confectionery."

ACTIVITY 4.8

(Adapted from The Guardian, October 2006)

1. Identify the market in which Cadbury Schweppes operates.
2. Using a demand and supply diagram, explain what impact rising production costs are likely to have on the market for chewing gum.
3. Explain why producers like Wrigley's produce more than one brand of chewing gum.
4. Explain how a hot summer could be blamed for weaker-than-expected confectionery sales.
4. Using demand and supply analysis, explain the impact concerns over obesity are likely to have on the UK confectionery market.
6. How might a company like Cadbury react to this change in market conditions?
7. Explain what is meant by the term 'Price Elasticity of Demand' (PED).
8. Explain why knowing the PED of its products would be useful to Cadbury Schweppes when making pricing decisions.

KNOWLEDGE REVIEW

- **DEMAND** is defined as the quantity of a good or service that a consumer is willing and able to buy at a given price in a given time period.
- **SUPPLY** is defined as the quantity of a good or service that producers are willing and able to supply onto a market at a given price in a given time period.
- **SUBSTITUTES** are goods which are in competitive demand and can be used in place of one another, eg Daz and Ariel
- **INFERIOR GOODS** are goods which are affected by a fall in demand due to an increase in incomes, eg second hand clothes.
- **COMPLEMENTS** are goods which are in joint demand and are used alongside one another, eg camera and film.
- **PRICE ELASTICITY OF DEMAND** measures how responsive the quantity demanded is to a change in price.

Chapter 5:

MARKET STRUCTURE AND THE DEGREE OF COMPETITION

In the previous chapter, we looked at how the demand for, and the supply of, a product interact to determine the equilibrium or market clearing price.

In this chapter, we will examine how the structure of the market in which the firm operates influences the power the firm has to determine the price of its goods and services.

The way in which a firm behaves and the strategies it adopts to achieve its objectives will very much depend upon the nature of the market in which it operates, and the level of competition it faces.

Taking account of the nature of the market, and the level of competition faced by a firm, is very important whenever a producer is contemplating a change in price or indeed any change to its **marketing mix** (more about this in chapters 8 and 9).

Economists single out a number of key characteristics, which will have a huge influence on the way individual firms behave. These characteristics determine the structure of the market and include:

1. The number of firms in the industry and their relative size
2. The extent to which the products produced by individual firms are similar
3. The ease or difficulty with which new firms can enter or leave the industry
4. The extent to which firms in the industry have the ability to earn abnormal or supernormal profits

We are going to look at four different market structures:

1. **PERFECT COMPETITION**
   A perfectly competitive market is characterised by a large number of small firms which produce goods, which are identical. There are no barriers to entry and supernormal profits can only be made in the short run.

2. **COMPETITIVE MARKET (MONOPOLISTIC COMPETITION)**
   A competitive market is characterised by a **relatively** large number of small firms which produce similar (but not identical) products. There are no barriers to entry and supernormal profits can only be made in the short run.

3. **OLIGOPOLY**
   In oligopoly there are several large firms who sell similar products. There are some barriers to entry and supernormal profits can be made in the long run.

4. **MONOPOLY**
   A monopoly is one large firm which produces all the output in the industry. Barriers to entry exist, which prevent other firms entering the industry. Supernormal profits can be made in the long run.

BARRIERS TO ENTRY

One of the most important factors in determining the structure of a market, and therefore the conduct and behaviour of firms in that market, is the ease with which firms can enter or leave the industry. If firms find it difficult to enter an industry, then we would say that 'barriers to entry' exist.

Barriers to entry are those characteristics of an industry, which prevent potential competitors from entering an industry.

Barriers to entry include:

1. GOVERNMENT RESTRICTIONS

Firms sometimes find it very difficult to enter a particular industry because it is illegal to do so without a government licence. For example, a government licence is required before a firm can engage in radio broadcasting, or the sale of alcohol. This therefore acts as a barrier to entry.

A patent is another example of a barrier to entry since it gives the firm which owns it the sole right to produce a product for a given period of time.

2. ADVERTISING

In some industries, firms spend huge amounts on advertising in an attempt to deter possible entrants. If new firms wish to compete with the more established businesses they will have to spend similar amounts on advertising. However, this level of spending is often beyond the means of most small firms.

3. SUNK COSTS

In certain circumstances it can be very difficult to leave an industry whenever things go wrong. If firms know that they will find it difficult to leave an industry when they are experiencing difficult trading conditions they may be reluctant to enter the industry in the first place. For example, in some industries a large amount of capital has to be invested, which is not recoverable if things go wrong; these unrecoverable costs are known as sunk costs. Therefore, firms may be reluctant to enter an industry that requires these sunk costs.

Barriers to entry are the key factor in determining whether firms can earn supernormal profits in the long run. If barriers to entry exist in an industry then the firm will have the ability to earn long-run supernormal profits. If, however, there are no barriers to entry then the firm might be able to make supernormal profits in the short run but will be unable to earn supernormal profits in the long run.

CASE STUDY

NORTHERN IRELAND LIQUOR LICENSING UNDER REVIEW

Under current liquor licensing law, the granting of a new public house or off-sales liquor licence in Northern Ireland is conditional on the surrender to the court of an existing licence. This provision exists nowhere else in the UK and is unique to the island of Ireland and indeed to the licensed trade. This surrender principle has generated a lucrative trade in licences in Northern Ireland with the average licence selling for about £140,000.

CASE STUDY...

Among interested parties, opinion is divided on the subject of surrender. To many, its continued existence constitutes a barrier to entry into the market and stands as an anti-competitive mechanism amidst an ever-increasing tide of market liberalisation measures occurring at local, national and international levels.

They believe that if the surrender principle was abolished and licences were granted on the basis of need, then competition in the pub trade would increase, which would result in a better deal for consumers.

Conversely, many of those in the licensed trade support the surrender principle as they believe that it protects Northern Ireland from the overprovision of alcohol which they feel exists in Great Britain. They argue that abolishing the surrender principle would lead to an increase in the number of outlets selling alcohol and in turn lead to greater problems of alcohol abuse and under-age drinking.

SUPERNORMAL PROFITS

Supernormal profits are defined by economists as any profit over and above the minimum required to keep an entrepreneur producing in that industry. Supernormal profits are profits which exceed what an entrepreneur would normally be expected to earn through the employment of a similar combination of factors of production elsewhere.

In 2005 the international banking corporation HSBC reported an operating profit of £11.5bn, which represents a profit of approximately £22,000 per minute.

In 2006 the oil exploration company Shell reported a second quarter profit of £3.7bn, which is equivalent to approximately £28,000 per minute.

For many people these profits could be described as excessive and there were calls in the national press for government action to curb the supernormal profits of these companies, with some economists calling for a windfall tax on the profits of banks and oil companies.

However, both companies claimed that these huge profits were a result of sound business practice and were therefore not excessive. Indeed, the CEO of one of the UK's other major banks is reported to have stated that he "did not know what supernormal profits were and that no level of company profit could be described as excessive".

HOW DO WE DETERMINE IF PROFITS ARE NORMAL OR SUPERNORMAL?

To determine if supernormal profits are being earned by a firm, economists could compare the firm's profits with other firms in the same industry. However, if all firms in the industry are making supernormal profits then this comparison will reveal very little.

Another approach is to compare the firm's profits with those of similar-sized firms in other industries. The problem with this comparison however, is that it does not allow for differences in management efficiency or market conditions.

Therefore, we can see that trying to determine the level at which profits can be considered supernormal is fraught with difficulty and is open to individual interpretation.

MARKET STRUCTURES

As stated earlier, the term market structure refers to the characteristics of a market, which determines a firm's conduct and behaviour. We will now look at the four main market structures in more detail.

PERFECT COMPETITION

A market is said to be perfectly competitive when individually buyers and sellers believe that their own actions will have no influence on the market price.

Perfectly competitive markets rarely exist in the real world; however **agriculture, market gardening** and the **foreign exchange markets** are good examples of markets which closely resemble perfect competition.

CHARACTERISTICS OF A PERFECTLY COMPETITIVE MARKET

1. In perfectly competitive markets there is **a large number** of buyers and sellers who buy and sell such a small amount that they cannot affect market demand or supply.
2. All firms in perfectly competitive markets produce **homogeneous** or identical products.
3. In perfectly competitive markets there is **perfect knowledge** of market conditions for both buyers and sellers. What this means is that all buyers and sellers know everything about all products in the market at all times and therefore will always make the best decisions regarding production and purchase.
4. In perfectly competitive markets there are **no barriers to entry;** this means that firms are free to enter and leave the industry as they wish.

As a result of these characteristics, the perfectly competitive firm will be a **price-taker**.

This means that firms in perfect competition have no control over the price they charge for their output. They must accept the market price as determined by the forces of demand and supply in the market and sell all of their output at this market price.

WHAT HAPPENS IF THE FIRM CHARGES ABOVE THE MARKET PRICE?

It will lose all its custom since consumers have perfect knowledge of prices elsewhere and will simply shift their demand to those firms who are charging the market price. In addition, because the firm is such a small part of the overall industry it will have no incentive to lower its price since it knows that it can sell all its output at the market price. In other words, it will exhibit a perfectly elastic demand curve.

PROFITS IN PERFECTLY COMPETITIVE MARKETS

Firms which operate in perfectly competitive markets are able to make supernormal profits in the short run. However, due to the fact that there is perfect knowledge in the industry, other firms will see that this firm is making supernormal profits. Since there are **no barriers to entry**, other firms will enter the industry and produce the same product until only normal profits are made by every firm. Therefore, in the long run, firms in perfect competition are only able to make normal profits.

ACTIVITY 5.1

DAIRY FARMING: A PERFECTLY COMPETITIVE MARKET?

Milk is a product we all take for granted. Almost every household in Northern Ireland buys milk on a regular basis, but how many of us ever consider how the product is produced and sold?

Most people in Northern Ireland buy milk that is either full cream or semi-skimmed. An increasing number of people now buy their milk in four-pint plastic bottles in supermarkets when they do their weekly shopping, with a decreasing amount of milk being delivered to the doorstep by milkmen.

The price of a pint of milk has not changed significantly in the last 10 years even though the demand for milk is relatively price inelastic over a certain price range. The price that the dairy farm receives is only a fraction of the actual price paid by consumers. A pint of milk typically costs the consumer about 40 pence whereas the dairy farm receives only eight pence per litre.

Table 1. Number and size of dairy farms in Northern Ireland 1993–2003	1993	2003
Total Number of Dairy Farms	6,179	4,742
Total Number of Dairy Cows '000	273	291
Average Herd Size	44	61
Average Milk Yield Per Individual Cow	4,930	6,290

1. Use the information in the last sentence to calculate what percentage of the price of a pint of milk is received by dairy farmers.
2. Explain what is meant by the statement "the demand for milk is relatively price inelastic over a certain price range".
3. What characteristics of a perfectly competitive market does the dairy farming industry possess?
4. How much influence would an individual dairy farm have on the price it charges for its milk?

COMPETITIVE MARKETS

A competitive market is defined as 'the market structure where there are a relatively large number of firms offering similar but differentiated products'.

Competitive markets have characteristics that are similar to perfect competition and some which are common to monopoly. The competitive market model is a more realistic model of the behaviour of firms in the real world and examples of competitive industries include:

1. Pubs and clubs and hotels in a city centre
2. Chip shops
3. Clothes shops and shoe shops
4. Estate agents
5. Local builders/plumbers

CHARACTERISTICS OF A COMPETITIVE MARKET

1. In a competitive market there is a **relatively** large number of buyers and sellers.
2. The firms in a competitive market sell **differentiated** products, ie the goods are not perfect substitutes for each other, but are differentiated through branding. The closer the products are, the more elastic the demand curve.
3. In competitive markets there is freedom of entry and exit into and out of the market. In other words, there are **no barriers to entry**. Since there are no barriers to entry, the firm will only be able to make normal profits in the long run.
4. There is imperfect information on behalf of buyer and sellers. Imagine the difficulty involved in trying to determine the price, quality and reliability of every plumber in the Yellow Pages.

Since firms in competitive markets produce products that are slightly different from those of their competitors, then they will have a certain amount of market power and so will have some influence over the price at which they sell their products.

Firms in competitive markets will not be price-takers, because they do have some market power. Yet because there is a large number of firms producing similar products, this market power will be small. Therefore, the demand curve facing the firm will be relatively **elastic**.

PROFITS IN COMPETITIVE MARKETS

In the short run it is possible for the competitive firm to make supernormal profits. However, since there are no barriers to entry, new firms will enter the industry until only normal profits are made by each firm.

When new firms enter the industry they increase the supply of similar products, and this decreases the demand for each individual firm's products. Therefore, the demand curve for each individual firm shifts inwards. In addition, because there are now more firms producing similar products the firm's demand curve becomes more elastic.

This increase in the supply of similar products puts downward pressure on prices until eventually only normal profits are made by each firm.

ACTIVITY 5.2

THE BELFAST HOTEL MARKET

A simple search on the internet for hotels in Belfast produces a result which lists over 50 hotels in the Belfast area. Some of these hotels are owned by large hotel groups and have accommodation for up to 200 people with a number of bars and restaurants available on site.

Conversely, many of the hotels are smaller family-owned businesses with only a few rooms and limited entertainment.

The hotel industry is thriving at the moment with tens of thousands of visitors staying in Belfast each year and accommodation rates in excess of 60%.

1. Explain how one hotel might differentiate its product from that of its rivals.
2. What characteristics of a competitive market does the hotel industry possess?
3. Explain what would be likely to happen in the hotel industry if many of the hotels in Belfast were making large profits.

KNOWLEDGE REVIEW

- **BARRIERS TO ENTRY** are those characteristics of an industry, which prevent potential competitors from entering an industry. Examples include government restrictions and sunk costs.

- **SUPERNORMAL PROFIT** is any profit over and above the minimum required to keep an entrepreneur producing in that industry.

- **PERFECT COMPETITION** is the market structure where there is a large number of small firms selling identical products. There are no barriers to entry and the firm can only make normal profits in the long run. Examples include agriculture and the FOREX markets.

- **A COMPETITIVE MARKET** is the market structure where there is a relatively large number of firms offering similar but differentiated products. Again there are no barriers to entry and therefore the firm can only make normal profits in the long run. Examples include estate-agents and shoe shops.

ACTIVITY 5.3

MCDONALD'S FACING COMPETITION

Fast-food chain McDonald's is closing 25 branches in a bid to improve profits at its struggling UK operations.

The closures were listed in McDonald's annual accounts, which showed that poor British sales were dragging down its profits.

This reduction in profits has caused the company's share price to collapse from a high of $48 in 1999 to just over $12 today (2004).

In the accounts, the firm said its UK stores were "experiencing a highly competitive informal eating-out market and low consumer confidence levels".

A source close to McDonald's stated that profits had been severely hit in the UK as a result of concerns about health, greater price competition from other fast food restaurants and the entrance into the market of gourmet sandwich stores.

Others in the industry suggest that McDonald's decline is a result of it becoming too big and becoming less customer-focused. One industry insider stated that "McDonald's problems are of its own making, it has allowed its image and brand to become dated and as a result people are switching to cooler more hip restaurants, which sell more exotic foods".

However, the company is not giving up. McDonald's chief executive Ralph Alvarez, stated recently, "the world has changed; our customers have changed; we need to change too".

The plan to reverse the trend of falling sales includes:

Cutting costs by reducing the number of new restaurants opened from an average of 1700 per year to around 350. This will slash capital spending and the money saved can be used to reduce the company's debt burden.

Action will also be taken to improve management and staff productivity through monitoring standards – something which has been avoided in the past to prevent trouble with franchisees.

The image of the restaurants is to be improved through the introduction of a quality control system to ensure cleanliness and customer service standards are being maintained.

The menu is also to be slimmed down with a greater emphasis on healthy products such as salads and sliced fruit.

And finally the advertising focus is to get an overhaul with a greater emphasis on young adults.

1. Using the information in paragraph 3 calculate the percentage change in share price between 1999 and 2004. (4)
2. Analyse three reasons why sales and profits at McDonald's have declined in recent years. (9)
3. Explain why a fall in profits would also cause a fall in the share price of McDonald's. (4)
4. The article refers to McDonald's franchisees. Explain what is meant by the term 'franchisee'. (4)
5. What evidence does the article provide which suggests that McDonald's is operating in a competitive market? (4)
6. McDonald's have an ambitious plan to reverse the decline in sales and profits. Critically evaluate the strategies outlined in the plan. (15)

OLIGOPOLY

An oligopolistic market is defined as 'the market structure where the supply of a good or service is dominated by a few producers each of whom has some control over the market'. Oligopoly is often simply referred to as **'competition among the few'.**

The Competition Commission define an oligopolistic industry 'as the market structure where the top four firms have more than 60% of the market'.

Oligopolistic markets are quite common in reality and examples include:

1. Petrol retailing and production, eg BP, Shell, ExxonMobil
2. The chemical industry
3. The telecommunications industry, eg BT, NTL
4. The Northern Ireland banking market: Ulster Bank, First Trust, Bank of Ireland and the Northern Bank.

CHARACTERISTICS OF AN OLIGOPOLISTIC MARKET

1. In oligopolistic markets, supply must be concentrated in the hands of relatively **few** firms.
2. In oligopoly, firms produce similar products, which are **differentiated** through branding.
3. In oligopolistic markets, **barriers to entry** exist and so firms will be able to continue making supernormal profits in the long run.
4. There is **imperfect knowledge** in the industry. Again, consider trying to determine the rates of interest paid and the fees charged for all the different financial products offered by the four main banks in Northern Ireland.

Since firms in oligopolistic markets produce products that are differentiated from those of their competitors, they will have a certain amount of market power. Consequently, they will have some influence over the price at which they sell their products.

Since they have some market power, firms in oligopolistic markets will not be price-takers. However, because there are other firms producing similar products, this market power will be limited. How much market power an oligopolistic firm has will depend on how successful it is at convincing the consumer that its product or service is different from that of its rivals.

PROFITS IN OLIGOPOLISTIC MARKETS

In oligopolistic markets firms are able to continue making supernormal profits over a long period because there are barriers to entry into the industry. It is often the case that if one firm in an oligopolistic market is making supernormal profits, entrepreneurs may see this and attempt to enter the industry in an attempt to gain some of the available profit. However, because barriers to entry exist in the industry they are unable to do so, and thus the oligopolistic firm can continue to make these supernormal profits in the long run.

THE MUSIC INDUSTRY

The market for the recording, sale and distribution of popular music is becoming increasingly concentrated as a result of a number of high-profile mergers and takeovers in the last five years.

Although there are many thousands of small independent record labels in the UK, the market could still be described as oligopolistic.

The vast majority of successful recording artists have deals with the five main music companies and many of the so-called independent labels have commercial ties with the big five.

The chart below shows the market share enjoyed by the main recording companies in the UK.

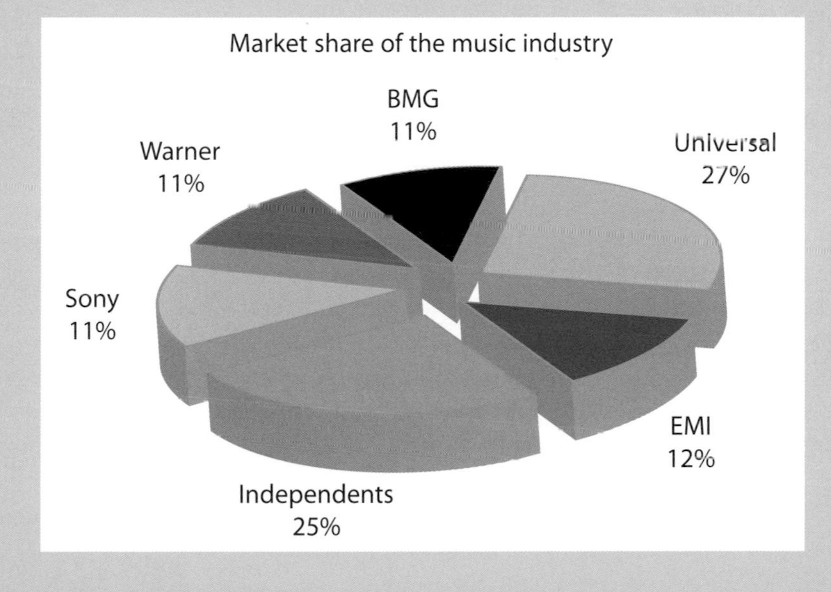

1. Explain what is meant by the term 'Oligopoly'.
2. What characteristics of an oligopolistic market does the music industry possess?
3. Why might further concentration in the UK music industry be bad for consumers?

COMPETITION IN OLIGOPOLISTIC MARKETS

Studies of oligopolistic markets have shown that prices are often very stable and tend not to change significantly even when demand or supply conditions change.

Consider the music industry, where the price of a CD has not changed significantly over the last ten years even though production costs have fallen and demand has fallen as a result of the growth of the MP3 market.

One possible reason for price stability in oligopolistic markets is that there might be an accepted price leader in the industry or what economists call a **barometric leader**. Any price changes in the industry would be initiated by the leader, and then other firms would follow suit.

There is evidence of price leadership in many industries, where smaller firms wait for the larger firms to initiate a price change and then they take similar action.

Another possible explanation of the relative price stability in oligopoly is that oligopolistic firms might reach a collusive agreement. A collusive agreement (or collusion) occurs when rival firms agree to set a common price or common conditions of sale in an attempt to manage the level of competition in a market.

Collusion is illegal in the UK and in the EU; however it is very difficult to prove.

PRICE WARS

Whilst prices in oligopolistic markets often appear to be stable, at other times they can be highly unstable.

Sometimes firms in these markets engage in **price wars** (when one firm cuts prices low in an attempt to destroy its rivals and gain their market share). This is a common strategy when demand for the product or service is falling.

For example, in the mid 1990s the Mirror newspaper initiated a price war with the other tabloids in an attempt to increase its market share. It initially cut its price from 38p to 20p, but the Sun newspaper soon followed suit, cutting its price to 20p as well. As a result both papers lost money and the Mirror was forced to increase its price back to its original level.

CASE STUDY

CARPHONE WAREHOUSE LAUNCHES NET PRICE WAR

Carphone Warehouse has launched a calls and internet service which it claims will cut residential phone bills by 60%.

Customers using the phone operator's TalkTalk service will be able to make unlimited local and national calls from their home phone for £20.99 a month.

The package includes a broadband internet connection and unlimited calls to 28 countries.

A spokesman for Carphone Warehouse said the company expects to make a loss of £50m on the business this year, but hopes to make a £40m profit after two years.

By then the firm also plans to have paid off the start-up costs for the service, estimated at £110m.

Analysts predict the latest offer could spark a price war between UK telecoms providers and described it as a "land-grab" on the broadband market, increasing the pressure on BT to follow suit.

However Richard Ireland, head of telecom for Ernst & Young, warned that the price-cutting strategy is a risky one and that "price wars do not always work in favour of the cheapest players".

(Source: Adapted from BBC News, 11 April 2006)

NON-PRICE COMPETITION

The existence of price wars is evidence of competition in oligopolistic markets. However, even when prices are stable, this does not mean that there is no competition. Non-price competition between firms in oligopoly is often intense.

Non-price competition refers to all forms of competition other than through the price mechanism.

Examples of non-price competition include: branding; advertising; product placement; product endorsement; free gifts and promotions.

Giving 50% extra free does not qualify as an example of non-price competition, since the consumer is getting more for the same price and so the average price of the product is reduced.

WHY DO FIRMS USE NON-PRICE COMPETITION?

One reason for using non-price competition is that firms find that their cost structures are very similar and that there is little scope to compete on the basis of price.

For example, if you consider the costs faced by sports retailers like JD Sports and JJB Sports. Both sell a similar range of branded goods, both have stores in towns and cities, and wages and other running costs are likely to be similar for both firms.

Such firms tend to avoid price competition because they fear it may lead to price wars. So they tend to keep prices unchanged and compete in other ways.

In some cases firms simply believe that consumers are more sensitive to changes in style or quality rather than changes in price. This is typical in the clothing industry, so clothes retailers tend to compete in these areas, rather than on price.

MONOPOLY

A monopolistic market is defined as the market structure where there is a single seller of a good or service which has no close substitute.

In Northern Ireland the electricity company NIE could be described as being a monopoly in that it is the only company in Northern Ireland with a licence to generate and supply electricity.

This pure monopoly, as defined above, is actually very rare in reality, as most firms will face some competition. However, this does not mean that monopolies do not exist; in Northern Ireland there is a number of firms that produce almost all of the output in their industry and therefore they should still be considered monopolies.

If one large firm dominates an industry then it can still be regarded by economists as being a monopoly even if it faces competition from other firms. This is because it will still have significant monopoly power.

The Competition Commission defines a monopoly as “any firm having more than 25% market share”. Using this definition, the supermarket chain Tesco could be described as a monopoly since it has a 29% share of the UK grocery market.

The Competition Commission also has a stronger definition for a firm which dominates an industry. They define a **dominant firm** as “any firm having more than 40% market share”. Microsoft would be described as being a dominant firm since it has 90% share of the UK computer operating systems market.

CHARACTERISTICS OF A MONOPOLISTIC MARKET

1. In a monopolistic market there is only **one firm** that sells all the output in the industry.
2. In a monopolistic market the product or service is **unique** to the monopolist and has no close substitutes with which to compare it.
3. In monopolistic markets **barriers to entry** exist, which keep would-be competitors from entering the market. Consequently, monopolistic firms will be able to make supernormal profits in the long run.

These characteristics mean that the monopolist will have a significant amount of market power and will therefore be able to set the price at which its products are sold. For this reason monopolists are often referred to as **price-makers**.

However, it should be remembered that the power of the monopolist is not absolute since it is still constrained by the demand curve. In other words, if the monopolist decides to increase its price it must be willing to accept that there will be a reduction in the quantity demanded.

PROFITS IN MONOPOLISTIC MARKETS

In monopolistic markets barriers to entry exist and therefore the firm will be able to continue making supernormal profits in the long run. If the monopolistic firm is making supernormal profits, entrepreneurs may see these profits and attempt to enter the industry in an attempt to gain some of the available profit. However, due to the fact that barriers to entry exist in the industry they are unable to do so, and thus the monopolistic firm can continue to make these supernormal profits in the long term.

ACTIVITY 5.5

THE MARKET FOR COMPUTERS

The computer market is often quoted as a good example of a monopolistic market. Monopolies are said to exist in both the manufacture of computers and in the market for computer software.

In the computer hardware market, Dell is the preferred choice of the Northern Ireland consumer and in the software market, research has shown that Microsoft is the largest company, with its Windows operating system being used on over 80% of Northern Ireland's computers.

The table below gives the market share of the major computer manufacturers.

Computer manufacturer	Market share (2006)
Dell	31%
HP	19%
IBM	6%
Apple	6%
Others	38%

ACTIVITY 5.5

1. Using the information in the table opposite, state which firm could be described as having a monopoly in the manufacture of computers. (2)
2. Explain why some economists might consider the market for computers in Northern Ireland as being oligopolistic. (3)
3. Explain why Microsoft could be described as having a dominant position in the Northern Ireland software market. (2)
4. Explain why monopoly power is regarded as being bad for consumers. (3)

KNOWLEDGE REVIEW

- **THE TERM OLIGOPOLY** refers to the market structure where the top four firms have more than 60% of the market. Barriers to entry exist and therefore the firm is able to earn supernormal profits. Examples include *telecommunication and banking*.

- **COLLUSION** occurs when rival firms agree to set a common price or common conditions of sale in an attempt to manage the level of competition in a market.

- **NON-PRICE COMPETITION** refers to all forms of competition other than through the price mechanism. Examples include: *branding; advertising; product placement; product endorsement; free gifts and promotions.*

- **A MONOPOLY** is a single seller of a good or service that has no close substitute, or alternatively any firm with more than 25% market share. Examples include *Microsoft* and *NIE.*

Chapter 6:

COMPETITION AND GOVERNMENT POLICY

In the previous chapter we looked at how the structure of a market influenced the conduct and behaviour of the firms who operated in it. In this chapter we will analyse the impact that the level of competition has on consumers and we will look at government policy designed to ensure that markets work well for consumers.

MERGERS AND ACQUISITION

As we saw in the last chapter, the level of competition in a market has a huge impact on the ability of firms to influence the price they charge for their output and in turn on their ability to make profits.

In order to manage the level of competition they face, firms often engage in mergers or takeovers as a competitive strategy.

The Competition Commission defines a merger as occurring when "two or more firms cease to be distinct" and occurs when two firms agree to join together to form one larger company. On the other hand, an acquisition or takeover occurs when one firm takes over or buys another firm.

Takeovers can be classified as hostile or friendly. A friendly takeover occurs whenever the bidder informs the target of its intention to acquire it. If the board of the target company feels that the bid represents good value for the shareholders they will recommend acceptance of the bid. If not, the board will reject the bid and the takeover attempt will be classified as hostile. Furthermore, if the bidder makes the initial bid without first informing the board it would also be considered to be hostile.

In the UK, mergers and takeovers are strictly regulated by the 'city code on mergers and takeovers' and the EU directive on takeovers.

Mergers can also be classified as horizontal, vertical or conglomerate.

HORIZONTAL INTEGRATION

Horizontal integration occurs when two firms which produce similar products merge. The firms must be at the same stage of production in the same industry. Examples of horizontal mergers include the merger of Halifax and the Bank of Scotland to form HBOS in 2001 and the takeover in 2006 of Grove Services by its main competitor Maybin.

VERTICAL INTEGRATION

Vertical integration occurs when two firms who are in the same industry merge, but the two firms are at different stages in the production process.

There are two types of vertical integration:

BACKWARDS-VERTICAL

This occurs when a company takes over a firm supplying its raw materials; an example of backwards-vertical integration would be a **pub buying a brewery**. A high profile example of a backwards-vertical merger was the purchase of Time Warner in 2001 by the internet service provider AOL.

FORWARDS-VERTICAL

This occurs when a firm takes over a company further along the production chain; an example of forwards-vertical integration would be **a brewery buying a pub**.

Essentially, if a company takes over another company, which is further back in the production chain and therefore closer to the source of raw materials then it is described as backwards-vertical.

However, if a company takes over another company, which is further forward in the production chain and therefore closer to the final consumer then it is described as forwards-vertical.

CONGLOMERATE INTEGRATION

Conglomerate integration occurs when firms in different industries merge. The goods and services they produce are not directly related. An example of a conglomerate takeover would be the merger of a cheese-processing plant with an electronics manufacturer.

The term 'conglomerate' is used to describe a company that is made up of a number of unrelated businesses. An example of a conglomerate is the Quinn group which has a range of businesses operating in diverse industrial sectors such as quarrying and cement manufacture, financial services and hospitality.

The various different types of integration are illustrated in the diagram below.

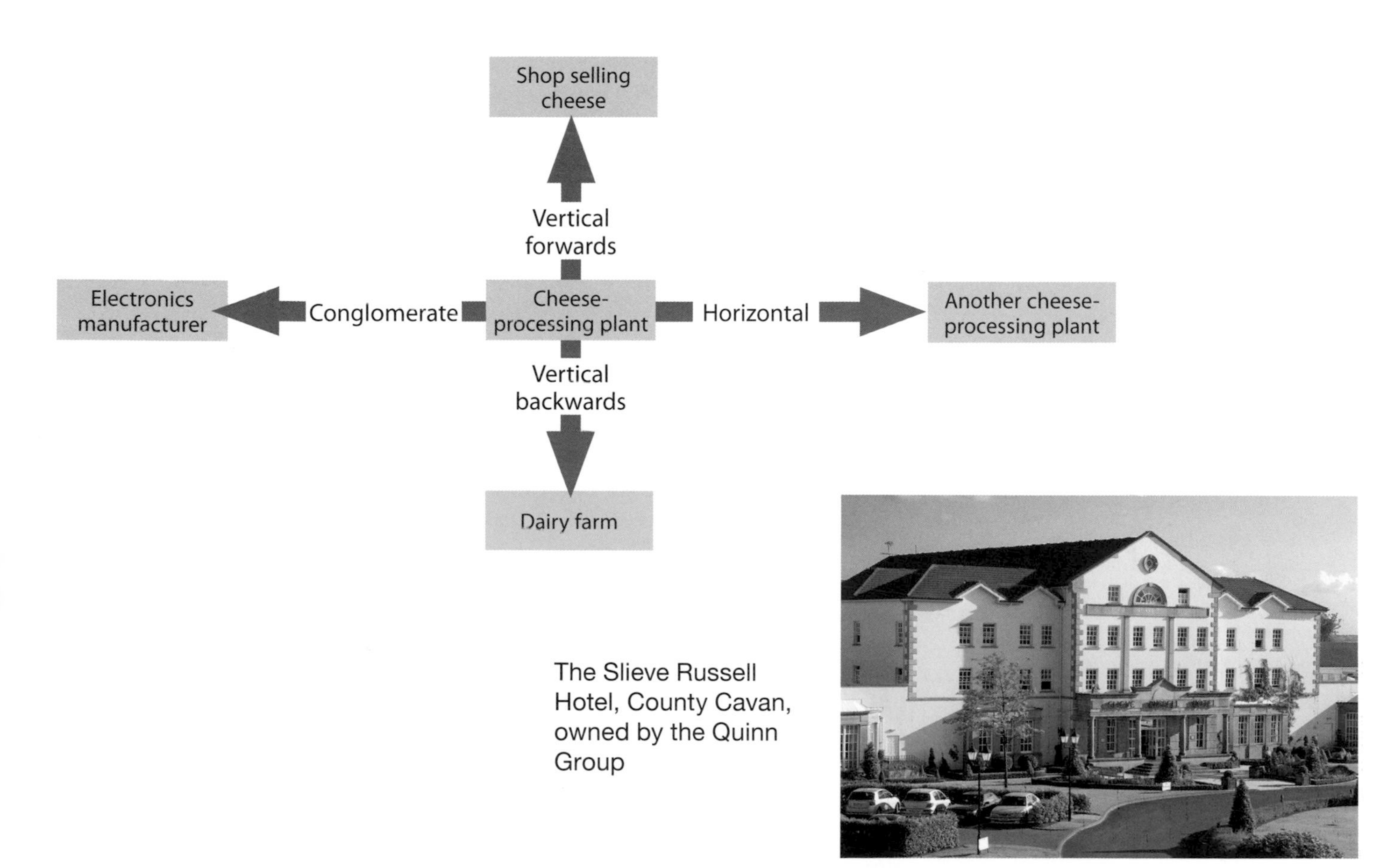

The Slieve Russell Hotel, County Cavan, owned by the Quinn Group

ACTIVITY 6.1

CLASSIFYING MERGERS

Classify each of the following examples of integration as either horizontal, backwards-vertical, forwards-vertical or conglomerate.

(a) Two dentists merge into a single practice
(b) A computer software company takes over a firm producing soft drinks
(c) Tayto purchases Golden Wonder
(d) Coca-Cola merges with C&C
(e) A clothing manufacturer purchases a clothes shop
(f) An oil refinery purchases a number of petrol forecourts
(g) A supermarket purchases a food processing plant
(h) Halifax purchases Bank of Scotland
(i) Disney purchases PIXAR films

BENEFITS OF MANAGING COMPETITION THROUGH MERGERS

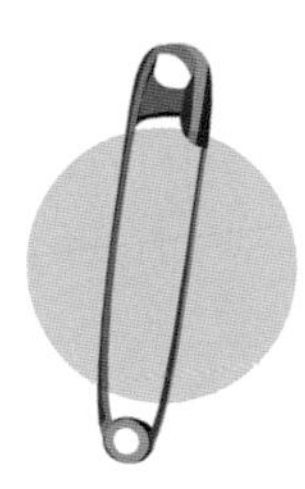

Growing the firm through merger and acquisition can lead to a number of benefits for the business. These benefits include:

1. ECONOMIES OF SCALE
Merging with or acquiring another firm will allow a company to grow quickly and gain economies of scale. Economies of scale are those advantages that large firms have over small firms which lead to falling average costs. For example, large firms are able to purchase their raw materials in bulk and so secure larger discounts than their smaller rivals.

2. DIVERSIFICATION
Growing the firm, particularly through vertical or conglomerate integration, will enable the firm to diversify its output and so will help to reduce the risk to the firm of changes to demand conditions. If the demand for one product falls then the firm can rely on sales of the other products to secure profits.

3. MARKET POWER
Growing the firm through horizontal integration will automatically increase the firm's market share and its market power. This increase in market power may allow the firm to increase price and profitability.

4. GAIN SPECIALIST KNOWLEDGE
Merging with another company allows the firm to bring new skills and specialised departments into the business which will complement the skills and expertise of the original business.

DRAWBACKS OF MANAGING COMPETITION THROUGH MERGERS

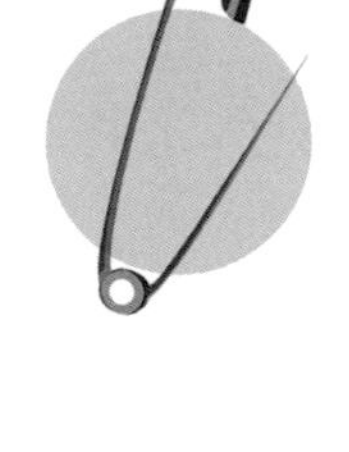
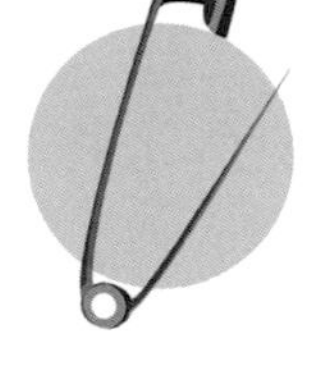

The completion of a merger or takeover is no guarantee of success; indeed growing the firm through merger or acquisition can lead to a number of difficulties and can actually lead to a net loss in value rather than a gain. Experience would seem to suggest that a large number of mergers do in fact result in a loss of value to the acquiring company.

The difficulties created through merging include:

1. DISECONOMIES OF SCALE

Merging with or acquiring another firm may lead a company to grow too large too quickly and therefore experience diseconomies of scale. Diseconomies of scale are those disadvantages of increased size which lead to increasing average costs. For example, large firms often experience managerial problems with regard to communication channels and staff motivation. The result is that the merged company becomes less efficient and average costs increase.

2. INCOMPATIBLE CORPORATE CULTURES

Different companies have different cultures and different ways of getting things done. Bringing two firms together can cause a clash of cultures. As a consequence, resources may be diverted away from new investment or research and development, towards measures to correct this conflict of cultures.

3. LACK OF EXPERTISE

When a firm merges with, or takes over a firm which operates in another industry, it may lack the specific expertise needed to be a success in that industry. This problem is often exacerbated through the laying-off of key personnel in the absorbed firm in an attempt to achieve synergies or economies of scale.

4. ATTRACTS REGULATION

Growing the firm through horizontal integration leads to an increase in the market share enjoyed by the merged firm. However, if this market share becomes too large this may lead to an investigation by the competition authorities, which can be both expensive and time-consuming.

KNOWLEDGE REVIEW

- **A MERGER** occurs when two firms agree to join together to form one larger company.
- **HORIZONTAL INTEGRATION** occurs when two firms who produce similar products merge. The firms must be at the same stage of production in the same industry.
- **VERTICAL INTEGRATION** occurs when two firms who are in the same industry merge, but the two firms are at different stages in the production process. Vertical integration can be both forwards and backwards.
- **CONGLOMERATE INTEGRATION** occurs when firms in different industries merge.
- **ECONOMIES OF SCALE** are those advantages that large firms have over small firms, which lead to falling average costs.
- **DISECONOMIES OF SCALE** are those disadvantages of increased size which lead to increasing average costs.

ACTIVITY 6.2

ADIDAS AND REEBOK

ADIDAS RUES COST OF REEBOK WOES

German sports group Adidas has cut its forecast for profit growth in 2007 as a result of plans to spend more money on revamping its ailing US arm, Reebok.

Adidas, the second largest sports firm worldwide after US firm Nike, cut its forecast for net income growth from 20% to 15% for 2007.

The news sent its shares down 8%, the biggest drop on Germany's Dax index.

Adidas bought Reebok in 2005 because it believed the acquisition would boost its trade in the US, but recent figures show Reebok sales have fallen.

"Reebok's orders are disappointing and the outlook is lacklustre. It will take longer to put Reebok on track," said Nils Lesser, an analyst with Merck Finck.

Adidas reported a net loss of €4.0m ($4.8m; £2.74m), blaming the costs of its takeover of Reebok.

The fourth-quarter loss compares with a net profit of €20m a year earlier, and was worse than forecast.

1. How would you classify the merger which took place between Adidas and Reebok in 2005?
2. Give three possible reasons why Adidas might have wanted to acquire Reebok.
3. Why might the merger between Adidas and Reebok not have been as successful as was hoped?

THE DEGREE OF COMPETITION AND ITS EFFECTS ON CONSUMERS

The degree of competition in an industry will have a significant impact upon the conduct of firms who operate in that industry but it will also have significant effects on the wider economy.

Most economists consider high levels of competition to be beneficial to an economy.

However, it should also be remembered that high levels of competition can have some detrimental effects on the economy.

We will now consider both the positive and negative effects of competition.

BENEFITS OF COMPETITION

Having a significant degree of competition between firms in an industry will lead to benefits in four key areas.

1. PRICE

The level of competition will have a huge impact upon the price that consumers pay for the output produced by an industry.

As a general rule, those firms that face limited competition will have greater scope to influence their price and will charge higher prices.

Those who face competition from a large number of firms producing similar products will have less scope to influence price and will, as a result, charge lower prices.

2. QUALITY

The level of competition in an industry will also have a significant impact upon the quality of goods and service produced by that industry. Firms who face limited competition will have little incentive to maintain quality and may therefore produce poor quality goods and services.

On the other hand, firms that face a lot of competition will be forced to produce high quality goods for fear of losing their customers to competitors.

3. CHOICE

A lack of competition in a market can also lead to a lower level of choice for consumers. In those markets where output is produced by a sole supplier, consumers have no choice over where to purchase their product. Consequently, in markets where there is significant competition the consumer may be able to choose from a range of differentiated products.

4. EFFICIENCY

In highly concentrated industries, firms with significant market power are in a position to charge prices that are considerably higher than would be the case in highly competitive markets. In this way, there will be less incentive to introduce cost-saving innovations to since the firm can respond to higher costs simply by raising prices. Consequently, organisational slack and inefficiency are common in markets with limited competition.

Conversely, firms that face a lot of competition will be forced to become efficient if they wish to remain competitive.

NEGATIVE EFFECTS OF COMPETITION

Having a high level of competition between firms is generally regarded to be in the public interest, since firms are more likely to produce high quality goods at lower prices.

However, in an attempt to gain a competitive advantage over their rivals, firms may engage in activities that produce undesirable consequences for both the internal and external stakeholders.

These undesirable consequences can be illustrated by looking at the case studies overleaf, which have been taken from local and national newspapers during November 2006.

CASE STUDY A

FRUIT OF THE LOOM CLOSES DERRY PLANT

The clothing company Fruit of the Loom has announced the closure of its sewing operation in Londonderry with the loss of 150 jobs.

The firm said the reasons for the shutdown included the cost pressures on Ireland as a base coupled with substantial overproduction of certain garments for coming seasons.

Kevin Daley, the local trade union representative, stated: "The company has been shaving jobs over the last two years in the Republic (of Ireland). But I had been told there would be no further job losses here in the next year".

More than 4,000 jobs have been lost in the textiles industry in the province over the last two years.

CASE STUDY A illustrates how increased levels of competition can lead to a **higher risk of unemployment** for some workers, with over 4,000 textile workers losing their jobs in the last two years as a result of increased levels of competition in this industry.

Experience would suggest that the greater the competition that exists in an industry, the more likely a firm is to try and reduce costs in an attempt to remain competitive. While most people would consider this to be a positive step it may have negative consequences for some employees. This is because one of the most common cost-cutting strategies used by firms is to reduce their workforce.

While cutting the workforce obviously has a detrimental impact upon the employees, it also negatively affects other stakeholders such as the wider community and the government.

CASE STUDY B

OIL COMPANY HAS BEEN FINED £25,000 FOLLOWING A POLLUTION ALERT IN THE NORTH SEA

A major oil company was prosecuted after diesel gushed into the water as a supply vessel refuelled an oil platform, about 160 miles east of Aberdeen.

It was a "routine operation", but 6.5 tonnes of fuel – intended to power the platform's generators – were discharged into the sea. The investigation found that "environmental best practice procedures for the transport of large quantities of oil were not being followed by the company".

A spokesman for the oil company "regretted" the accident.

He added that the firm had carried out its own investigation, along with an inquiry conducted by the authorities. The official stressed that the energy giant had learned lessons and "remedial action" had been taken in an effort to prevent a similar spill.

CASE STUDY B illustrates how increased levels of competition can lead to **increased levels of pollution** and have a negative effect on the local and national environment.

It also illustrates how firms, in an attempt to reduce costs, will often look to use the cheapest method of production. However, as the case study demonstrates, the production process that has the lowest cost may not always be the most environmentally friendly.

CASE STUDY C

SOLAR HEATING FIRM FINED 40K FOR COOKING UP LIES

A solar heating firm has been fined £40,000 for exaggerating the benefits of "going green".

The company claimed household energy bills would be slashed by 70% – when the truth was just 8%. In the first prosecution of its kind in Britain, the £5m-a-year company was found guilty of misleading the public under the Trade Descriptions Act.

Ivan Hancock, of Dorset Trading Standards, said: "All we are asking is that firms like this one stick to the facts so consumers can make a decision based on correct facts."

CASE STUDY C illustrates how higher levels of competition can lead to an **increased risk of unfair trade.**

In a situation where consumers have imperfect knowledge about the qualities of a product, producers may be tempted to exaggerate or lie about the merits of their product in an attempt to secure a sale.

CASE STUDY D

SPORTSWEAR MANUFACTURER CONDEMNED FOR USING SWEAT-SHOP LABOUR

The international aid agency, Oxfam Community Aid Abroad, has released a new report condemning conditions at dozens of factories in Indonesia supplying a top sportswear manufacturer.

The report says tens of thousands of employees are still living in extreme poverty and work in dangerous conditions.

CASE STUDY D illustrates the **social and ethical** problems associated with high levels of competition.

In an attempt to maintain a competitive advantage and increase profits in an increasingly competitive marketplace, firms may be tempted to move production to low wage countries where labour laws are more relaxed than in the UK.

Many of the high street's biggest names have been accused of sourcing their products from companies who use child labour or who force employees to work in dangerous conditions.

These case studies highlight the main problems associated with increased levels of competition and illustrate the need for government policy to correct these problems.

ACTIVITY 6.3

CHANGING SHOPPING HABITS LIFT VALUE MARKET TO £7.8BN

Adapted from The Telegraph, 31 October 2006

Shoppers' love affair with discount clothing retailers like Primark continues unabated, with Verdict Research predicting that nearly £1.00 of every £4.00 spent on clothing this year will be with a value retailer.

The growth of retailers like Primark and supermarket clothing brands over the last decade has fundamentally changed the way people shop for clothes.

Maureen Hinton, senior analyst at Verdict Research, said: "Not only have discount retailers been the main drivers of price deflation in the market – in the process causing a fundamental price shift across the whole market – they have also been almost entirely responsible for any new growth over the past two years."

The value market is now worth £7.8bn, says Verdict Research in its latest report, UK Value Clothing Retailers 2006. In 2001, the value sector accounted for 16% of the overall clothing market; today it is almost a quarter.

Table 1: Market share of Value retailers

Market share %	2005	2006
George@Asda	17.8	17.3
Primark	12.9	15.7
New Look	10.7	11.4
Tesco	10.3	11
Matalan	11.8	10.7

(Source: Competition Commission)

However, Verdict warns that not every discount retailer is benefiting from the boom. Mrs Hinton said:

"Not all value retailers are prospering. More than 90% of their growth this year will come from four operators: Primark, New Look, Tesco and George, and of these Primark accounts for the lion's share, at 42.8%."

She added: "With clothing market growth at its lowest since the turn of the millennium, and operating costs rising, smaller operators are struggling as larger players intensify the competition with aggressive space growth."

"Both smaller operators and new entrants have little opportunity to build the scale necessary to run a profitable price-led proposition. The value model relies on scale, cost efficiencies and high footfall to support its low price position and high volume sales," added Mrs Hinton.

ACTIVITY 6.3

However not everyone is happy with the growth in the value clothing market. Sofia Minney of People Tree stated: "If the UK shopper is paying two pounds for a T-shirt - how much is the person who's making it being paid"?

"Fashion can and should be used as a development tool to help people escape from poverty".

Many High Street stores – including Primark and Peacocks – now belong to the Ethical Trading Initiative (ETI), which makes sure they stick to a code of conduct covering working conditions, wages and the right to belong to a union.

However, unless clothes are advertised as ethical there is no way of knowing how they were made. This has led to growing calls for a label that would show fashion-lovers they can hand over their few pounds for the latest fashion and still have a clear conscience.

1. Use the information in paragraphs 1 and 4 to calculate the approximate value of the UK clothing market. (2)
2. Use the information in the table to determine which retailer has experienced the greatest growth and the greatest fall in market share between 2005 and 2006. (2)
3. Explain why small operators and new entrants are finding it difficult to compete in this sector of the clothing market. (6)
4. How might intense price competition in the UK clothing market impact upon wages and working conditions in the factories which produce the clothes? (4)
5. Explain how ethical labelling might mitigate against these problems. (4)
6. Examine three types of non-price competition used by the UK clothing industry. (9)

GOVERNMENT INTERVENTION IN THE MARKET

As a result of these negative aspects of competition, the government often intervenes in the market to protect the various stakeholders and to provide a healthy competitive environment in which businesses can prosper.

This government intervention can take various forms, from the introduction of regulations and laws to the imposition of taxes and other charges. Which form this intervention takes depends upon the reasons for the intervention and the nature of the market involved.

ENSURING FAIR TRADE

One of the main reasons for government intervention in a market is to ensure fair trade in the market. We learned earlier in this chapter how some firms may be tempted to mislead consumers in an effort to secure higher profits. For this reason the UK government has passed a number of laws that protect consumers from unscrupulous traders. These laws include the Sale of Goods Act, the Trade Descriptions Act and the Weights and Measures Act.

CONTROLLING COMPETITION

Another reason why governments intervene in a market is to control the level of competition to ensure that individual firms do not gain too much market power.

COMPETITION POLICY IN THE UK

The UK government has passed a number of laws aimed at encouraging greater competition in markets. These laws include the Fair Trading Act, the Competition Act, the Restrictive Trade Practices Act, and more recently the Enterprise Act. These laws are all designed to stop large firms abusing their market power and to try and make UK industry more competitive.

WHO ENFORCES THESE LAWS?

1. THE OFFICE OF FAIR TRADING (OFT)

The Office of Fair Trading is an independent non-ministerial government department which acts as the UK's primary competition and consumer protection authority. It is led by a Board of Directors, which consists of a chairman, an executive director and five non-executive members.

The aim or mission of the OFT is to **"make markets work well for consumers".**

It pursues this aim through:

- encouraging businesses to comply with competition and consumer law and to improve their trading practices through self-regulation
- studying markets and recommending action where required
- empowering consumers with the knowledge and skills to make informed choices and get the best value from markets, and helping them resolve problems with suppliers through Consumer Direct.

The OFT has a wide range of enforcement tools at their disposal. For instance, they can impose heavy financial penalties on companies guilty of breaching competition law. They also have the power to take court action against rogue traders, refuse and revoke consumer credit licences, and ban estate agents if they find them guilty of unethical behaviour.

With regard to mergers, the OFT have the power to investigate mergers and takeovers and if they believe that action is needed to improve competition they can refer the case to the Competition Commission.

2. THE COMPETITION COMMISSION

The Competition Commission is an independent public body, which carries out investigations into monopolies and mergers. It was established by the Competition Act 1998 and replaced the Monopolies and Mergers Commission on the 1st April 1999.

Every inquiry conducted by the Competition Commission is undertaken in response to a reference made to it by another authority, usually by the Office of Fair Trading (OFT), but in certain circumstances the Secretary of State, or by the regulators under sector-specific legislative provisions relating to regulated industries. The Competition Commission does not have the power to conduct inquiries on its own initiative.

ENTERPRISE ACT

The introduction of the Enterprise Act in 2002 changed the Commission's role and gave it increased powers to deal with competition issues. Since 2002 the Commission has been responsible for making decisions on competition questions and for implementing appropriate remedies. Previously, it could only make recommendations to the Secretary of State, who then decided whether or not to implement them.

The Enterprise Act also changed the Commission's terms of reference. Previously the Commission had to determine whether matters were **against the public interest.** Since the Enterprise Act it now concentrates specifically on competition grounds; in other words, it judges each case on the impact it will have on competition.

The aim of the Competition Commission is to increase the level of competition in the UK economy, and by doing so improve the UK's economic performance and productivity in the international economy.

CASE STUDY

POOLS MERGER REFERRED TO THE COMPETITION COMMISSION

Attempts by the owner of Littlewoods Pools to buy its biggest rival Vernons hit a snag when the Office of Fair Trading referred the proposed tie-up to the Competition Commission.

Sportech, which bought Littlewoods Pools in 2000, revealed in March that it had entered exclusive talks with Ladbrokes about the acquisition of its Vernons Pools business. The OFT said a tie-up would mean Sportech owning all three football pools operators, since it already owns Zetters.

Simon Pritchard, OFT director of mergers, said a deal would create a monopoly supplier and he voiced concerns that football pools players would face higher prices or lower payout ratios after the merger.

"Many pools players switched to the National Lottery after its 1994 launch but remaining customers are mostly dedicated players spending almost £80m a year," he said. "Other evidence before us clearly supported the large number of consumer concerns we received, and suggested that too few of these customers would switch to alternatives to discipline Littlewoods if it reduced value for money."

The Competition Commission will now investigate and is expected to issue a report by October 2007.

Sportech said it was disappointed by the OFT's decision and it promised to make a further announcement once it had considered what action to take.

(Adapted from The Guardian, 3 May 2007)

3. INDUSTRY WATCHDOGS

All of the major privatised utilities have an industry regulator, such as:

- The Office of Communication **OFCOM** for the communications industry (including internet, TV, Radio etc)
- The Office of Rail Regulation **ORR** for railways
- The Office of Water Services **OFWAT** for water.

In Northern Ireland, the **Utility Regulator** (formerly known as **OFREG**) has responsibility for the regulation of the electricity, gas and water markets.

These watchdogs have the power to limit the share of the market any one firm can control and they can impose price controls on firms. In practice this means that the watchdogs have the power to limit the price that firms, in the industries they regulate, can charge.

CASE STUDY

OFCOM PLANS MOBILE PHONE SPECTRUM AUCTION

OFCOM plans to grab back a third of the mobile phone spectrum that Vodafone and O2 have been using in the UK for 22 years and auction it to at least three other companies, in a repeat of the dramatic 3G auction of the dot.com era.

The original mobile phone companies Vodafone and O2, formerly Cellnet, were given 2G spectrum when the UK mobile industry was founded in 1985. But OFCOM wants to release part of it to new entrants so they can run wireless broadband services, especially in rural areas.

Vodafone and O2 will receive no compensation for losing a massive chunk of the airwaves and will not be allowed to bid in the auction, proposed for 2009, to try to retain it.

The last time mobile phone spectrum came up for auction for 3G networks during the dot. com boom in 2000, five networks – including new entrant 3 – paid £22.5bn. While the new auction is unlikely to attract those prices, OFCOM estimates that 'liberalising' the spectrum used by Vodafone and O2 could bring benefits to the UK economy of up to £6bn.

ANTI-COMPETITIVE PRACTICES

The competition authorities in the UK are concerned with mergers and monopolies but they are also concerned with large firms who may not technically be monopolies but who are large enough to have some power over the market.

For example, if a group of companies together have more than 25% and they adopt similar practices which restrict trade, then they can be classified as a **complex monopoly** and be dealt with as if they were a monopoly.

The competition authorities also try to ensure that these firms do not abuse their market position by using anti-competitive practices.

Anti-competitive practices are strategies used by producers with the aim of restricting competition in the market.

Examples of anti-competitive practices include:

1. DESTROYER/PREDATORY PRICING

This occurs when a dominant firm cuts price so low that other firms have to make a loss in order to match the low price. The aim of destroyer-pricing is to force competitors out of the market and therefore strengthen the firm's monopoly position.

CASE STUDY

BUS COMPANY ACCUSED OF PREDATORY PRICING

Cardiff's main bus company has been accused of "predatory behaviour" in an investigation by the Office of Fair Trading (OFT).

Cardiff Bus offered a service which operated below cost and was withdrawn after a rival firm left the market, the OFT has provisionally found.

It said the firm operated the service at a loss forcing 2Travel plc out of the local market.

Cardiff Bus denied it had infringed competition law.

A spokesman said: "Cardiff Bus confirms that it has today received a statement of objection from the Office of Fair Trading.

"Cardiff Bus will be vigorously defending this allegation as it does not believe that it has infringed competition law."

Their response followed a statement issued by the OFT, which said it had provisionally found the company "engaged in predatory behaviour designed to eliminate a competitor".

It said that between April 2004 and February 2005, the firm deliberately made a loss after another bus company 2Travel plc began to operate services.

"Cardiff Bus is accused of providing a new no frills bus service, which operated below cost and was withdrawn once 2Travel left the market," said the OFT.

The OFT found that the Cardiff Bus Company, which carries an estimated 80,000 people each weekday in Cardiff, used its dominant position to run its no frills services with revenues so far below costs that it was impossible for its competitor to remain in the market."

Robin Finer, OFT assistant director, said: "Dominant companies have every right to compete vigorously but they have a special responsibility not to distort competition.

"Though consumers might see a short term fall in prices, ultimately they will lose out if a dominant company can exercise its market power without constraint or regard to normal competitive pressures."

(Adapted from BBC News, 15 May 2007)

2. DOMINANT DISPLAY CONDITIONS

Large manufacturers often refuse to supply a retailer unless the retailer agrees to display the product in a prominent position at the expense of a rival firm's products. A prominent soft drinks company has been accused of using this strategy in Northern Ireland's main supermarkets.

3. PRICE-FIXING

This occurs when competitors agree to maintain prices within a certain limited range so as to avoid competition on the basis of price. Ultimately consumers suffer because prices will tend to be higher where price-fixing occurs than would otherwise be the case.

CASE STUDY

FIRMS FINED FOR PRICE-FIXING

Fines totalling nearly £19m have been imposed on ten firms including Manchester United, JJB Sports and Umbro for fixing the price of replica football shirts.

The Office of Fair Trading (OFT) found that the firms fixed prices for top-selling short-sleeved adult and junior shirts of the England team and Manchester United.

Price agreements were also made among some retailers for the short-sleeved adult and junior shirts for Chelsea, Glasgow Celtic and Nottingham Forest, the OFT said.

The OFT says most of the price-fixing agreements covered key selling periods such as the launch of new kits and England's participation in Euro 2000.

The retailer JJB Sports was fined £8.3m, one of the largest fines ever imposed by the OFT.

Sheila McKechnie, director of the Consumers' Association, applauded the OFT's move.

"The fact that the OFT has handed out such a sizeable fine shows that it means business," she said.

"It is also particularly cynical that sports businesses have been exploiting one of the key family markets and have been in effect taking advantage of parents under pressure from children eager to get their hands on the latest kit."

But JJB Sports, which received the biggest fine, vehemently denied any wrong-doing and said it would be appealing against the OFT fine.

"JJB is very disappointed that the OFT have found it to be guilty of price-fixing; a charge which it believes is totally unfounded.

"JJB today reiterates that it has never been involved in any form of price-fixing and will launch an immediate appeal against the decision of the OFT to the Competition Appeal Tribunal."

(Adapted from BBC News, 1 August 2003)

4. RESALE PRICE MAINTENANCE

This occurs where a manufacturer and a retailer agree that the retailer will sell the good at or above a pre-agreed price. Resale price maintenance prevents retailers from competing on the basis of price and therefore increases the profits of both the retailer and the manufacturer.

MARKET SIZE, SHARE AND GROWTH

The term **market size** refers to the number or value of units sold to a particular market in a given period of time (normally a year). The term **market growth** refers to the increase in sales in the market over a particular period. By comparing changes in market size and growth over a particular period firms are able to identify trends in the market which will help them when they are making important commercial decisions.

The chart below shows the size and growth of the UK leisure market between 1995 and 2005 expressed in terms of sales value. We can see from the chart that the market has grown on average by about 6% each year and currently the market is valued at £198.6bn.

Growth of the UK leisure market, £bn at current prices

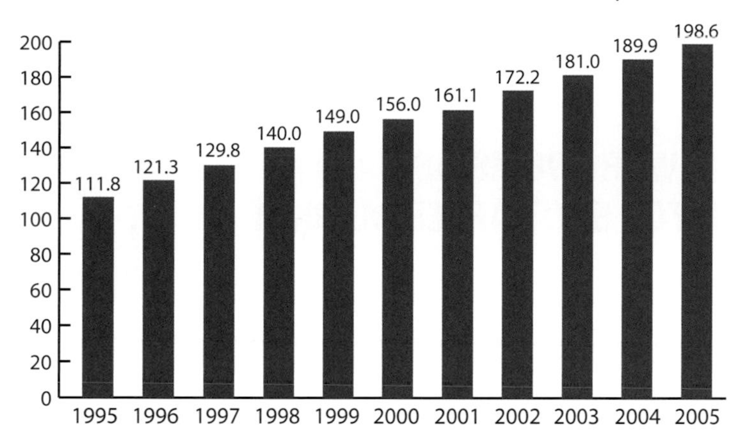

Market Share, on the other hand, is defined as the proportion of total sales in a market that is held by a particular brand, product or company. It is normally calculated by taking a company's sales revenue and dividing it by the total value of sales in that particular market. Alternatively, it can be calculated by taking the company's total volume sales and dividing it by the total volume of units sold in that market.

Clearly, the figure for market share will vary according to whether it is based on the value of sales or the volume of sales. To illustrate, consider the likely market share for Mercedes. It should be fairly obvious that a calculation of market share based on the value of sales would give a much higher figure than one based on the volume of sales. This is because Mercedes is likely to sell significantly fewer cars than firms such as Ford. However, each unit sold by Mercedes is likely to be of a much higher value.

MEASURING MARKET SHARE

When trying to get an accurate measure of market share it is important to first clearly define the market we are dealing with in terms of the geographical boundaries and the product boundaries.

For example, when trying to measure the market share of a company like Tesco we need to consider whether the market we are measuring is for food, groceries or consumer goods.

We also need to consider whether the market we are measuring is a local market, a regional market or a national market.

When we have clearly defined the boundaries of the market, we can calculate market share through the following formula:

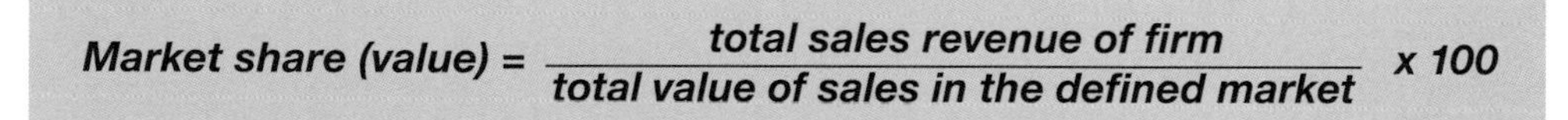

$$\textit{Market share (value)} = \frac{\textit{total sales revenue of firm}}{\textit{total value of sales in the defined market}} \times 100$$

For example, if the UK sales of Next in a particular year were £1.750m and the total value of the UK clothing market in the same year was £30.121m, then Next's market share would be £1.750 / £30.121 x 100 = **5.8%.**

CASE STUDY

MORTGAGE PRICE WAR LOOMS AS HALIFAX VOWS TO REGAIN TOP SPOT AFTER MARKET SHARE HALVES

HBOS is launching a range of new, tactically priced mortgages every three or four weeks as it fights to regain its crown as the country's biggest mortgage lender. The bank admitted yesterday that its share of new mortgage business had more than halved to 8% in the first six months of the year – its lowest level for seven years.

Halifax, owned by HBOS, has traditionally enjoyed a market share of 21% of home loans but it made a series of pricing errors in the first part of the year that led to lower sales.

Fears that HBOS could spark a price war, knocked shares in the mortgage lenders yesterday and unsettled the FTSE 100. HBOS shares fell by 39p to £10.31 while Northern Rock dropped by 29p to 997p, Alliance & Leicester lost 23p to £11.04 and Bradford & Bingley was down 9.25p to 397p.

A full scale mortgage price war, which last erupted in 2001 when HBOS and Nationwide went head to head for customers, seems highly unlikely this time round. Indeed, HBOS was quick to reassure its investors that it was not intending to launch products that would erode its profit margins.

(Adapted from The Guardian, 13 June 2007)

CONCENTRATION RATIOS

Concentration ratios are the most common method of measuring the combined market share of the top firms in an industry and are therefore used to measure the degree of concentration in an industry.

Concentration ratios typically measure the proportion of the market that is owned by the leading brands or companies in the market. For example, they measure how much of total output the top 5, 10 or 15 firms produce.

If the market leaders own a large proportion of the market, the market is described as highly concentrated. By contrast, where the market leader has a small proportion of the market, the market could be described as highly competitive.

Concentration ratios can be based on a range of variables including the total volume of output in the industry or the total value of output produced.

1. AGGREGATE CONCENTRATION RATIO

The aggregate concentration ratio takes, for example, the top five firms and measures the **volume** of output they account for.

In the construction industry the top five firms account for only 4% of total output, (source OFT) and therefore the construction industry could be described as highly competitive.

2. MARKET CONCENTRATION RATIO

The market concentration ratio is based on the **value** of output and measures the share of the market enjoyed, for example, by the largest five firms. For example, in the sugar market the two largest firms (Tate & Lyle and British Sugar) account for over 70% of the market, and therefore this market could be described as highly concentrated.

Concentration ratios can also be calculated for other variables; for example, the **employment concentration ratio** would measure the percentage of total employment taken by the top five firms.

Calculating a concentration ratio can help to tell us what type of market structure we are dealing with and they are used by the Competition Commission to determine if an industry is monopolistic, oligopolistic or competitive.

If the top four firms account for more than 60% of the market, then we would class the market as oligopolistic.

If one firm had more than 25% of the market share, then we would class that firm as a monopolist.

If one firm had more than 40% of the market share, then the firm would be regarded as having a dominant position.

ACTIVITY 6.4

TOP 20 UK ACCOUNTANCY FIRMS 2007

Ranking 2007	Name of firm	UK fee income (£m)
1	PricewaterhouseCoopers LLP	£1,980.0
2	Deloitte	£1,790.0
3	KPMG LLP	£1,454.0
4	Ernst & Young LLP	£1,130.0
5	Grant Thornton UK LLP	£387.1
6	BDO Stoy Hayward	£330.0
7	Baker Tilly	£200.4
8	Smith & Williamson	£152.6
9	PKF (UK) LLP	£130.4
10	Tenon Group plc	£123.6
	Industry total	*£8,700.0*

(Source: Accountancy Age top 50 firms)

1. Use the figures in the table above to calculate the share of the market enjoyed by:
   - Deloitte
   - KPMG
   - Tenon Group
2. Calculate a three firm, a four firm and a five firm concentration ratio for this industry.
3. What does the answer to question 2 suggest about the structure of this industry?

ACTIVITY 6.4

4. Given that the industry total figure in the table above, is calculated using only the top 50 firms in the industry, how might this influence the accuracy of your results to question 1 and 2?
5. Give one other measure on which the concentration ratio might be based.

KNOWLEDGE REVIEW

- **THE OFFICE OF FAIR TRADING** is an independent non-ministerial government department which acts as the UK's primary competition and consumer protection authority.

- **THE COMPETITION COMMISSION** is an independent public body, which carries out investigations into monopolies and mergers.

- **ANTI-COMPETITIVE PRACTICES** are strategies used by producers with the aim of restricting competition in the market. Examples include destroyer-pricing and dominant display conditions.

- **PRICE-FIXING** occurs when competitors agree to maintain prices within a certain limited range so as to avoid competition on the basis of price.

- **MARKET SHARE** is defined as the proportion of total sales in a market that is held by a particular brand, product or company. It is normally calculated by taking a company's sales revenue and dividing it by the total value of sales in that particular market.

- **CONCENTRATION RATIOS** are a method of measuring the combined market share of the top firms in an industry and are therefore used to measure the degree of concentration in an industry.

COMPETITION POLICY AND NORTHERN IRELAND BANKS

(Adapted from BBC News, April 2006)

Bank customers in Northern Ireland appear to be paying higher charges than those in Britain, a report has said.

The Competition Commission said it may be due to a lack of proper competition between the big four Northern Ireland banks.

A so-called super-complaint over the charges was lodged with the Office of Fair Trading and the Commission has been investigating bank services.

It said customers may be paying higher charges and getting lower rates of interest than they should.

The level of charges imposed by the 'Big Four' Northern Ireland banks – Bank of Ireland, Ulster Bank, First Trust and Northern Bank – on current accounts sparked complaints by consumer groups.

The problem has arisen due to a lack of competition in the banking industry in Northern Ireland. The Big Four banks hold a combined market share of over 80%, meaning the market structure is a highly concentrated oligopolistic market.

This high market concentration gives the four banks the power to push up charges to customers, enabling them to earn high levels of supernormal profit.

The banks are able to get away with these huge charges and profits because there are high barriers to entry into the banking sector.

Firstly, a new bank must have sufficient finance to establish a wide network of branches, expanding into small towns, and rural areas.

Secondly, it must be able to afford expensive advertising, for example on TV, or in daily newspapers.

Another barrier to entry is reputation – it takes many years for a bank to establish itself and to gain the trust of new customers.

But a significant problem for new entrants is customer inertia – it is well known that people often do not bother to change their bank account, even though better deals may be on offer, because it is seen as a hassle. In Northern Ireland people are more likely to divorce than to switch banks!

Other UK banks have attempted to enter the Northern Ireland market, but with little success so far. For example, both Abbey and Alliance and Leicester have set up branches in Belfast.

However, these banks do not have the capital to expand into rural areas or to develop their network of branches to provide sufficient competition to the established banks.

In addition, recent security scares with on-line banking continue to deter people from using Internet Banking, and thus reduces the impact of another source of competition.

ACTIVITY 6.5

The Big Four banks do defend their higher charges. They argue that Northern Ireland has a much more dispersed population and that maintaining their rural branch network causes their costs to be much higher than in the rest of the UK.

However, others doubt the extent to which these higher costs can fully explain the difference in the bank charges.

Using the information above answer the questions below:

1. The Northern Ireland banking market has been described as Oligopolistic. Explain what this means.
2. Why might the existence of oligopolies be bad for consumers?
3. Why have other banks not been able to compete with the 'Big Four' in Northern Ireland?
4. Explain the role that the OFT and the Competition Commission could play in this case.
5. Explain what is meant by the term 'supernormal profit'.
6. Examine some of the ways in which an economist might determine whether a firm was making supernormal profits.
7. Examine some of the forms of non-price competition used by banks in Northern Ireland.

Chapter 7: MARKETING AND MARKET RESEARCH

7

MARKETING

Marketing is a difficult concept to define precisely as there is a wide range of activities that are considered to be part of the marketing process. Indeed, a search for a marketing definition on the internet will lead to over one hundred different results, which vary from short concise definitions of fewer than twenty words, to the more detailed definitions, which run to several paragraphs.

Essentially, marketing is the term used to describe all the different activities a firm undertakes when it attempts to identify and meet the wants and needs of its customers.

Many people assume that marketing is only about the advertising of goods and services to consumers; however advertising is only a tiny part of the overall marketing process. The process of marketing involves a wide range of different activities ranging from market research to product design, promotions, and pricing strategies.

One of the best and most commonly used definitions of marketing is the Chartered Institute of Marketing's definition, which is as follows:

Marketing is the management process responsible for identifying, anticipating and satisfying consumers' requirements profitably.

Another commonly used definition of marketing is ***the process involved in putting the right product in the right place at the right time at the right price.***

Getting the right product to market, at the right time and price sounds very easy. All you have to do is provide a good or service that consumers want, at a price they are willing to pay, sell it in a place they are willing to buy it and do it all at the right time.

Nevertheless, it is not as easy as it seems; many firms have failed because they have got one element of the marketing mix wrong.

For example, consider how successful this book is likely to be if it was priced too high or if it was released after the beginning of the school year.

In order to ensure that they do not fail in this way, firms need to consider all the different elements of the marketing process.

Marketing plays a key role in determining the success of a business. High quality marketing enables a firm to identify the wants and needs of consumers at the right time and allows them to provide consumers with the goods they require at a price that is acceptable and in a location which is convenient.

Marketing is a multi-faceted process and involves everyone in the organisation. Indeed, a famous quote on marketing that is often attributed to David Packard, the founder of the Packard computer company is **"Marketing is too important to be left to the marketing department".**

MARKETING OBJECTIVES

When firms engage in the process of marketing it is generally done to achieve some particular goal or aim. There are a number of different marketing goals or objectives that a firm might have. The specific marketing objective adopted by a firm will depend on a range of factors which include: the nature of the product itself, the number of potential customers and the level of competition in the industry.

The most common marketing objectives include:

1 INCREASING SALES

The most widespread marketing objective adopted by firms is to generate a greater level of sales. The primary reason for adopting this objective is the belief that greater sales will lead to greater profits.

It should be noted however that increasing sales will not always lead to higher levels of profits. In some cases the increase in costs associated with higher levels of production may be larger than the extra revenue generated through greater sales.

For example, if a firm is experiencing diseconomies of scale any further increases in output will cause average costs to increase and could therefore lead to lower levels of profit.

CASE STUDY

ADVERTISING BLITZ INCREASES SALES FOR LASTMINUTE.COM

The travel website Lastminute.com has announced its first set of results since it was floated on the stock market. A spokesman for the company said it was growing fast and following its business plan.

He added that Lastminute.com had doubled the number of registered users to 1.4m, and sales had increased sharply as its advertising blitz appeared to have paid off.

The company increased its sales to £11.4m for the half year compared with £300,000 for the same period a year ago.

The company spent £4.8m on advertising in the second quarter, almost four times its gross profits of £1.25m.

Chief executive Brent Hoberman told the BBC he was confident that the company could see off its rivals.

"We feel we're doing something very different and the vast majority of (travel companies) are working with us ... while we watch very carefully what others are doing ... we are doing something very different on a global scale," he said.

(Adapted from BBC News, 4 May 2000)

2 INCREASING MARKET SHARE

For a large number of firms it is not the actual levels of sales which is important but rather the level of market share, where market share is defined as the proportion of total sales in a market that is held by the firm's brand or product. This is because, in some cases, firms believe that the best way to compete effectively is to become the market leader in the industry.

Indeed, the renowned business writer Michael Porter claims that if a business organisation "can claim the lion's share of the market then profits will follow".

While this may be true most of the time, in some cases firms may be happy with their current position in the market and have no desire to become the market leader. If this is the case, then their aim will be to maintain market share at its current level and their marketing strategy will be designed with this in mind.

Where a firm designs its marketing activities to maintain market share, the firm is described as engaging in maintenance marketing.

3 ENHANCE THE BRAND IMAGE

In many cases marketing activities are carried out, not to increase sales or market share in the short term, but rather to improve the image of the company, the brand or the product.

Many of the largest companies organise marketing activities that are designed to simply raise the profile of the company or to improve its image in the eyes of potential consumers.

Marketing activities used for this purpose often include some form of promotional activity such as sponsorship or product endorsement.

For example, firms such as Sony sponsor marquee events such as the Champions League in the hope that the quality of the sporting event will improve the perception consumers have about the quality of their PlayStation console.

Clearly, this type of marketing strategy is carried out in the hope that it will ultimately lead to a greater level of sales. However, this is not the primary short term objective.

CASE STUDY

BP CHANGES ITS IMAGE

The UK multinational, formerly known as British Petroleum and now known simply as BP, unveiled a new "green" brand image in 2000, in an attempt to win over environmentally aware consumers.

A new green, white and yellow logo replaced the BP shield and a new slogan, 'Beyond Petroleum' was adopted. Both of these changes were designed to show the company's commitment to the environment and solar power.

The re-branding exercise did not come cheaply with the company spending £4.5m in researching the new brand and over £100m supporting the brand change.

However, the new image and logo was part of a total re-branding exercise aimed at improving the company's image, which BP hoped would ultimately boost profits.

Why the new image?

Oil is one of the world's dirtiest industries and one that provokes the most environmentalist anger. The changes were intended to highlight the company's interest in alternative and environmentally friendly fuels. About 40% of the company's business is now in natural gas and its solar business is one of the world's largest.

In its new advert, BP is recognising the importance of the environmentalist pound.

CASE STUDY...

"Is it possible to drive a car and still have a clean environment? Can solar power become mainstream? Can business go further and be a force for good? We think so" the advertisement says.

All the same, environmentalists have yet to be convinced and have accused BP of green-washing, a process whereby a company improves its environmental image while maintaining unsound environmental practices.

A spokesman for the environmentalist group Greenpeace said:

"This is a triumph of style over substance. BP spends more on their logo than they do on renewable energy".

The discussion of marketing objectives, above, covers only a few of the most common objectives adopted by firms. Each individual marketing campaign will have its own specific objectives and the marketing strategies used by a firm will be specially designed to meet those particular objectives.

Once a firm has set its marketing objectives, the next stage in the marketing process is to carry out market research.

In the rest of this chapter we will discuss the different forms of market research and look at the reasons why firms undertake market research.

MARKET RESEARCH

Market research is the first stage of any marketing campaign and refers to the systematic collection and analysis of information on a particular product or market.

In other words, market research is the process whereby firms attempt to discover what consumers require from a good or service so that they are better placed to satisfy those requirements.

For example, if a firm is developing a new product or service they will generally carry out some form of market research before bringing the product to market. This is to ensure that the firm does not commit large quantities of its scarce resources to the production of a good or service which does not satisfy the requirements of its consumers and therefore does not sell. Indeed, many otherwise successful firms have suffered as a result of failing to carry out effective market research.

Market research can be both time-consuming and costly and therefore it is not possible for a firm to carry out market research prior to making all commercial decisions.

However, with markets throughout the world becoming more and more competitive, there is an ever-increasing incentive for firms to engage in effective market research, which in turn will help the business to make informed commercial decisions and make them more competitive.

The market research industry in the UK is huge, and is estimated to contribute about £1.2bn to GDP.

PURPOSE OF MARKET RESEARCH

Firms will undertake market research for a number of reasons.

1. TO IDENTIFY MARKETS

One reason why firms engage in market research is to identify potential markets. When a company attempts to sell a product they need to be aware of the type of consumer who is likely to purchase that product, since no one product is likely to satisfy the requirements of all consumers. For instance, products which are likely to be popular with teenage girls are unlikely to be as popular with middle aged men.

It is therefore essential that firms are able to identify their target market so that they can fine-tune their products to suit the needs of a particular market segment. Having a clearly identified target market also allows the firm to focus its marketing budget much more closely on its potential customers.

CASE STUDY

HAIR-CARE FIRMS WISE UP TO ETHNIC POUND

Black women in the UK spend six times more on hair-care products than white women, according to research carried out by L'Oreal, the French company which produces hair and beauty products.

This translates into a significant financial opportunity and explains why several hair-care companies, which already target ethnic markets in the US, are getting ready for major efforts in the UK and Europe.

Marketing Week, which is running its first Diversity Marketing Forum in June, says Britain's diverse communities – including ethnic, religious and sexual minorities – now make up a £120bn market. Obviously any firm which targets these consumers and can produce a product that meets their needs has the potential to make a lot of money.

One of the approaches L'Oreal is taking is to build links with black hair salons, through providing seminars and training and attending black hair and beauty exhibitions.

It has also run road-shows, giving advice and makeovers to customers in ethnic areas like Shepherd's Bush in London. It is hoped that by producing products which meet the specific needs of these groups L'Oreal will gain a significant competitive advantage over its rivals.

(Adapted from BBC News, 2 May 2005)

2. TO TEST NEW PRODUCT OR SERVICE CONCEPTS

If a firm is planning to launch a new innovative product or service onto the market it would be prudent to test that product or service on a small scale before it is launched nationally. Carrying out this form of test marketing ensures that firms do not spend time and energy producing a product that consumers have no desire to purchase. Confectionery firms often trial new products and their associated marketing campaigns in particular regions to gauge consumer reaction before launching the product nationwide.

3. TO FIND OUT ABOUT COMPETITORS

Carrying out market research allows firms to gather information on the number and relative size of competitors that they are likely to face in the market. If the business carries out detailed market research it will also allow them to get information on the relative strengths and weaknesses of their competitors and will therefore enable them to identify strategies that will make their business more competitive.

4. TO IDENTIFY CONSUMER PERCEPTION ABOUT A COMPANY

In recent years consumers have become much more cognisant of how products are made and the commercial activities that businesses engage in. As a result, firms need to be aware of how consumers perceive the company and the adverse impact that a negative perception can have on a company's brand.

Carrying out market research will enable a firm to determine how consumers view the company, and therefore assist in the planning of marketing activities to manipulate those perceptions.

CASE STUDY

QUEEN SEEKS THE OPINION OF THE PEOPLE

The Queen has commissioned pollsters MORI to interview 'focus groups' about how the Royal Family is perceived by the public.

Focus groups have already been asked for their opinion about the Royal Family and MORI is now preparing a report that will be seen by the Queen and other members of the family.

The decision to appoint MORI was "entirely the initiative of Buckingham Palace", said a spokeswoman.

She said: "The Palace has commissioned MORI to undertake some opinion research on its behalf so it can find out how it is perceived by the public and how it can ensure the Royal Family's work is suited to the interests and concerns of the people."

(Adapted from BBC News, 5 January 1998)

TYPES OF MARKET RESEARCH

Market research generally involves some form of data collection and can be classified as either primary research or secondary research.

PRIMARY RESEARCH (also known as field research) involves the collection of original data for a specific purpose and is normally collected directly from the source.

To collect primary research, an original research plan must be devised, which encompasses the process of collecting the data, inputting the data and producing and analysing the final results. Examples of primary research include surveys, focus groups, consumer panels and interviews.

ADVANTAGES OF PRIMARY RESEARCH

Because the research is original, the results gathered will generally be more relevant to the needs of the business that commissioned the research. If the firm devises a detailed research plan prior to carrying out the market research the data collected should answer all of the questions it was designed to answer.

In addition, since primary research involves the collection of new information for a specific purpose, the data should be more accurate and up-to-date.

DISADVANTAGES OF PRIMARY RESEARCH

The main disadvantage of primary research is that it often takes a long time to plan and carry out effectively. This can be a particular problem in fast-changing markets where firms need accurate information quickly.

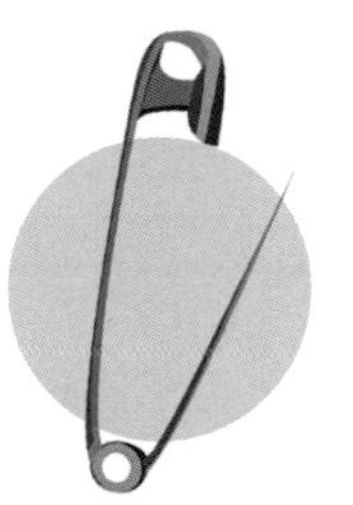

Furthermore, because primary research generally requires a great deal of marketer involvement it can be very expensive to carry out and in some cases may end up costing many thousands of pounds.

Finally, if the market research is not planned properly or is carried out by someone who lacks the experience required, it may yield results that are inaccurate or biased, which could in turn lead to the firm making poor commercial decisions.

SECONDARY RESEARCH involves the processing of data that has already been collected. Also known as desk research, secondary research is the most common research method employed by businesses in the UK today. To collect secondary data, market researchers will typically consult previously published material such as government reports, press articles or previous market research projects, which have been carried out for some other purpose.

ADVANTAGES OF SECONDARY RESEARCH

Because it is generally easier to search out secondary sources of data than it is to mount a primary research programme, secondary research is often quicker to complete than primary research. In recent years the development of the internet has made accessing secondary data much simpler.

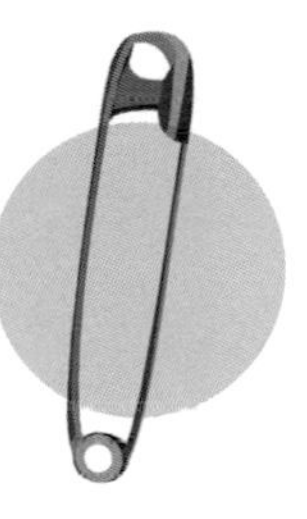

The other main advantage of secondary research is its relatively low expense in comparison to field research. Since the data used in secondary research has been collected already for some other purpose, the cost involved in obtaining it should be lower than would be the case with primary research.

Furthermore, collecting secondary data can be useful in that it can highlight general trends and specific areas of interest and can therefore guide researchers in their primary data collection.

DISADVANTAGES OF SECONDARY RESEARCH

The main disadvantage of secondary research is that previous studies may not have targeted the exact issue that the current research requires and therefore the data may be of limited use.

Secondly, even when the secondary data is relevant to the current study, it may be out of date and therefore the results achieved may be inaccurate. This is a particular problem for firms who operate in fast changing industries.

One further problem associated with secondary data is that the data may be biased. In some cases data may be collected to serve a situation in which either the commissioners or the researchers had a vested interest. It is important when using secondary data that this potential bias in the data is considered.

ACTIVITY 7.1

USING PRIMARY AND SECONDARY RESEARCH: BEIERSDORF

The multinational cosmetics company Beiersdorf uses both primary and secondary research as a part of its international market research function.

The company, which is based in Hamburg, Germany, and produces products under the well known brands of Nivea and L'Oreal, has a separate market research department which is responsible for supplying the company with detailed up-to-date information on its products, customers and markets.

Examples of primary research include product usage tests, where carefully selected individuals are given an unbranded sample of a product, which is under development and asked to use the product for a week. The consumers are required to record in a diary when they used the product and to score the product on a number of set criteria. This information is then used to highlight the product's strengths and potential areas of concern.

Secondary research is also often used by the firm. For example, prior to the introduction of the Nivea pearl and beauty deodorant range, Beiersdorf consulted a Consumer Usage and Attitude Survey, which was collected in the USA and the UK, as well as a study on fragrances, which was originally commissioned by one of the major Fragrance Houses.

1. With reference to the case study, explain what is meant by primary research.
2. Explain two benefits that a firm gains from using primary research.
3. Evaluate the view that secondary research is a much more economical form of market research.

QUANTITATIVE AND QUALITATIVE RESEARCH

Another way to classify market research is to classify it as either quantitative research or qualitative research.

QUANTITATIVE RESEARCH

This form of market research is typically used to determine **how many** people behave, act or think in a particular way.

Quantitative research involves the collection of numerical data, which can then be analysed statistically to identify general trends or patterns. It normally involves large numbers of respondents ranging from small samples of 50 or so to larger samples with many thousands of respondents.

Quantitative research is a very structured form of market research where every respondent in the sample is asked exactly the same series of questions in exactly the same order. Quantitative research does not allow for any development or elaboration of the answers, by way of exploring the possible reasons for a respondent's choices, and therefore does not generally address the how or why of consumer behaviour.

Typical quantitative techniques include questionnaires, telephone surveys, and random street surveys, all of which classify as primary research. However, quantitative research can also be secondary in nature and can include the analysis of a company's sales data, advertising spend or market share.

QUALITATIVE RESEARCH

Qualitative research, on the other-hand, is used to determine **how** people feel and **why** people act in a particular way.

Unlike quantitative research, qualitative research does not include a fixed series of questions, but rather a discussion guide, which is used to steer the conservation on a particular path. The actual content of the interview or discussion will be determined to a large degree by the responses of the interview.

For this reason qualitative research is often referred to as 'touchy-feely' research and generally requires researchers to interpret the information collected without the support of any statistical techniques.

Furthermore, qualitative research typically involves much smaller samples than quantitative research and therefore the results obtained may not be as representative or accurate as would be the case with quantitative research.

As is the case with quantitative research, there are a number of qualitative methodologies most of which are done face-to-face and include focus groups, in-depth interviews and consumer panels. All of the above examples would be classified as primary research but qualitative research can also be secondary in nature and can include the analysis of previously collected qualitative data.

KNOWLEDGE REVIEW

- **MARKETING** is the management process responsible for identifying, anticipating and satisfying consumers' requirements profitably.

- **MARKET RESEARCH** refers to the systematic collection and analysis of information on a particular product or market.

- **PRIMARY RESEARCH** (also known as field research) involves the collection of original data for a specific purpose and is normally collected directly from the source.

- **SECONDARY RESEARCH** (also known as desk research) involves the processing of data that has already been collected by some other person or organisation.

- **QUANTITATIVE RESEARCH** involves the collection of numerical data which can then be analysed statistically to identify general trends or patterns.

- **QUALITATIVE RESEARCH** Involves the collection of non numerical data and generally requires researchers to interpret the information collected without the support of any statistical techniques.

MARKET RESEARCH METHODS

There are a number of different research methods that companies can use to obtain the information they require. The most common of these are considered below:

SURVEYS

One way to find out what consumers require from a product is to simply ask them! This is normally done using a questionnaire, where each respondent is asked a number of questions relating to a product or market.

These surveys can be carried out via e-mail, the internet, the telephone, by post or face-to-face. Each of these methods has its own particular strengths and weaknesses, which we will consider below.

(A) FACE-TO-FACE SURVEYS

A face-to-face survey typically involves a set number of questions in a set order with respondents being selected at random either through a high street intercept or via a door-to-door process with streets or house numbers being selected at random.

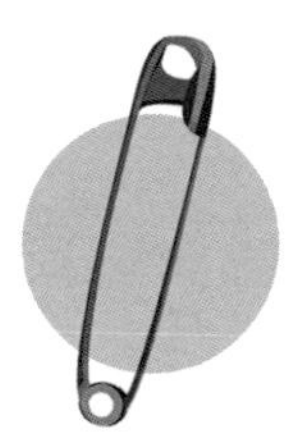

ADVANTAGES

- Face-to-face interviews help to break the barriers between the researcher and the respondent and therefore should lead to higher response rates and less respondent error.
- In face-to-face interviews researchers are able to ask for clarification if the initial answer is ambiguous or unclear.
- Face-to-face interviews allow the researcher to use pictures or images to stimulate responses from the interviewee.
- Having an experienced researcher carry out the survey allows for the use of a large number of routing questions, which may be deemed too complicated for a postal survey.

DISADVANTAGES

- Face-to-face interviews are extremely time-consuming and as a result the cost per interview is very high particularly when compared to telephone or internet questionnaires.
- Face-to-face interviews may lead to a hidden bias in the choice of respondents particularly if done via a high street intercept.
- Face-to-face interviews normally involve small samples due to the time and cost involved in completing them. This clearly can have an impact on the value of the results produced.

(B) TELEPHONE SURVEY

The telephone survey is becoming an increasingly popular alternative to the face-to-face interview. In a telephone survey respondents are normally selected at random from a telephone directory or in some cases via random number dialling.

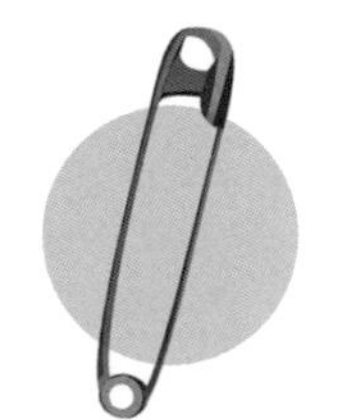

ADVANTAGES

- The main advantage of a telephone survey is its low cost when compared to a face-to-face interview since all researchers can be housed in a central location, which reduces the time and cost associated with travel.

- Telephone interviews allow researchers to draw their sample from a wide geographical area, which should help to make the results more representative of the whole market.
- Telephone surveys generally provide results much more quickly than postal or face-to-face surveys. This is particularly true if the results are being entered directly onto a computer during the actual interview process. This can be done with the use of a Computer-Assisted Telephone Interview (CATI) system, which can log and analyse results instantaneously.

DISADVANTAGES

- Since not everyone has a telephone or has their number listed on a directory the sample may not be truly representative of the whole population.
- Telephone interviews do not allow for the use of picture or images to stimulate responses from the interviewee.
- The increased use of telesales and identity fraud has meant that individuals are less likely to take part in telephone interviews for fear of being sold something or giving away personal information.

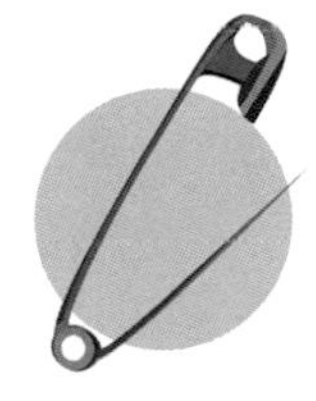

CASE STUDY

MILLIONAIRES PREFER GAP TO GUCCI

Britain's millionaires are careful spenders who would rather snap up high street bargains than splash out on designer labels, a survey commissioned by BBC 2's Mind of a Millionaire has revealed.

The survey was conducted by wealth research specialists, Tulip Financial Research Ltd, who carried out 300 thirty minute phone interviews in February 2003 with a representative sample of UK millionaires.

The extensive survey is broken down into statistics on millionaires who own their own companies, female millionaires, millionaires from poor backgrounds and multi-millionaires.

The research, which was the biggest of its kind, found that 42% of those interviewed said that they spent less than £500 a year on clothing.

The survey also found that a third of millionaires (38%) spend under £60 a week on their weekly food shopping.

However, the survey found that millionaires do like their holidays – they take at least three a year. Multi-millionaires take five a year and they spend on average £14,000 annually on breaks, Nonetheless, their number one spending priorities are saving and investing.

(Adapted from Mind of a Millionaire: www.bbc.co.uk)

(C) POSTAL SURVEY

In a postal survey a questionnaire is sent by post and the respondent has to complete the questionnaire independently and return it to the organisation carrying out the research. Estimates suggest that approximately 100 million questionnaires are posted out in the UK each year.

ADVANTAGES

- Postal surveys reduce the need for research staff and therefore the cost of each completed questionnaire is low when compared to face-to-face or telephone surveys.

- Postal surveys allow the research to cover a much larger geographical area, which in turn should help generate a more representative sample.
- In a postal survey respondents can complete the questionnaire in their own time and therefore they can refer to files or data if the questions are of a precise or technical nature.
- Postal surveys also reduce the possibility of interviewer bias or error since they are completed independently.

DISADVANTAGES

- With a postal survey there is no way of knowing who has completed the questionnaire. Even when they are addressed to a particular person someone else may complete and return the questionnaire.
- Because there is no interview to explain the questions or to ask for elaboration in answers, the questions must be straightforward and easy to answer.
- Questionnaires which are long, or appear to be time-consuming tend to have very low response rates as respondents are reluctant to spend the time completing them.
- If the response rate is very low the cost per completed questionnaire increases significantly.

(D) E-SURVEY

An increasingly popular method of carrying out primary market research is via an E-survey. With this method a questionnaire is sent to selected individuals via e-mail, with the respondents then completing the questionnaire in their own time and returning it to the sender. Alternatively, the questionnaire can be posted on an organisation's website with invitations sent to individuals to encourage them to complete it.

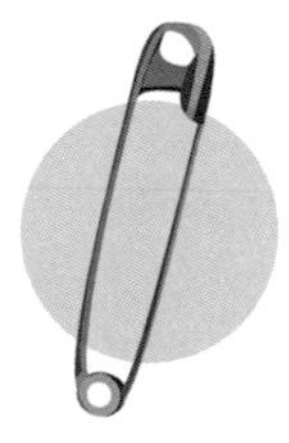

ADVANTAGES

- The main advantage with an E-survey is the speed with which it can be sent, completed and returned.
- Electronic surveys are also much cheaper to complete than postal or face-to-face surveys.
- Where the survey is sent via e-mail only the intended respondent can receive the questionnaire.

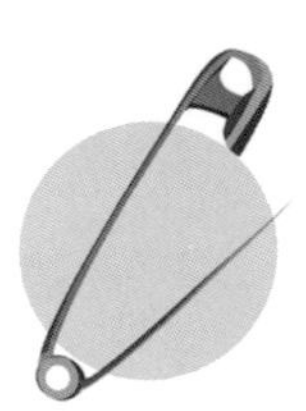

DISADVANTAGES

- Response rates tend to be very low with E-surveys as potential respondents often delete unsolicited mail or route it to bulk or trash folders.
- Problems with internet security mean that electronic surveys can be less secure than traditional methods of communication.
- Since not everyone has an e-mail account or access to the internet the sample may not be representative of the whole population.

FOCUS GROUPS

A focus group is a form of qualitative research in which a group of individuals is asked to share its thoughts, attitudes and feeling on a particular product or concept.

Focus groups normally contain between six and ten people who are typically screened to ensure that they form part of the relevant market segment.

Focus group discussion generally lasts for anything up to two hours and respondents are asked a set of questions, which are used to guide the discussion. The discussion is loosely structured and respondents are free to discus with other members of the group any area relevant to the focus of the research.

Traditionally, focus group discussions were carried out at some central location with all participants being present in the same physical space but with developments in ICT, many focus groups now take place on-line.

ADVANTAGES

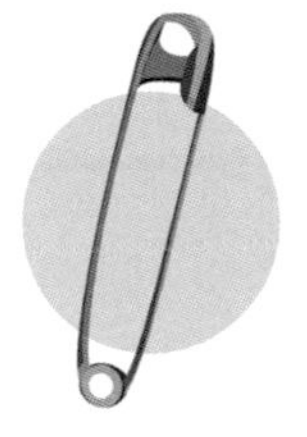

- One of the key advantages of a focus group is that it is quick and easy to assemble and the results can be produced in a fairly short period of time.
- Focus groups are particularly useful in the collection of the vital qualitative information that firms often require to explain why people hold particular tastes or preferences.
- In a focus group discussion people are able to build on the answers of others. This can lead to a much freer discussion and often results in more complex and detailed answers than would be the case with one-to-one interviews.
- Focus groups are particularly good for obtaining data from children or people who would not normally be able to complete other forms of survey.

DISADVANTAGES

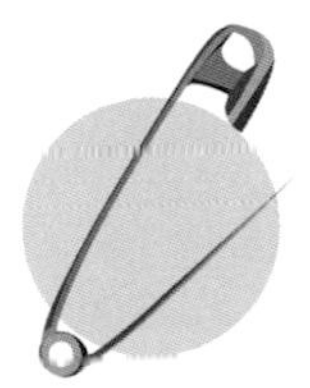

- The main disadvantage of focus groups is that they are conducted on a small scale and therefore the results may not be truly representative. This is especially true if the group contains a few dominant members who may have an undue influence on the discussion and the responses of others.
- The data collected in a focus group is much more difficult to analyse as the results are of a qualitative nature.
- The results obtained by a focus group also often depend on the researcher who is moderating and leading the discussion. For example, the timing of a question and the manner in which it is asked can have a large impact on the responses received.

CONSUMER PANELS

Consumer panels are very similar to focus groups in that they consist of a number of members who form part of a particular market segment. Each member of the panel is asked to contribute their thoughts and feelings on a particular product or service.

The key difference between a consumer panel and a focus group is that the consumer panel is used on an ongoing basis and members are called upon on a frequent basis to analyse a range of products and concepts and provide data for the firm, whereas focus groups are normally dissolved after the initial research is completed.

ADVANTAGES

- As with focus groups, consumer panels are particularly useful in the collection of vital qualitative data.
- Because consumer panels are used on an ongoing basis, respondents gain experience and confidence and therefore supply more useful data.

DISADVANTAGES

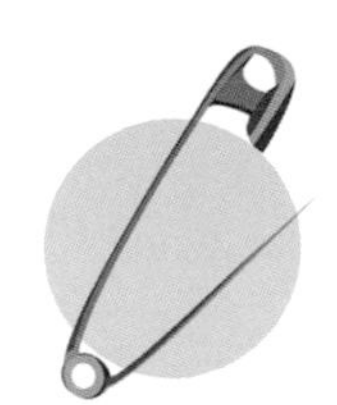

- As is the case with focus groups, the main disadvantage of consumer panels is that they are conducted on a small scale and therefore the results may not be truly representative.
- Because of the qualitative nature of the data the results can be very difficult to analyse and therefore require the analytical skills of an experienced researcher.

TEST MARKETING

Test marketing is the process of trialling a new product, service or concept on a section of the market prior to a full scale roll out. The products are generally trialled in a particular geographical area or TV region and are often supported by a full advertising and marketing campaign to gauge consumer reaction before the product is launched nationally.

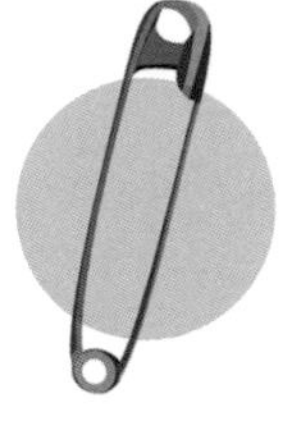

ADVANTAGES

- Carrying out test marketing ensures that firms do not waste valuable resources producing a product that consumers are unlikely to purchase.
- Test marketing can be used to test all aspects of the marketing mix and can provide valuable quantitative and qualitative data, which can be used by the firm prior to a full scale launch.
- Because products are usually tested in a large geographical area the sample is likely to be much more representative than would be the case with many other forms of market research.

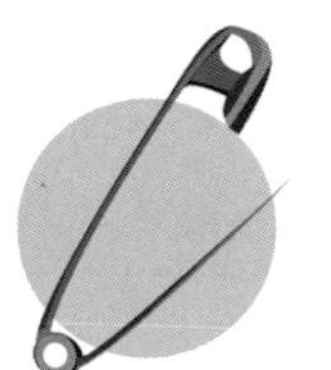

DISADVANTAGES

- Test marketing can give a firm's competitors vital information about their products and could lead to competitors releasing their own product nationally in advance of the original firm.
- Although test marketing is designed to reduce the cost involved in launching a product that subsequently proves unpopular, it is in itself a time-consuming and costly process.
- Because of the nature of test marketing it is normally carried out quite late in the market research process. In most cases the firm will already have made significant investment in the product prior to the testing process and therefore the reduction to risk and cost may be minimal.

CASE STUDY

THE INDEPENDENT TESTS THE MARKET

The Independent newspaper has chosen London as the test market for a new tabloid edition, the latest ploy in the daily's effort to boost its anaemic circulation figures.

The content, editorial style and 60p cover price of the new publication - billed by the paper as "Britain's only quality tabloid" will be exactly the same as its broadsheet namesake's.

But the Independent is hoping that the new paper's easy-to-handle format will win over fans of serious news among London's army of commuters, many of whom have difficulty grappling with broadsheets on cramped tubes and trains.

"Our readers, particularly those who commute to work, have long expressed a desire for a more convenient format for their newspaper," said Independent editor Simon Kelner.

To begin with, the new-look Independent will be sold alongside its bigger sister in the London area. If the tabloid goes down well in the capital, it will be introduced in other regions at a later date.

The decision to target the commuter market is thought to have been influenced partly by the success of Associated Newspapers' Metro, a daily tabloid distributed free of charge at public transport hubs in several UK cities.

(Adapted from "Tabloid transformation" BBC News, 29 September 2003)

INTERVIEWS

An interview is similar to a face-to-face survey in that each respondent meets with an interviewer and is asked a set of questions. The interview differs, however, in that respondents are normally selected on the basis of meeting predetermined criteria.

Furthermore, interviews have a fairly loose structure when compared to face-to-face surveys and because they are used to collect in-depth qualitative data, respondents are encouraged to give full and detailed answers.

Interviews are a very popular form of market research with approximately 15 million being conducted each year in the UK.

ADVANTAGES

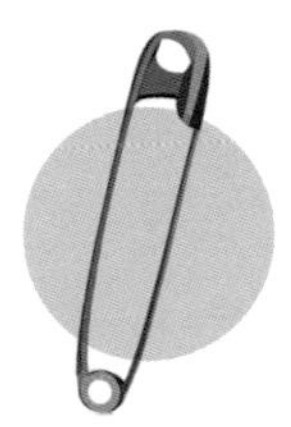

- Interviews allow the researcher to collect rich qualitative data, which can be extremely useful in explaining why consumers behave in the ways they do.
- Having a less structured set of questions allows a rapport to build between the researcher and the respondent, which leads to more in-depth answers and therefore higher quality data.
- Because the interview is conducted on a one-to-one basis, the responses are not influenced by dominant group members as might be the case with focus groups or consumer panels.

DISADVANTAGES

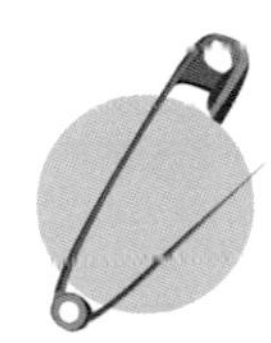

- In-depth interviews are extremely time-consuming and are therefore very expensive to carry out.
- Because of the time and cost involved, interviews are normally conducted with relatively small samples and therefore may not be truly representative.
- One-to one interviews are open to interviewer bias and therefore it can be difficult to compare the results collected by different researchers.

OBSERVATION

In this form of market research, firms try to examine how consumers actually behave as opposed to trying to analyse their responses to questions that are designed to determine how they would behave.

Observation is important since the answers that respondents give in interviews and focus groups may not actually reflect their true behaviour. For example, evidence suggests that when individuals are asked about their diet or drinking habits the answers they give suggest they have healthier eating and drinking habits that is actually the case. This is not to suggest that respondents are lying; it may simply be the case that they think their diet is healthier than it actually is.

The most common forms of observation include the use of in-store CCTV to track the movements of customers, or the use of bin audits to study the products people actually buy.

ADVANTAGES

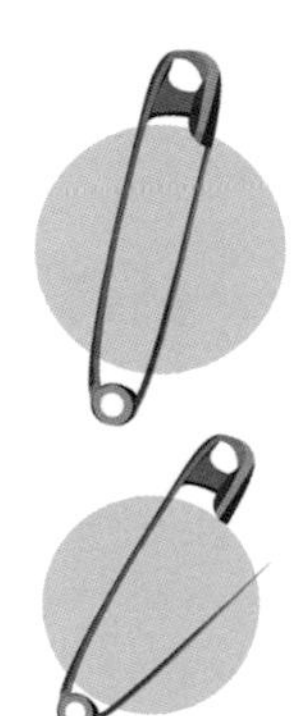

- The main advantage of observation is that it yields accurate results, particularly if the individuals are not aware they are being observed.
- Observation is also free from any researcher bias or undue influence.

DISADVANTAGES

- Trying to analyse the results of observation can be both difficult and expensive since it requires the skills of highly trained professionals.

- Observation does not allow for any interaction between the researcher and the individual under scrutiny.
- Social libertarians argue that this type of covert surveillance by firms can raise moral and ethical questions about how the data is used.

STORE LOYALTY CARDS

On the face of it, a store loyalty card is simply a device through which firms reward their loyal customers with discounted prices or points that can then be used to purchase an item at a reduced price.

However, in reality store loyalty cards are an excellent device for the collection of primary data on the behaviour of consumers.

Every time a consumer purchases a product from a store the card is swiped and details of exactly what was purchased are stored on computer.

This information allows firms to build a very accurate picture of the shopping habits of its customers both at an individual and at a macro level.

This information can then be used by the firm to assist it in its marketing decisions.

Store loyalty cards have proven to be very popular with stores in the UK, with approximately 160 store loyalty card schemes operating, the biggest of which is the Nectar card used by firms such as Sainsbury's and BP.

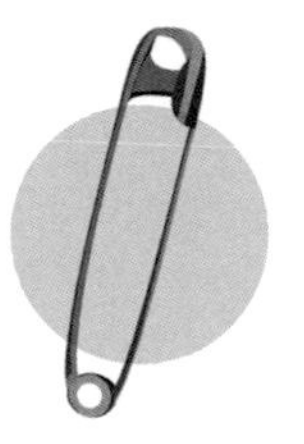

ADVANTAGES

- As with other forms of direct observation, the main advantage of store loyalty cards is that they produce large quantities of accurate information.
- The data produced by store loyalty cards can be used to look for regional or local trends in shopping habits and therefore enable firms to specifically target certain geographical areas.
- Once the card system is set up it is extremely easy to run.
- Evidence suggests that those stores which have loyalty cards find that customers spend a longer time and more money in their stores than those which don't use loyalty cards.

DISADVANTAGES

- A store loyalty card system can be very expensive to start up and run. Indeed, the UK supermarket Safeway (which was taken over by rival Morrisons in 2006) estimated that its store card had cost the firm approximately £35m per annum.
- The data produced is quantitative in nature and therefore does not explain the reasons behind the behaviour.
- As with observation, concerns have been raised about how this information is used and who has access to it.

CASE STUDY

LOYALTY CARDS PROVE VERY VALUABLE

Supermarket loyalty cards are a valuable tool for the big name stores, according to new research by the Economic and Social Research Council, which tracked the spending of two matched groups of consumers for four months. Shoppers were asked to keep a diary of where they shopped, how long they shopped, and what they spent their money on.

CASE STUDY...

The researchers at Stirling University found that, per visit, card-holders spent much more time in their chosen store, 38 minutes against 13 minutes, and much more money, £34 against £14, than non-cardholders.

They were not, however, noticeably more loyal, as defined by repeated visits, than non-cardholders.

Professor Leigh Sparks, head of the Department of Marketing at Stirling University, commented on the findings: "This doesn't mean that you get a card and you immediately spend more. Cardholders were probably already more committed to the store before they applied for a card. The supermarkets have not been able to make people 100% loyal to their stores. People still shop around in all sorts of different ways."

Professor Sparks noted that the second thing the programme found was that retailers were getting a vast amount of data from their card schemes.

"The best of the retailers were able to exploit their data, analyse it at very detailed levels, and apply it to the merchandising of goods, the set-up inside stores, and the set-up of individual stores."

Professor Sparks said it had been agreed not to name the shops involved in the study, but it was clear that the major supermarkets were making major strides in the way they were using their data and analysing it.

(Adapted from BBC News, 6 May 1999)

ACTIVITY 7.2

TESTING TIMES FOR YOUNGSTERS

The testing of consumer products on children has become an essential part of the development process of anything from toys and fast-food, to electronic equipment and cars.

With parents reduced to cash cows who feed their children's consumer habits, it has become vital for firms to find out what children want. As one market researcher stated "I don't see how you can develop something that is directed at children without the children being involved".

Companies like Lego have tested their products on very young children for years.

Rather than asking questions, Lego will take its products to nurseries in Denmark to observe the children while they play.

"When we talk about children, it's the intuitive play that is interesting," said Jens Maibom, vice president of the toy-maker Lego's educational department.

Such observations, as well as focus groups involving teachers, parents and children, help Lego understand its customers.

From the age of four, a child begins to influence consumer decisions, and by the age of six "the parents are only providing the money", according to Mr Maibom.

By the time they are seven, children are seen as consumer voices in their own right, said Dave Lawrence of Logistix Kids, a company that specialises in child market research.

The young's growing influence or 'pester power' has led to a sharp, parallel increase in child market research budgets.

ACTIVITY 7.2

Logistix Kids – one of many firms researching the markets for toys, fast-food, drinks and snacks – says it spends more than £500,000 each year to investigate trends in the child marketplace.

However, the ethical implications of such research are potentially enormous.

And there is much confusion about exactly what methods are acceptable.

To clear up the confusion, the Market Research Society (MRS) has drawn up a set of guidelines to protect children's rights and to ensure they are not exploited.

Nonetheless, many argue that the guidelines do not go far enough and that using children in this way is immoral and should be banned.

(Source: BBC News, 29 June 2001)

1. The case study refers to the use of focus groups by Lego. Explain how focus groups operate and assess their benefit as a method of market research.
2. Analyse three alternative forms of market research that a firm could use in order to understand its child customers.
3. Explain why some people might be concerned about the increased use of child-centred market research.

ACTIVITY 7.3

RESEARCH METHODS

Read the situations below and for each one select two research methods which you feel would be most appropriate. In each case justify your choice and explain whether the research method could be classified as primary or secondary and quantitative or qualitative.

- Bass Ireland is contemplating introducing a new alco-pop onto the UK market.
- A local restaurant owner is planning to open a new Thai restaurant in the town centre.
- One of the major supermarkets is contemplating expanding its opening hours to 24 hours a day seven days a week.
- An entrepreneur wants to investigate the possibility of opening a Curves gym franchise in the city centre.
- A UK engineering firm is considering supplying its products to the Asian market.
- An on-line retailer is considering changes to its website.

SAMPLING

In an ideal world a business would like to know as much as possible about the tastes and preferences of all its potential customers. However, due to the time and cost involved in collecting this information firms often use a representative sample. For example, if a TV company wanted to know the views of teenagers on a particular programme they could select a sample of 500 or so and ask them, rather than trying to ask every single teenager in the UK.

THE PROCESS OF SAMPLING

To ensure that the information obtained from the market research project is accurate, it is vitally important that the firm selects the sample in the correct manner. A poorly-selected sample can yield inaccurate and unrepresentative results, which can in turn lead to the firm making poor commercial decisions.

To select an appropriate sample, firms should follow the following four steps:

1. DEFINE THE SAMPLING FRAME

A sampling frame is simply a list from which the actual sample will be taken. Common sampling frames include the telephone directory, the electoral register or a firm's full customer list.

2. CHOOSE A SAMPLING METHOD

There are different sampling methods which a firm can use to select its actual sample. These include:

(A) RANDOM SAMPLING

Also known as probability sampling, random sampling involves selecting a sample through chance, either via a lottery system or a system of random number selection. For example, if a firm is using a telephone survey it can select its respondents through the use of a programme that selects numbers at random or via a system which chooses actual phone numbers at random from a telephone directory.

The main advantage of a random sample is its relative ease of use as a selection process.

Furthermore, random sampling allows firms to accurately estimate the size of any potential sampling error as this will be based on the laws of probability.

The main disadvantage of random sampling, on the other hand, is that it may yield results that are unrepresentative since the selection process is completely down to chance.

(B) STRATIFIED SAMPLING

In stratified sampling the population is divided into mutually exclusive strata or layers with random sampling taking place within each stratum.

For example, if a school was carrying out research to gauge the opinion of its students it could divide the total school population into separate strata based on year group and sample a number of students in each year group.

In order to ensure that the sample is representative the school must ensure that the number of pupils surveyed in each year group is proportional to the number of students in that year group. For example if there are twice as many students in year 10 as there are in year 9 then the sample from year 10 must be twice that of year 9.

In some special cases, however, disproportionate stratified sampling may be used.

For example, if the school was researching an issue that would have a greater impact on Year 9 students they may decide to survey a greater proportion of Year 9 students.

As with all forms of probability sampling, stratified random sampling allows researchers to accurately calculate the size of any sampling error. However, because it requires a separate sampling frame for each stratum, stratified sampling can be an expensive process.

(C) CLUSTER SAMPLING

Cluster sampling is sometimes confused with stratified sampling, but they are two different techniques. In cluster sampling the population is again divided into sub groups, though in this case they are referred to as clusters rather than strata.

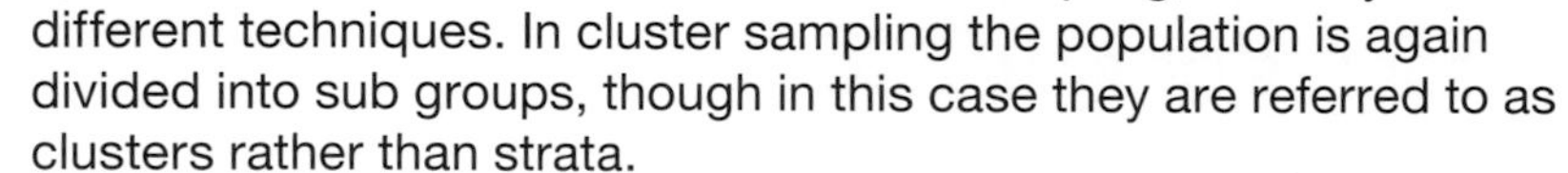

The key difference between cluster sampling and stratified sampling is that whereas in stratified sampling a sample is taken from all strata, in cluster sampling only a selection or cluster of sub-groups is selected.

To illustrate the difference, consider again the example of a school that is carrying out market research on the views of its pupils. In stratified sampling a sample was taken from each year group whereas in cluster sampling only a number of year groups, for example year 8, 9 and 11, would be selected and a sample taken from them.

Cluster sampling is often used when the sample population is geographically dispersed. For instance, if the government wanted to survey farmers it would be much cheaper to survey a number of farmers in a cluster of a few counties than to try and survey farmers from all over the country.

However, if a small geographical area is used it reduces the accuracy of the results as the clusters may not be truly representative of the whole population. For example, the views of farmers in North Down may be very different from those of farmers in West Tyrone.

(D) QUOTA SAMPLING

In quota sampling researchers are given a certain quota of subjects of a specified type to recruit for the research project. For example, a researcher may be asked to gauge the opinions of 20 males and 20 females from three separate ethnic or socio-economic groups. The researcher is free to select these subjects in whatever manner he or she prefers.

The main advantage of quota sampling is that it is easier and cheaper to carry out than any of the probability sampling techniques considered above since it does not require the use of a sampling frame.

The main drawback of quota sampling however, is that it is open to researcher bias and, since it is not based on the laws of probability, it is not possible to estimate the size of the sampling error.

3. DECIDE ON THE SIZE OF THE SAMPLE

Once a firm has come to a decision on which type of sampling method to use it must then decide on the size of the sample. Clearly, the larger the sample the more likely it is that the sample will be a fair reflection of the population. However, collecting a large sample can be very time-consuming and costly, so the firm has to find a compromise between a sample that is large enough to be representative and small enough to represent value for money.

4. SELECT THE SAMPLE

The final stage of the sampling process is the selection of the actual sample. If the firm has given due consideration to all of the previous stages in the sample selection process, it can carry out its market research secure in the knowledge that the results it obtains will be a fair reflection of the views held by the target population.

- **A FOCUS GROUP** is a form of qualitative research in which a group of individuals is asked to share its thoughts, attitudes and feelings on a particular product or concept.
- **CONSUMER PANELS** also consist of a number of members who form part of a particular market segment. However, consumer panels are used on an ongoing basis, whereas focus groups are normally dissolved after the initial research is complete.
- **TEST MARKETING** is the process of trialling a new product, service or concept on a section of the market prior to a full scale roll out.
- **SAMPLING** is the process of selecting a representative group from a larger population. Sampling methods include random, quota, stratified and cluster.

THE LIMITATIONS OF MARKET RESEARCH

As stated earlier in this chapter, market research is the process whereby firms attempt to discover what consumers require from a good or service so that they are better placed to satisfy those desires.

However, no market research process is foolproof and errors can occur at any stage of the research process, which can result in inaccurate or misleading results.

The aim of market research is to help companies make the right decisions by giving them some insight into their market. Nevertheless, the accuracy and therefore the usefulness of market research is limited by a number of factors.

1. THE SIZE OF THE SAMPLE

As stated earlier, the larger the sample the more accurate the results of the market research are likely to be. However, it is not always possible for firms to carry out market research on a large sample. For most firms cost will be a major consideration and therefore they must choose a sample large enough to be accurate yet small enough to be economically viable.

Most market research is carried out on the basis of a 95% confidence level. What this means is that the results will be accurate 95 times out of every hundred. But this still means that results will be inaccurate five times out of every 100.

2. RESEARCH BIAS

It is incredibly difficult to design any form of market research that contains absolutely no bias. Firms need to be very careful when using market research to ensure that the results are as free from bias as possible. It is often the case that poorly designed market research produces exactly the results that the business expected or hoped for rather than results that truly reflect consumer preferences.

3. FAST CHANGING MARKETS

In some industries, for example the fashion industry, consumer tastes and preferences change so rapidly that it is difficult for market research to keep up. Carrying out market research in these industries often produces results that are dated and therefore of limited use.

Despite these limitations, it is very rare that a business would make any significant decision without first carrying out some form of market research. As long as firms take the time to carefully plan their research they should find that it acts as a vital source of information, which can assist them in the decision-making process.

CASE STUDY

THE BEST JUST GOT BETTER?

An example often used to illustrate the limitations of market research was the decision of The Coca-Cola Company in 1985 to change the flavour of its flagship product Coke. The company had carried out extensive market research including focus groups, surveys and taste tests, all of which suggested that the new flavour would be a big hit.

However, when the new Coke was released under the slogan "the best just got better" sales were less than impressive.

The change in flavour annoyed many of Coke's loyal customers and in the first month after the change the company received over 400,000 complaints.

What the market research had failed to uncover was the emotional attachment many Americans had to the original Coke brand.

Indeed, the negative reaction of consumers was so strong that Coca-Cola was forced to reintroduce the original formula under the brand name Classic Coke just three months after it was taken off the market.

ACTIVITY 7.4

SAMPLING

The headmaster of a large secondary school is considering changing the school's uniform and dress code. He wishes to conduct a survey to gauge the views of the pupils but is unsure as to the best way to select an appropriate sample. He has asked you to write a report explaining the different sampling methods he could use to select his sample.

The number of pupils in each year group is given below:

Year	Male	Female	Total
9	84	85	169
10	77	82	159
11	87	91	178
12	90	95	185
13	68	62	130
14	66	62	128

Chapter 8: THE MARKETING MIX: PRODUCT AND PRICE

As we saw in the previous chapter, there are a wide range of activities which could be considered to be part of the marketing process. These activities range from market research to product design, promotions, and pricing strategies.

In the previous chapter we looked at the first stage of the marketing process, which is market research. In this chapter we will begin to look at the other stages of the marketing process which are collectively described as the marketing mix.

THE MARKETING MIX

The marketing mix is the term used to describe the range of marketing activities that a firm can use to ensure that its output meets the needs and wants of its target market.

The traditional marketing mix consists of four key elements which are often referred to as the 4 Ps: Product, Price, Promotion and Place.

The diagram below illustrates the main elements of the traditional marketing mix.

The marketing mix

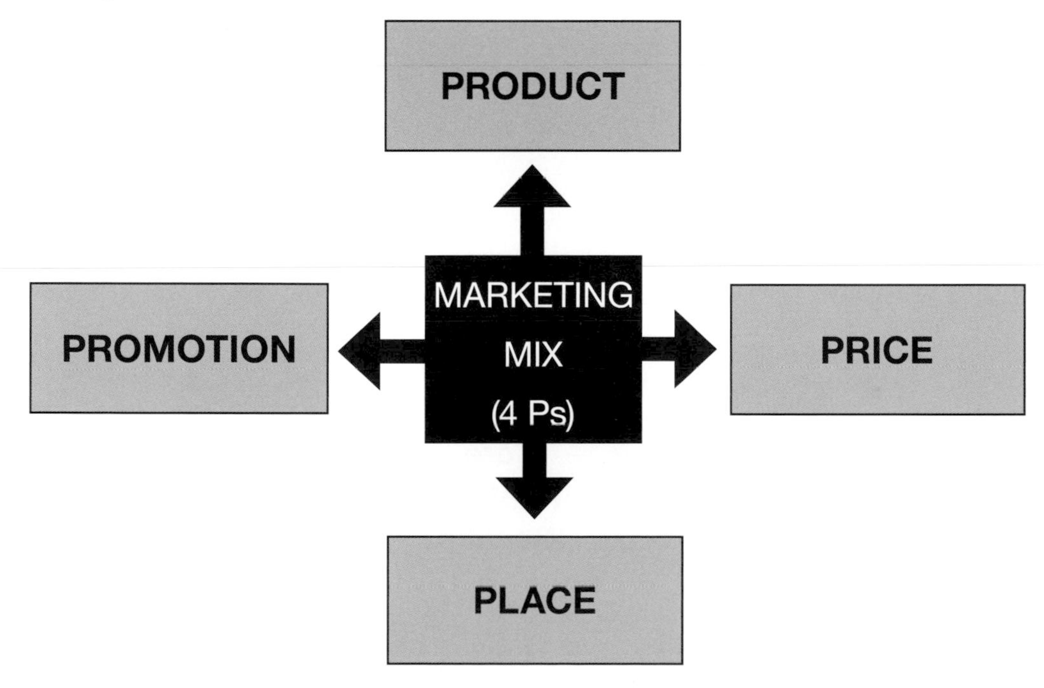

It should be noted that the marketing mix has been expanded in recent years to include three further elements: Processes, People and the Physical environment. We will discuss these three elements in more detail later when we deal with the extended marketing mix in chapter 9. For the rest of this chapter we will focus on the first two elements of the marketing mix – Product and Price.

PRODUCT

The term 'product' is used to refer to anything which is offered for sale on a market that is capable of satisfying consumer wants and needs. It includes not only physical objects, such as a car or bar of chocolate, but also services, such as banking and legal advice, as well as places and ideas.

Product is often regarded as the most important element of the marketing mix; if a firm producing a product does not satisfy a need or a want it will generate no sales, regardless of how it is priced or promoted.

When defining their product, firms often find it useful to consider their product in three different stages which are referred to as the **layered product model**.
At the centre of the layered product model is the **core product**. The core product does not refer to the actual product which the company makes but rather to the benefit consumers gain from buying the product. For example, if Nestle are considering the layered product model for one of their chocolate bars, the core product will refer to the benefit a consumer gets from consuming a bar of chocolate: the satisfied hunger and the pleasure associated with a sugar rush.

The next layer in the model is the **actual product** layer. This layer refers to the actual product made by the company and includes the specific ingredients and packaging which makes one bar of chocolate different from others. At this stage the product is not only concerned with satisfying hunger or giving a sugar rush but includes the added value provided by that particular product such as its distinctive flavour, shape and packaging.

The final layer in the model is the **augmented product** layer which adds more value to the product through activities such as after sales service, quality guarantees and warranties.

The layered product model can be illustrated in a diagram as shown below.

The layered product model

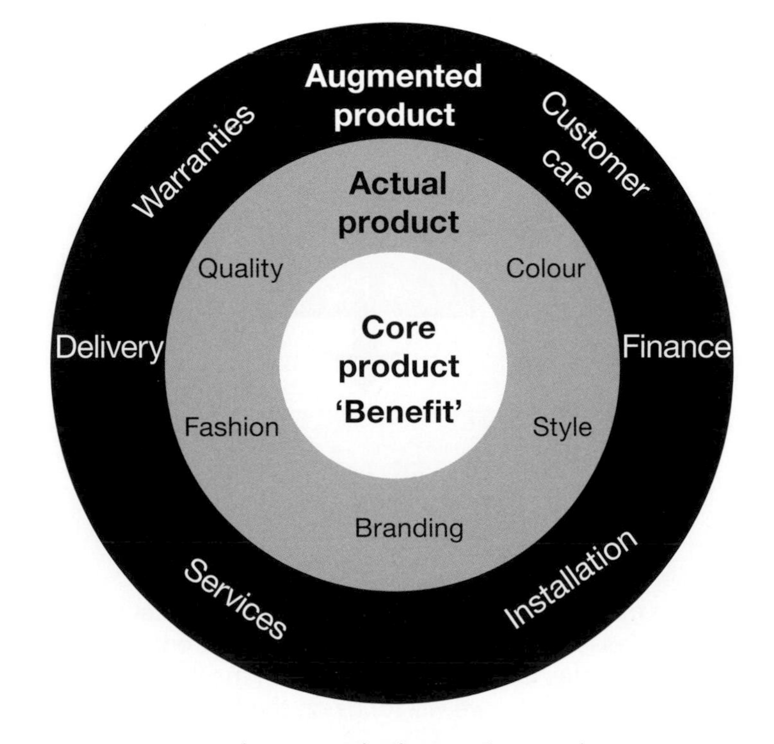

The Three Levels of a Product (www.marketingteacher.com)

PRODUCT LIFE CYCLE

Another practical tool which is often used by firms to analyse both their product and their marketing activities is the product life cycle.

The product life cycle is a model which charts the stages a product will typically go through over its lifespan and measures the sales it is likely to have over this period.

The life cycle of a product can be divided into five key stages: Development; Introduction; Growth; Maturity; and Decline.

At each of these stages, the level of sales, and consequently the revenue generated by the product, will be different.

Most products will follow a similar pattern in that their sales will increase, often quite rapidly, after the initial launch before levelling off and eventually declining.

If we plot sales on the vertical axis against time on the horizontal axis we can plot the life cycle curve of a product. The diagram below illustrates the life cycle for a typical product.

The product life cycle

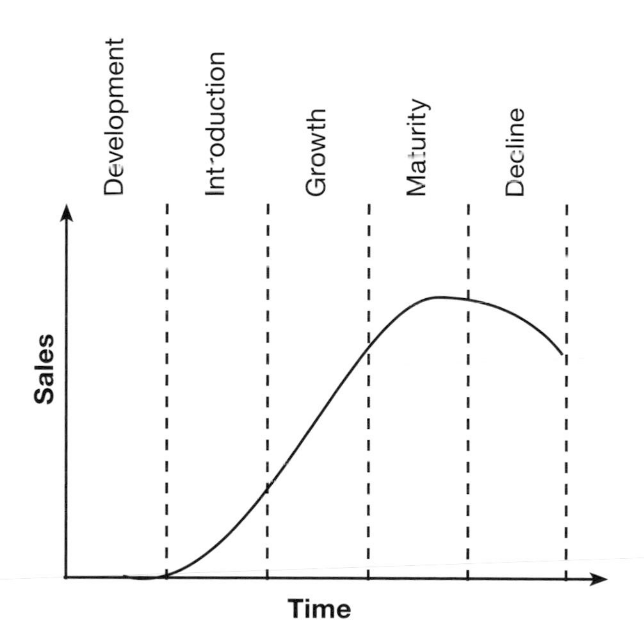

Although it is widely accepted that most products will follow this pattern, the exact duration of each stage and the level of sales achieved in each stage will differ widely between products.

Some products will have a longer, flatter curve which reflects a gradual increase and decrease in sales while others will have a much sharper shape which reflects rapid growth and equally rapid decline.

Rubik's Cube is probably the most popular mechanical puzzle of the twentieth century. Erno Rubik, a Hungarian designer, invented the Cube in 1974 as a design exercise for his interior design students.

Rubik patented the Cube and went on to build and market it in Hungary under the name Magic Cube. In 1979, he approached a big game company, IdealToy Corporation, and they

CASE STUDY...

agreed to make the Cube and market it in the West, under the name of Rubik's Cube.

When the Rubik's Cube was introduced to the West in 1980 its sales soared very quickly, reaching ten million by 1982, but they fell away just as quickly to virtually zero by 1983.

Fad items like the Rubik's Cube have a very sharp life cycle where sales increase very quickly and the saturation point is reached in a short space of time.

The product life cycle curve for a fad item such as the Rubik's Cube is shown in the diagram below.

The life cycle of a fad

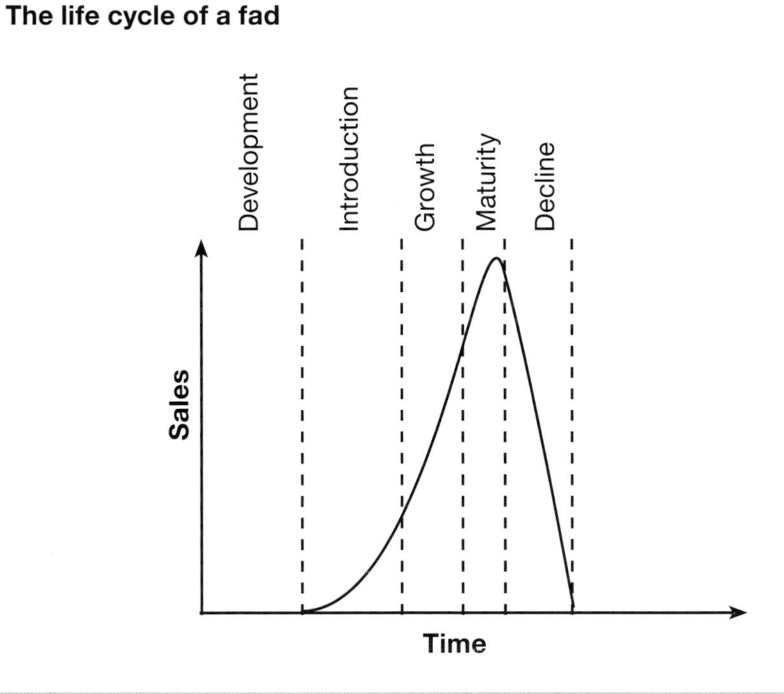

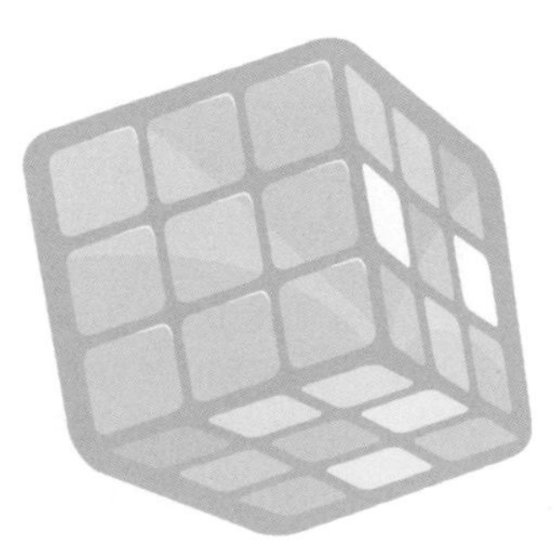

The first stage of the product life cycle is the **development stage.** This stage takes place before the product is put onto the market and therefore at this stage in the cycle, sales are zero. During this stage the idea for the product is refined and extensive market **research** is carried out which may include test marketing.

The duration of this stage will vary significantly between products; high tech products such as aeroplanes or pharmaceuticals will have a development stage of up to ten years, whereas fashion items such as clothing or pop music would have a very short development stage. In such cases firms would be keen to get the product to market before fashions change.

The next stage in the typical product life cycle is the **introduction stage.** This stage only begins when the product is fully launched onto the market, since any small scale test marketing launch would be considered to be part of the development stage. This stage is typically characterised by slow sales growth because consumers are often reluctant to try new products or ideas.

Advertising costs are typically high during this period as firms try to increase awareness of the product and attract the **early adopters**. During this stage the firm is also likely to incur additional costs associated with trying to persuade retailers to stock the product and give it favourable display space. In addition, the low production volumes mean that the firm is unlikely to benefit from economies of scale (see chapter 11).

This combination of low sales growth and high costs mean that the firm is likely to experience negative profits (or losses) during this period.

The exception to this rule occurs in the life cycle of innovative products such as the Nintendo Wii, where firms are able to charge high initial prices to the small group of **innovators** who are prepared to pay in order to gain the kudos associated with purchasing a truly ground-breaking product.

The third stage of the product life cycle is the **growth stage.** At this stage sales begin to increase quite rapidly as the product gains market acceptance and the early adopters purchase the product. These early adopters will be joined later in this growth stage by a group of consumers known as the **early majority.** The early majority are those consumers who wish to be fashionable and purchase new products. However, they are trend followers rather than trend setters.

During the growth stage, retailers will become keen to stock the product and consumers will begin to ask for it. The advertising and promotional activities carried out by the firm will also change, with a greater emphasis on persuasive advertising rather than informative advertising.

During this stage, firms will generally begin to make profits as even though costs remain quite high they now represent a much lower proportion of total sales.

Towards the end of the growth stage, competitors will enter the market, attracted by the increasing sales and as a result the firm may begin to experience downward pressures on price.

The next phase of the product life cycle is the **maturity stage**. This is the longest and most common stage for most markets and is often the most profitable. During this stage a group of consumers known as the **late majority** enter the market and begin buying the product.

Sales continue to grow during this phase but at a much slower pace as competition intensifies in the market.

Firms are often able to reduce their advertising spend during the early part of this period because brand awareness is already quite high. They may instead begin to look at ways to modify the product in order to differentiate it from other products in the market.

At the end of the mature stage the **saturation point** is reached. This is the point at which sales are at their peak and very few new customers can be found. At this stage firms may begin to reduce prices in an attempt to stimulate further sales and some of the less popular brands may drop out of the market.

Eventually the sales of all products will begin to fall and the product will reach the last phase of its life cycle: the **decline stage.**

In the decline stage sales and revenue will fall, possibly as a result of the product becoming obsolete or as a result of competitors producing a product which represents much greater value.

Those consumers who purchase the product during this stage are commonly known as **laggards.** Laggards are consumers who are not concerned with being fashionable and therefore do not buy the latest products, but are more concerned with finding a bargain.

Profits will fall during the decline phase because unit costs increase as a result of lower production volumes, and prices are reduced in an attempt to stimulate sales.

In most cases the product becomes unprofitable and the firm ceases production.

In some cases, however, the decline phase does not lead to the end of the product. If a product has built up sufficient loyalty, its sales may stabilise at a profitable level after the initial decline and the firm may continue producing the product for a long time thereafter.

To illustrate this, consider the market for music. In the early 1990s, vinyl discs were considered by many to be a thing of the past because music fans switched to CD as their preferred format. Indeed, some music companies ceased the production of vinyl completely. Nevertheless, a significant number of music fans remained loyal to the vinyl format and as a result vinyl has remained a profitable segment of the music industry.

The PLC and the innovation adoption model

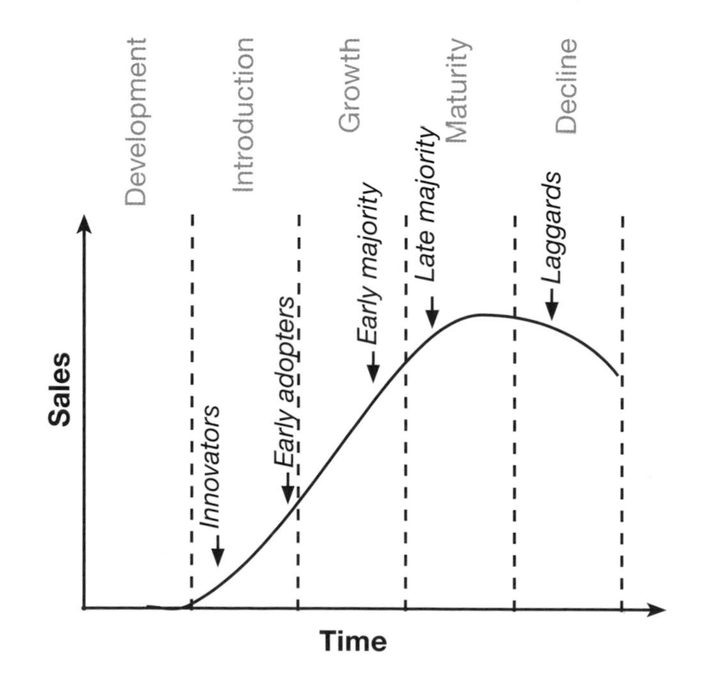

KNOWLEDGE REVIEW

- **THE MARKETING MIX** refers to the range of marketing activities that a firm can use to sell its products. It typically consists of four key elements: Product, Price, Promotion and Place.

- **THE PRODUCT LIFE CYCLE** is a model which charts the sales and revenue that a product will typically achieve over its lifespan.

- **INNOVATORS** are those consumers who are prepared to pay a high price in order to gain the kudos associated with purchasing a truly ground-breaking product.

- **THE EARLY MAJORITY** are those consumers who wish to be fashionable and purchase new products but who are trend followers rather than trend setters.

- **LAGGARDS** are consumers who are not concerned with being fashionable and therefore do not buy the latest products, but are more concerned with finding a bargain.

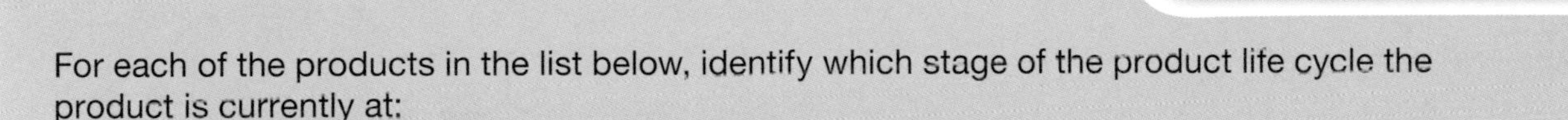

ACTIVITY 8.1

For each of the products in the list below, identify which stage of the product life cycle the product is currently at:

EXTENDING THE PRODUCT LIFE CYCLE

Businesses are always looking for ways to increase their sales and consequently maximise the profits they receive from selling their goods or services. One way to do this is for the firm to customise its marketing strategies to try and extend each of the stages of the product life cycle.

The exact nature and type of strategy used by the firm to extend the product life cycle will depend on a range of factors including: the type of product sold, the stage to be extended, the type of consumer targeted and the level of competition the firm faces.

Examples of extension strategies include:

1. Product modification

A common strategy often used by firms to extend the life cycle of their products is to modify the products in some way in order to make them appear different or superior to the original product.

When this strategy is used early in the maturity stage the modifications can be purely cosmetic but as the product proceeds through the maturity stage, the modifications need to be more fundamental in order to attract additional custom.

This strategy is very popular with car manufacturers who regularly attempt to extend the product life cycle of their cars by adding new features and branding the cars as the Sport version or the TDI version.

CASE STUDY

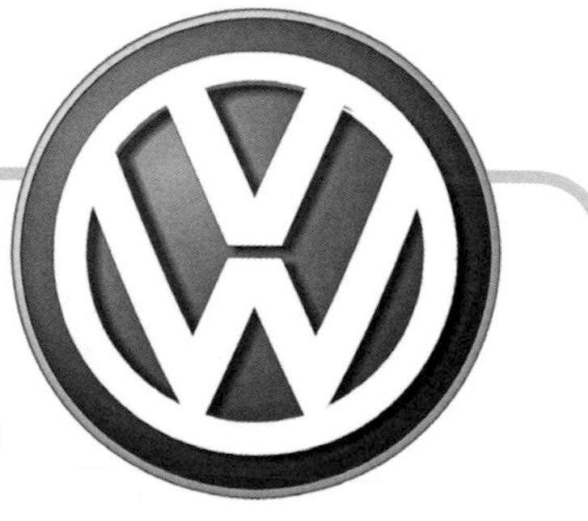

THE VW GOLF

The Volkswagen Golf began life in 1974 and was an attempt by Volkswagen to replace the VW Beatle which had fallen into the decline phase of its product life cycle.

The Mark 1 Golf, which was marketed in the US as the VW Rabbit, proved to be extremely popular among consumers in Europe and the US, with over 25 million cars being built by 2007, making it Volkswagen's best selling model and the world's third best selling car behind the Toyota Corolla and the Ford F-Series.

Over the last 30 years the Golf has been modified extensively in an attempt to prolong its life cycle and is now on its fifth platform (the Mark 5).

The fifth generation Golf now comes in a choice of six models, which are adapted to suit a wide range of lifestyles and budgets.

The entry model in the Golf series is the Golf S which retails at around £12,000. Next in the range is the Match, followed by the GT Sport, the GTI, the GTI edition 30 and at the top of the range the R32 which retails at a little over £26,000.

Within this range a wide choice of engine types is also available including the TSI 1.4, the 2.0 litre TDI and the 3.2 V6.

It is through this process of continuous modification that Volkswagen have been able to extend the life cycle of the Golf into its 33rd year with little sign that it is about to enter a period of decline.

2. Find a new use for the product

Another policy often used by firms in an attempt to extend the life cycle of their products is to find alternative uses for the product.

If a firm is able to convince consumers that their product can be used in a number of different ways then the firm may be able to extend the mature stage significantly longer than would otherwise have been the case.

In recent years the manufacturers of mobile phones have managed to maintain a high level of sales through adding features that allow their phones to act as cameras, personal organisers and even music players. Indeed, Sony Ericsson have branded one of their mobile phones as the Walkman phone.

3. Repositioning

When products reach the mature stage their image may begin to suffer as a result of new, more modern products entering the market.

To prevent the onset of the decline phase, firms often attempt to reposition their products by changing the image of the product in an attempt to alter the consumer's perception of those products.

This repositioning plan may involve simple cosmetic changes to the advertising or marketing strategy or may involve more radical changes to the actual product.

Either way, the objective is the same: to enhance the image of the product in the minds of consumers in order to generate a greater level of sales.

CASE STUDY

Lucozade is the umbrella name for a range of energy and sports drinks, which are produced by GSK plc in the UK. The original Lucozade, now known as Lucozade Energy, was first manufactured in 1927 by a Newcastle chemist who produced it as a source of energy for those who were sick.

Lucozade was originally sold only in hospitals and chemists and was packaged in a large glass bottle with an orange cellophane rap. This changed in 1983 when advertising agency Ogilvy & Mather set about repositioning Lucozade as an energy drink. A new slogan was introduced and the product was repackaged in the smaller, more convenient PET bottle. The repositioning proved extremely popular and sales rocketed as a result, reaching almost £100 million in 1989.

The product range was expanded in the 1990s with the introduction of Lucozade Sport and Lucozade Hydro active, and sales have continued to go from strength to strength.

4. Repackaging

Making alterations to a product's packaging can be a very simple but useful strategy when trying to extend the life cycle of a product. Repackaging is very common in the retail sector where the introduction of new labels, new colour schemes or new containers have all proven to be successful at extending the product life cycle.

5. Re-branding

The term 're-branding' refers to the process of selling the same product or service under a new or different brand identity.

The purpose of re-branding is to disassociate the product from its previous brand and hence remove any negative perceptions associated with the previous brand. Re-branding is a fairly drastic measure and often involves radical alterations to the logo, image and marketing strategy, and for this reason is often very costly.

While re-branding can be extremely successful in extending the life cycle of a product, it contains a significant element of risk and has often proven to be of limited use.

CASE STUDY

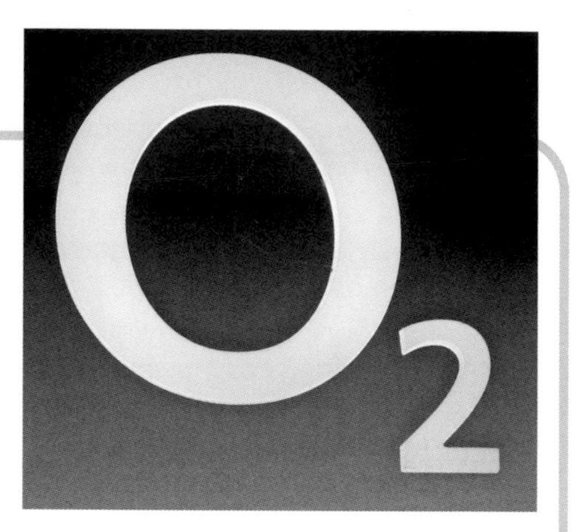

BT CELLNET BECOMES 02

In September 2001, UK mobile phone operator BT Cellnet announced it was getting rid of its brand name in favour of a new international identity.

The decision followed a continuous drop in its market share of call revenues. Furthermore, BT Cellnet's arch-rival Orange (often admired for its brand name) increased its revenues and knocked BT Cellnet into third place, behind both Orange and Vodafone.

The new brand name was O2, the chemical symbol for Oxygen. "We chose a name that was modern and universal and you don't have to teach people to spell it," said Peter Erskine, chief executive of the mobile business.

The owners of BT Cellnet felt the name-change would help to forge a clearer, more relevant identity. But did it?

The early signs were that it didn't. Indeed, despite a massive marketing campaign including sponsorship of the TV show Big Brother, many customers were unfamiliar with the name a full year after the change.

However, as time passed customer awareness increased and the performance of the company improved.

6. Reducing price

Reducing the price at which a product is sold is another strategy frequently used by firms to extend the life cycle of their products. A price reduction can be an effective tool in extending all of the stages of the life cycle because it is likely to attract additional custom. In turn, the level of sales achieved in each stage and the duration of each stage is likely to increase.

Firms can choose from a range of different pricing strategies, which we will explore on page 141 in the second element of the marketing mix – price.

CASE STUDY

CUT-PRICE OFFERS GAVE NEW CAR SALES A BOOST IN MAY

A total of 194,113 new cars were registered last month – a 10.4% rise on the figure for the same time last year according to data from the Society of Motor Manufacturers and Traders (SMMT).

"Car buyers are taking advantage of the spectacular deals on offer at dealerships throughout the UK," said SMMT chief executive Christopher Macgowan.

"With a strong economy and a host of innovative and exciting products, consumer confidence is healthy and as new car prices continue to fall, it is an exceptionally good time to purchase a car," he added.

The SMMT said sales were on course to reach a total of 2.2 million for the year, although the current level of demand was likely to ease slightly later in the year.

(Source: BBC News, 6 June 2000)

PORTFOLIO MANAGEMENT AND THE PRODUCT LIFE CYCLE

As stated earlier, it is not easy for a firm to predict with any certainty what the exact life cycle of a product is likely to be. The duration of each stage and the level of sales associated with each stage will differ from one product to another.

Nonetheless, from a marketing perspective the product life cycle is a very useful concept in that it provides valuable insights which can then be used by the firm to develop its marketing strategy. By using the product life cycle, the firm can plan its production and marketing strategy to ensure that it is able to survive if and when its products reach the decline stage. Ideally, firms should aim to have a range of products at different stages of the product life cycle so that when one product enters the decline stage other products will be entering the growth or mature stage. Diversifying in this way will allow the firm to spread the risk of declining sales over a range of products and make the firm more resilient to changing market conditions.

Business guru Peter Drucker argues that businesses need to keep a careful eye on all of their products to ensure that when today's successful products, or what he referred to as **today's breadwinners**, go into decline the firm has new products, or **tomorrow's breadwinners,** to take their place.

Drucker argues that the key to success is to use the profits generated by today's breadwinners to finance the development of tomorrow's breadwinners, thereby ensuring that the firm has a succession of new products coming onto the market at just the right time.

This type of product succession planning can be illustrated on the diagram overleaf.

Life cycle management

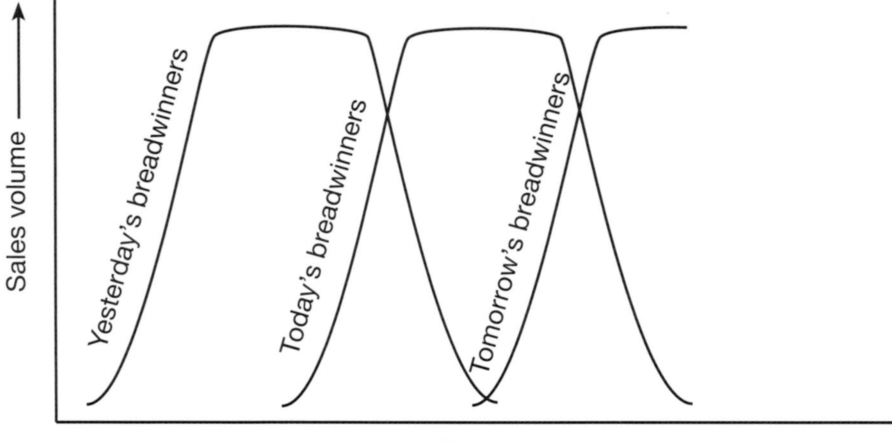

ACTIVITY 8.2

LAST ORDERS FOR GUINNESS

Guinness is one of Britain's best loved brands, yet sales of the famous black stout have been falling year after year, both in the UK and Ireland (see graph below).

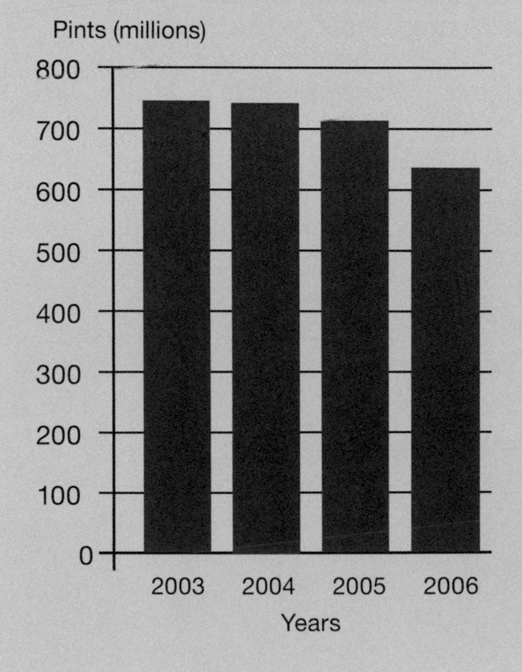

In the last two years Guinness sales have declined in volume by 13% in the UK and things are even worse in Ireland, where sales are down nearly 30% since 2001.

Guinness is, however, continuing to perform well in some markets, particularly Nigeria and America.

ACTIVITY 8.2

In the UK and Ireland, a growing taste for lighter, blander, more refreshing drinks and a long term shift to entertaining at home, have taken their toll on Guinness's sales.

Despite this, the brand is hopeful.

"You're talking about a company that's been around for 250 years and a brand that has been growing from strength to strength, not just in this market but all over the world over that time," says Philip Almond, marketing director for Guinness GB.

(Source: BBC News, 23 November 2007)

1. Identify the stage of the product life cycle reached by Guinness in 2007.
2. Explain some of the reasons why Guinness might have reached this stage.
3. Evaluate some of the strategies Guinness GB could use to reverse the decline in sales and extend the life cycle of their marquee brand.

PRICE

The term 'price' simply refers to the amount of money a firm requires in return for providing its goods or services.

When students are asked to consider the term 'marketing' they often ignore the pricing element, considering it more to do with the accounting or finance function than the marketing function. Yet, this is a mistaken view; price is a fundamental element of the marketing mix. Indeed, any marketing strategy which ignored the price element would be doomed to failure regardless of how well the other elements of the mix were considered.

PRICING STRATEGIES

There are a number of different strategies which a firm can use when deciding on the best price for its product. The strategy chosen will depend on a number of factors including:

The nature of the product being sold
The level of competition the firm faces (see chapter 5)
The price consumers would be willing to pay (see chapter 4)
The cost of producing the product

The following are the most common pricing strategies used by firms.

COMPETITIVE PRICING

Competitive pricing occurs when a firm sets its price at a level which is at or just below the price charged by its main competitors. The price is set at a rate which makes the goods appear competitive but at the same time does not have a detrimental impact on the image of the product.

Competitive pricing is a very common strategy and normally forms part of a wider promotional campaign.

The problem though with competitive pricing as a strategy for dealing with competition is that it could lead to a price war, which can be both risky and expensive for the business.

PENETRATION PRICING

Penetration pricing is often used when a new product is being introduced onto a market which is already relatively competitive. It occurs when a firm sets a low initial entry price to attract consumers to the product. The price is then increased towards the market price as consumer loyalty is built up. Penetration pricing is only useful for goods which generate repeat purchases, and is often used in the market for magazines and confectionery.

Penetration pricing is a very effective way of maximising sales and works best when demand is price elastic. Sometimes though, the low initial price associated with penetration pricing may be damaging to the product's reputation and may simply attract bargain hunters who will switch to another product whenever the price increases.

PREDATORY/DESTROYER PRICING

Predatory pricing occurs when a firm sells its products at a very low price with the intention of driving competitors out of the market, or to create a barrier to entry (ie to prevent potential competitors from entering the market).

If the firm is able to drive competitors from the market they will be able to raise their prices again to a level that would be above the original competitive level.

Predatory pricing is used by firms who have a degree of market power and can be very successful in the long run. However, in the short run the firm may lose money as a result of this strategy, and if the competition is not as weak as predicted the firm who engages in this strategy may itself be forced out of the market.

PSYCHOLOGICAL PRICING

Psychological pricing occurs when a firm sells a product at a price designed to convince the consumer that the product is cheaper than it really is. For example, when a product is sold at £39.99 consumers tend to ignore the 99p and subconsciously believe that the product is closer to £39 than £40. Psychological pricing is a very common strategy, with over 70% of all goods sold in the UK ending in either 99p or 95p.

Research has shown that psychological pricing is very effective and that consumers are more likely to round down than round up whenever prices end in odd numbers.

Nevertheless, as with any pricing policy which makes the product appear cheaper than that of rival products, psychological pricing may be damaging to the preconceived view that consumers have about the quality of the product.

SKIMMING/CREAMING

Skimming is often used by firms who are launching a new or improved product onto the market. The price of the product is set high initially to target those consumers who are likely to be willing to pay the higher price. These consumers, who are known as innovators or early adopters, are generally less sensitive to increases in price.

Consider the market for plasma screen televisions. Currently these products retail at very high prices, but early adopters will still be keen to purchase the plasma screen televisions and will be willing to pay the high price.

After a period of time the price of these TVs will be reduced in an attempt to attract other consumers into the market.

Skimming can be a very effective way of increasing sales revenue but it will only be successful if the demand for the product is inelastic. In addition, using a price skimming strategy is likely to draw competitors into the industry as they will be attracted by the high margins available.

COST PLUS PRICING

Cost plus pricing occurs when a firm calculates the average cost of producing a good or service and then adds on a percentage profit or mark-up to calculate the selling price. This is the most common form of pricing used by small firms and new businesses. The problem with this strategy is that it takes no account of demand and therefore there is no way of knowing if potential customers will purchase the product at the calculated selling price.

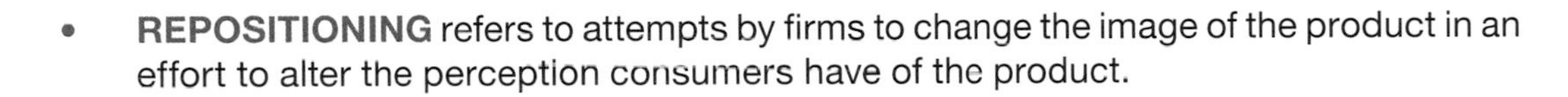

KNOWLEDGE REVIEW

- **REPOSITIONING** refers to attempts by firms to change the image of the product in an effort to alter the perception consumers have of the product.
- **RE-BRANDING** refers to the process of selling the same product or service under a new or different brand identity.
- **PENETRATION PRICING** occurs when a firm sets a low initial entry price to attract consumers to the product. The price is then increased towards the market price as consumer loyalty is built up.
- **PREDATORY PRICING** occurs when a firm sells its products at a very low price with the intention of driving competitors out of the market.
- **PSYCHOLOGICAL PRICING** occurs when a firm sells a product at a price designed to convince the consumer that the product is cheaper than it really is, eg £9.99.

ACTIVITY 8.3

WALKMAN PHONES ON THE INCREASE

Demand for mobile phones with Walkman music players helped first quarter profits more than triple at Sony Ericsson, the mobile-phone joint venture of Japan's Sony and Sweden's Ericsson.

The world's fifth largest mobile phone handset maker said 2.5 million Walkman-branded phones were shipped in the first quarter.

Miles Flint, president of Sony Ericsson, said: "With a total of eight Walkman phones

ACTIVITY 8.3

now announced or shipping, plus the introduction of Cyber-shot imaging phones, we are beginning to deliver the differentiation in our product portfolio which Sony Ericsson promised at the start of the joint venture."

The launch of Walkman phones in August 2005 has helped Sony Ericsson tap into the rising demand for music-enabled devices. The company has recently also moved to gain a greater share of fast-growing markets by introducing cheaper handsets in emerging markets.

First quarter net profits rose from €32m (£22m) to €109m in the three months ending March 31, on sales up 55pc to €1.99bn.

Sony Ericsson said the average selling price of its phones – a closely watched figure in the industry – was €149 in the first quarter, up from €143 in the fourth quarter of 2005, and €137 in the first quarter of last year.

Mr Flint said he didn't expect "average selling prices going any higher than this" in 2006. Nokia this week said its average selling price was €103 in the first quarter.

The joint venture had a global market share of about 6pc–7pc in the quarter. The company shipped 13.3 million phones, 41pc more than a year earlier.

"The W800, W550 and W600 Walkman phones were big sellers and we have sold 5.5 million Walkman-branded phones since mid-August, proving the success of our mobile music strategy," he added.

Global mobile-phone unit sales will exceed 900 million this year compared with an earlier forecast of 10pc increase from 780 million units, it said.

(Adapted from The Telegraph, 14 April 2006)

1. Explain what is meant by the term 'branded' as used in paragraph 2.
2. Paragraph 8 states that "the joint venture had a global market share of about 6pc–7pc in the quarter". Explain how the figures for market share are calculated.
3. Sketch a diagram showing the product life cycle for a typical product and identify which stage of the life cycle the Walkman phone has reached.
4. Explain why Sony Ericsson produce three different models of the Walkman branded phone.
5. Evaluate three alternative pricing strategies that Sony Ericsson could use when setting a price for their new phones.

Chapter 9: THE MARKETING MIX: PROMOTION AND PLACE

9

In the previous chapter, we looked at the first two elements of the marketing mix, product and price. In this chapter we will look at two further elements – promotion and place.

Before going on to look at the role of promotion or place in the marketing mix, it is important to note that no single element of the marketing mix is independent of the others. When planning the marketing mix for a product, firms must ensure that they do not consider any of the elements of the marketing mix in isolation because all the elements are interrelated. For example, if a firm was planning to modify its product in an attempt to extend its product life cycle then it would also be prudent to plan its promotional material to reflect this.
Likewise the use of, for example, penetration pricing by a firm, could be considered to be both a pricing strategy and a short term promotional strategy aimed at attracting new customers to the product.

PROMOTION

Promotion is the process by which businesses communicate information about their products in an attempt to persuade consumers to purchase them.

Promotion is a hugely important element of any marketing strategy because even the most innovative product will not sell if consumers do not know it exists or do not know where they can purchase it.

When communicating information about their product, firms must carefully consider the process a typical consumer will go through before he or she decides to make a purchase. There are a number of different tools which are used by firms to model this process, but the most commonly used tool is the AIDA customer response hierarchy.
A customer response hierarchy is a model which describes the stages a consumer goes through before making a purchase. The model suggests that in order to convince a consumer to purchase a product the firm must move the consumer through four key stages.

1. **Awareness:** the first thing a promotional campaign should do is raise awareness among consumers about the product or brand.
2. **Interest:** once consumers are aware of the product the firm must then make the consumer interested in finding out more about the product.
3. **Desire:** the firm must convince consumers that their product is the one they want or indeed need.
4. **Action:** this is the stage where the consumer actually purchases the product.

There are a wide range of different activities which fall under the heading of promotion. The four most common promotional methods are: advertising, sales promotions, sponsorship and public relations.

The specific combination of strategies that a firm uses to promote its product is often referred to as the promotional mix or more commonly the marketing communications mix.

Examples of promotional strategies include:

1. ADVERTISING

Advertising refers to the process of drawing attention to a product, a brand or a company.

Advertising is a hugely important element in the promotional mix and this is reflected in the huge sums of money spent on advertising by firms keen to gain a competitive advantage over their rivals. The Advertising Association estimate that over £19bn was spent on advertising in the UK in 2007.

Advertising is multi-dimensional and can take place across a wide range of different media. The most common advertising media are shown in the table below.

Regardless of the form of media used to advertise a product, the objective of the advertisement remains the same, namely to **inform** consumers about the product and to **persuade** those consumers to purchase the product.

Methods of advertising

Advertising method	Advantages	Disadvantages
TV	Can reach a wide audience. Can be adapted to suit audience.	Very expensive. Expansion of digital TV and resultant channel hopping has reduced effectiveness.
Radio	Cheaper than TV. Wider population coverage. Can target particular groups since less channel hopping.	Lacks visual impact and therefore less memorable. Only a limited amount of information can be carried.
Cinema	Relatively cheap. Captive audience since they can't switch channels.	Reach is limited to audience numbers.
Billboards/posters	Can reach wide audience. Relatively cheap.	Tend to be ignored. Can't target particular market segment. Carry limited amounts of information.
Newspapers/Magazines	Can be used to reach particular market segment. Can carry a lot of information.	Can be very expensive. An advert can be lost amongst a large number of other adverts.
Internet	Worldwide potential audience. Can contain large amounts of information.	Internet pop-ups can irritate consumers. Audience limited to those who use internet.

Methods of advertising

Direct mail	Wide audience coverage. Can be targeted to particular group.	Junk-mail can irritate rather than persuade. No guarantee it will be read.
Vehicles	Wide audience coverage. Relatively cheap if used on companies' own vehicles.	Carry limited amounts of information. Often ignored.

As we saw in chapter 4, an effective advertising campaign should lead to an increase in the demand for a product and should therefore make the firm more competitive.

Indeed, in the modern economy, advertising is one of the best methods a firm has of gaining a competitive advantage over its rivals.

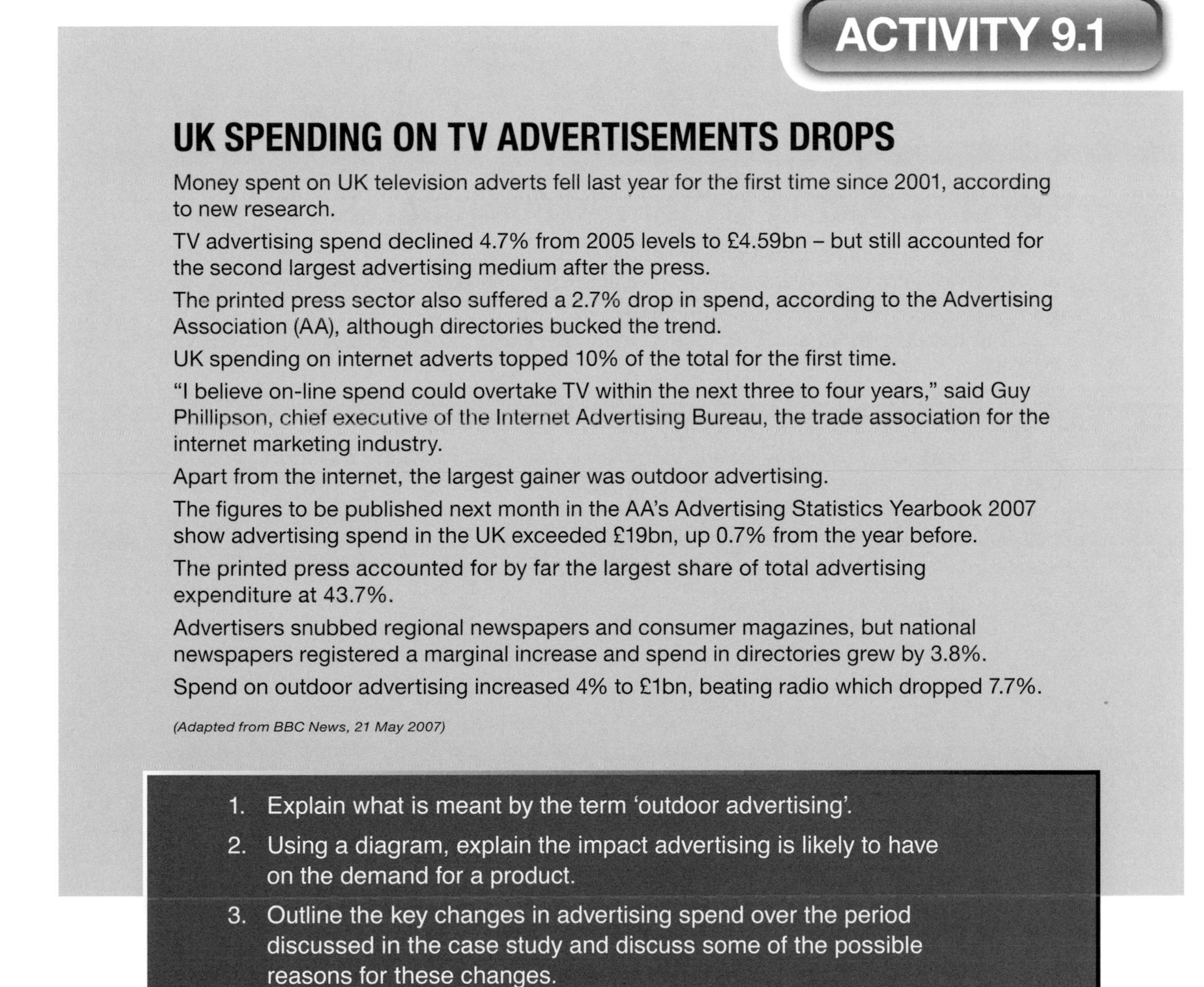

ACTIVITY 9.1

UK SPENDING ON TV ADVERTISEMENTS DROPS

Money spent on UK television adverts fell last year for the first time since 2001, according to new research.

TV advertising spend declined 4.7% from 2005 levels to £4.59bn – but still accounted for the second largest advertising medium after the press.

The printed press sector also suffered a 2.7% drop in spend, according to the Advertising Association (AA), although directories bucked the trend.

UK spending on internet adverts topped 10% of the total for the first time.

"I believe on-line spend could overtake TV within the next three to four years," said Guy Phillipson, chief executive of the Internet Advertising Bureau, the trade association for the internet marketing industry.

Apart from the internet, the largest gainer was outdoor advertising.

The figures to be published next month in the AA's Advertising Statistics Yearbook 2007 show advertising spend in the UK exceeded £19bn, up 0.7% from the year before.

The printed press accounted for by far the largest share of total advertising expenditure at 43.7%.

Advertisers snubbed regional newspapers and consumer magazines, but national newspapers registered a marginal increase and spend in directories grew by 3.8%.

Spend on outdoor advertising increased 4% to £1bn, beating radio which dropped 7.7%.

(Adapted from BBC News, 21 May 2007)

1. Explain what is meant by the term 'outdoor advertising'.
2. Using a diagram, explain the impact advertising is likely to have on the demand for a product.
3. Outline the key changes in advertising spend over the period discussed in the case study and discuss some of the possible reasons for these changes.

2. SALES PROMOTION

The term 'sales promotion' refers to any short term incentive used to encourage consumers to purchase a good or service. Firms can choose from a wide range of alternative sales promotion strategies which include:

PRICE REDUCTIONS/DISCOUNTS

Firms often use short term price reductions or discounts to encourage consumers to purchase a product. The aim of a price reduction is not only to increase sales in the short term but also to generate greater sales in the long term as a result of an increased customer base.

A variation on this strategy is the special offer where goods are sold in greater quantities but at an original price. Examples range from 25% extra free to buy one get one free (BOGOF).

HMV CUTS PRICE IN ATTEMPT TO BOOST SALES

HMV group, which owns Waterstone's, today said it was cutting the prices of music, DVD and books in an attempt to win back sales from supermarkets and on-line retailers.

At the start of the month, it reduced the prices of large amounts of its CD and DVD back catalogue to between £5 and £10, hoping the move would boost sales in the run-up to Christmas.

"We saw this as a very necessary correction, and it puts us in a position to be competitive at Christmas," the HMV Group chief executive, Alan Giles, told Reuters.

Tough competition from companies such as Amazon and Tesco saw HMV's like-for-like sales slide 3.7% for the 12 weeks to September 23, stripping out the benefit of its recent acquisition of the Ottakar's bookstore chain.

"The markets in which the group operates, particularly music, continue to experience very difficult trading conditions," the firm's chairman, Carl Symon, said.

(Adapted from The Guardian, 28 September 2006)

LOSS LEADERS

This is an alternative form of price reduction often used by large retail outlets. Loss leaders are items which are sold below cost (ie at a loss) to attract consumers into the store. It is hoped that when consumers enter the store to purchase the loss leader they will also purchase other full price items and therefore the retailer will recover the cost of the loss leader. For this reason loss leaders are often placed at the back of the store so that consumers must walk past other full price items which have higher profit margins.

This strategy is commonly used by supermarkets in the run-up to Christmas when certain items such as alcohol are sold at a loss.

COMPETITIONS

Firms often use competitions to encourage consumers to purchase a product. In many cases consumers have to purchase the product on a number of occasions to gain the required number of tokens to enter the competition. This is a strategy commonly used by the publishers of newspapers who require consumers to collect coupons over a number of days.

MONEY BACK/MONEY-OFF COUPONS

In some cases coupons are included on the packaging of a product which entitles the consumer to a discount when they purchase the product again. The aim of this strategy is to encourage repeat purchases and build customer loyalty.

FREE GIFTS

Some products include a free gift when a purchase is made. For example, the publishers of women's magazines often include gifts such as make-up bags or hair bands in an effort to encourage sales.

FREE CDS BOOST SALES

Getting a free CD with your daily newspaper is becoming an ever more regular occurrence. In one weekend in 2007 the British Association of Record Dealers calculated that 10 million CDs, with a market value of over £100m, were given away free with newspapers, four times as many as were sold in the preceding week.

Though they can cost over £300,000 to produce, cover-mounted CDs (as they are known in the trade) have been at the forefront of most newspaper's efforts to combat falling sales. The reason is simple: a free CD can add up to 20% to a newspaper's circulation.

Indeed, the Sunday tabloid newspapers can put on anything between 200,000 to 450,000 extra in sales depending on the giveaway.

But newspaper bosses say they are a mixed blessing – they are expensive to produce and do not bring in loyal readers, but the practice has to be maintained because of the intense rivalry in the market.

"They produce massive spikes in circulation, but the readers don't come back the next week. They are the anabolic steroids of the newspaper industry," said one newspaper executive.

(Adapted from The Guardian, 24 February 2005)

POINT OF SALE (POS) DISPLAYS

Special displays are sometimes erected inside shops in an attempt to encourage shoppers to purchase a product. Often these displays will include a demonstration or a free sample.

CUSTOMER LOYALTY CARDS

A customer loyalty card is a device through which firms reward their loyal customers with discounted prices or points which can be used to purchase other items at a reduced price. Loyalty cards encourage consumers to return to the same store again and again since they are able to build up points or reward.

3. SPONSORSHIP

Sponsorship can be defined as any commercial agreement whereby the sponsor provides financial or other support in return for the right to associate its brand or products with the sponsored event.

Sponsorship is becoming an increasingly common method of promotion with businesses now involved in sponsoring sporting events and teams, music concerts, school and charity events and even TV programmes. Examples of sponsorship agreements include Appletiser's sponsorship of the popular TV series Friends and the joint sponsorship of The Champions League by Heineken, Sony, MasterCard, Vodafone, PlayStation and Ford.

Firms are willing to spend huge sums of money to sponsor events such as the Champions League because not only is it an effective form of advertising but they also believe that their products will be viewed in a more positive light as a result of their association with such a high profile event.

CARPHONE WAREHOUSE EVICTS BIG BROTHER

Carphone Warehouse dropped its £3 million sponsorship of Channel 4's Big Brother in the wake of the row over alleged racist bullying in the show.

The firm temporarily suspended its sponsorship during the Celebrity Big Brother series in January 2007.

It followed allegations that Bollywood actress Shilpa Shetty was being bullied by fellow contestants.

The firm said the "huge publicity" had prompted it to look for alternative sponsorship opportunities.

Channel 4, which had been hopeful Carphone Warehouse would sponsor this summer's series, said it is now in talks with other companies to find a new sponsor.

Carphone Warehouse said it would continue to advertise during Big Brother commercial breaks and on the show's website, and would work with Channel 4 on other projects.

At the time, the firm's chief executive, Charles Dunstone, said: "Our concern has rapidly mounted about the broadcast behaviour of individuals within the Big Brother house.

"We are totally against all forms of racism and bullying and indeed this behaviour is entirely at odds with the brand values of the Carphone Warehouse."

1. Explain what is meant by the term 'sponsorship'.
2. Explain why firms are keen to sponsor programmes such as Big Brother.
3. What does the case study suggest about the difficulties associated with sponsorship agreements?

4. PUBLIC RELATIONS

The term 'Public Relations', or PR as it is more commonly known, refers to any activity which aims to establish and maintain goodwill and mutual understanding between an organisation and its public.

Public relations is a very important aspect of promotion and one in which businesses invest a large amount of time and energy.

Almost all large organisations will have a designated PR department, whose aim will be to create a positive image for the company in the hope that this will encourage consumers to purchase products from the company rather than from its rivals.

Examples of public relations activities include making donations to charity, supporting community projects and producing in an environmentally friendly manner.

The key to success with any PR strategy is to ensure that as many potential customers as possible are aware of the positive activities of the firm. To ensure that this is the case, firms often issue press releases in the hope that news organisations will use the press release as the basis for a positive story in their newspaper, magazine or news programme.

PLACE

As you will recall from chapter 7, a commonly used definition of marketing is *the process involved in putting the right product in the right place at the right time at the right price.*

Clearly then, if firms are to successfully market their products, they must ensure that they provide consumers with the goods they require at a price which is acceptable and in a location which is convenient.

The choice of method used to get goods and services to a location where consumers can purchase them is known as the **channel of distribution**.

Choosing an efficient and effective channel of distribution is vitally important if a firm is to meet its marketing objectives. Indeed, estimates suggest that, on average, distribution costs account for approximately one fifth of a product's overall costs.

CHANNEL OF DISTRIBUTION

The term 'channel of distribution' simply refers to the system of organisation through which goods and services are transferred from the manufacturer to the final consumer. The diagram below shows the three main distribution channels.

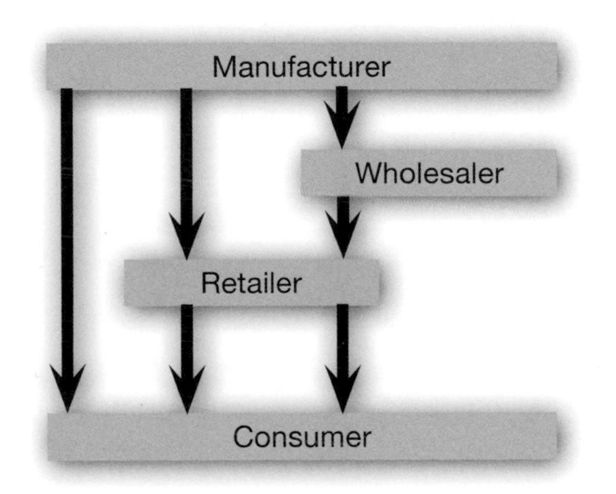

1. Manufacturer to consumer

This channel distributes goods from the producer directly to the end user. Sometimes known as a zero level channel, it is growing in popularity as a result of the increase in direct selling. Examples include farm shops, where the farmer sells directly to the consumer, or bespoke jewellery, where the jeweller makes a single item of jewellery to meet the exact specifications of the consumer.

2. Manufacturer to retailer to consumer

Also known as a one level channel, this is becoming the most common channel of distribution in consumer markets. This is as a result of the growth of large retail chains such as Tesco and M&S who prefer to buy directly from the manufacturer rather than from a middleman, as they can often secure better prices if they deal directly with the manufacturer.

3. Manufacturer to wholesaler to retailer to consumer

Two level channels such as these are still common in consumer markets, where small retailers do not have the buying power to purchase directly from the manufacturer and therefore must buy their stock from a wholesaler. As we saw in chapter 1, small retailers can group together to buy collectively in an attempt to reduce costs. For example, the retail chain SPAR acts as a wholesaler to its members and allows them to purchase stock at a lower price as a result of its increased buying power.

CHOOSING A DISTRIBUTION CHANNEL

The actual choice of distribution channel chosen by a firm will depend on a wide range of factors, which include: the cost of the distribution channel; the level of control that can be exercised over the channel; the geographical coverage of channel selected; and the reliability of the channel relative to product presentation, continuity of supply and the level of customer care or after sales service.

In most cases manufacturers will not stick rigidly to one distribution channel but will instead use a range of distribution channels as appropriate to the good or service they are producing.

For example, companies such as Tayto can distribute their goods via all three channels: sell their products directly to consumers through their website; sell to retailers such as Tesco; or sell to retailers via wholesalers such as Makro.

ACTIVITY 9.3

DISTRIBUTION CHANNEL

The companies described opposite, require advice as to which method of distribution to use when they expand into overseas markets. In each case suggest a method of distribution and justify your suggestions:

1. "Slice of life" – a UK Pizza company, which specialises in the production of small pizzas and pizza slices for sale in restaurants or convenience stores.
2. "Uisce Beatha" – A Northern Ireland based whiskey brewery which produces high quality Irish whiskey. Currently they only sell to a few bar and restaurant chains in the UK.
3. "Seamus O'Kane" – A bodhran maker in Northern Ireland who makes high quality bodhrans. He has recently noticed that people from other countries are interested in buying his drums and that there may be a market abroad.
4. "Home improvements" – A company which makes and sells household goods such as furniture and appliances.

METHODS OF TRANSPORT

Regardless of the channel chosen, the distribution of products will require the goods to be transported to their final destination. The method of transport selected is very important and will depend on a number of factors which include speed, cost and reliability.

The table below outlines the main methods of transport and considers the main advantages and disadvantages of each method.

Methods of transport

Method of transport	Advantages	Disadvantages
ROAD Most common method of transport in Northern Ireland. The province is well served by the road network with six main motorways.	• Allows door to door delivery. • Does not depend on timetables. • Secure because driver stays with the goods.	• Purchase and maintenance of vehicles is expensive. • Traffic congestion can cause delays and increase costs. • Cost associated with empty return journey.
RAIL Northern Ireland has a limited rail service of approximately 350 km run by NI railways.	• Faster than road transport in most cases. • Lower cost than road transport.	• Requires transhipment to and from train station which increases risk of damage. • Northern Ireland poorly served by rail network.

Methods of transport

AIR Northern Ireland has two main airports: the George Best Belfast City Airport and Aldergrove International Airport. A smaller airport operates from the City of Derry.	• Very fast. • Can be relatively cheap for small, light products.	• Very expensive for bulky or heavy products. • Requires transhipment to and from airport.
SEA Northern Ireland has two main seaports: Belfast and Larne.	• Cheap compared to air transport. • Roll-on/roll-off ferries reduce the need for handling or transhipment.	• Slow compared to air. • May require transhipment and therefore increases the risk of damage or loss.
PIPELINE/CABLE This method of transport is associated with the transportation of utilities such as oil, gas and electricity and in recent years electronic data such as music and video files (see case study below).	• Once the network is provided the cost of distribution is very low. • Advances in ICT make this a very attractive method of transportation for many industries.	• High initial fixed cost associated with providing network. • Not suitable for all types of product.

CASE STUDY

FOX FILMS 'FOR RENT VIA ITUNES'

Apple and 20th Century Fox studio are to announce a deal that will allow consumers to rent the studio's films through iTunes, media reports say. The service will work in the same way as Apples iTunes service where consumers can download music for a set fee.

However, customers will have a limited time to watch films downloaded from the iTunes store.

One industry watcher stated that "if the reports are true, this looks like a new assault on the video and movie market".

Apple shares rose above $200 for the first time on Wednesday in response to the news.

(Adapted from BBC News, 27 December 2007)

ACTIVITY 9.4

METHODS OF TRANSPORT

For each of the examples opposite, select the most appropriate method of transport and justify your selection in each case.

ACTIVITY 9.4

1. Fresh fruit coming from Argentina to Northern Ireland.
2. A daily paper being distributed all around Ireland.
3. Transport of live pigs from a farm in County Down to a market in County Armagh.
4. The transport of large generator units by FG Wilson to customers in the Middle East.
5. The transport of medicine and drugs from Pfizer to customers in USA.
6. A record company selling music to teenagers.

THE EXTENDED MARKETING MIX

The traditional marketing mix with the 4 Ps is a very effective method of analysing the marketing activities of firms that produce goods. However, as we learned in chapter 3, the service sector of the economy has been growing in recent years and is now the dominant sector of economic activity in the UK.

Therefore, the traditional marketing mix has been expanded in recent years to include three further elements: Processes, People and the Physical environment. These additional Ps have been added in an attempt to better reflect the marketing activities of service sector firms.

The diagram below illustrates the 7 Ps of the extended marketing mix.

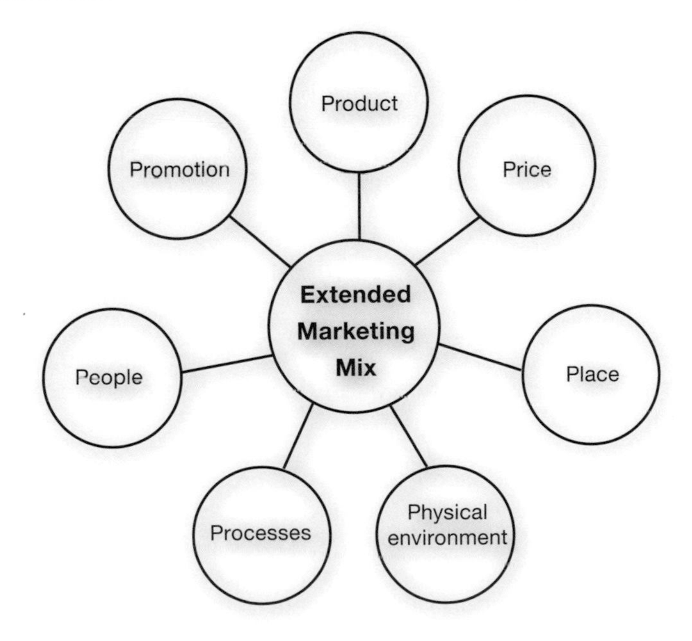

This extended marketing mix is an attempt to introduce a more integrated approach to marketing and endeavours to show how other functional areas within a business can contribute to the achievement of the firm's marketing objectives.

PEOPLE

In the provision of services, where there is no tangible product from which to derive utility, a vitally important factor in determining the level of satisfaction experienced by consumers is to look at the behaviour and attitude of the staff who are providing the service.

Customers are more likely to be loyal to a firm if the employees of the firm deal with their purchase or request in a pleasant and professional manner.

PROCESSES

The term 'processes' refers to the systems employed by the firm to ensure that their services are successfully delivered to their customers. This includes the system used to purchase the service, the distribution system used to deliver the service, and the processes used to deal with customer inquiries or complaints.

PHYSICAL ENVIRONMENT/EVIDENCE

In the past when manufacturing was the dominant sector of the UK economy, the physical layout of the factory which produced the goods was not important, at least not from the perspective of the consumer; after all, the consumer was unlikely ever to see the factory. However, in the provision of services, the actual physical environment is much more important. For example, in the retail sector the layout and design of the shop floor is often as significant a factor in determining the success of the business as the products being sold.

The term 'physical evidence' applies not only to the store or office but also to the company's website and indeed all of those aspects of the service that communicate the identity or values of the brand or company.

THE INTERNET AND E-COMMERCE

Developments in information and communications technology have fundamentally changed the way businesses sell and distribute their goods and services. New technology, such as the internet and broadband, has opened up a whole new world of opportunities for business. These opportunities range from the ability to undertake much more efficient market research to the ability to communicate more effectively with suppliers and customers.

Undoubtedly, the single most important development in this area over the last 20 years has been the introduction and growth of e-commerce.

E-commerce, or electronic commerce to give it its full title, refers to the distributing, buying, selling, marketing and servicing of products or services over electronic systems such as the internet.

The amount of trade conducted electronically has grown dramatically in the UK in recent years with over £100 billion worth of goods and services being traded electronically each year. Most firms in the UK (more than 70%) have their own website, and while many of these firms do not use this site to sell their products (only 15% have a full e-commerce site) they can use the internet to support other aspects of their marketing activities.

With the spread of broadband internet access and improving levels of consumer confidence in the security of on-line purchasing, e-commerce seems set to become an even more important feature of business activity in the UK.

ACTIVITY 9.5

ON-LINE SHOPPING EXPECTED TO SOAR

Christmas shoppers are expected to make Monday, 10th December, the busiest day of the year for on-line shopping.

Credit card firms are predicting a rise of more than 50% in on-line shopping this Christmas, compared with 2006.

Shoppers will spend £5.6bn on-line this month – more than 10% of all plastic card spending.

But consumers are being warned to protect their computers from fraudsters with anti-virus software and to examine sites carefully.

High Street retailers are facing a nervous Christmas, with stores worried that a dip in consumer confidence could hit sales.

But on-line retailers are expecting their peak day on Monday as shoppers try to make sure presents are delivered by Christmas.

In the past five years, the number of adults shopping on-line has doubled to 30 million.

Internet firm Play.com is preparing for an average 650 orders every minute.

The firm is expecting to ship more than 250 tonnes of goods during the day, while overall sales are likely to be up almost a third year-on-year.

(Adapted from BBC News, 3 December 2007)

1. Outline what is meant by the term 'e-commerce'.
2. Analyse some of the possible factors which have led to a 50% increase in on-line shopping.
3. Evaluate the impact that the internet and e-commerce are likely to have on UK businesses.

KNOWLEDGE REVIEW

- **PROMOTION** is the process by which businesses communicate information about their products in an attempt to persuade consumers to purchase them.
- **ADVERTISING** refers to the process of drawing attention to a product, a brand or a company.
- **LOSS LEADERS** are items which are sold below cost (ie at a loss) to attract consumers into the store.
- **SPONSORSHIP** can be defined as any commercial agreement whereby the sponsor provides financial or other support in return for the right to associate its brand or products with the sponsored event.

- **PUBLIC RELATIONS** are any activities which aim to establish and maintain goodwill and mutual understanding between an organisation and its public.

- **THE TERM CHANNEL OF DISTRIBUTION** simply refers to the system of organisation through which goods and services are transferred from the manufacturer to the final consumer.

- **E-COMMERCE** is the selling, marketing and servicing of products or services over electronic systems such as the internet.

ACTIVITY 9.6

THE MARKETING MIX

Choose a product (either a good or a service) and write a detailed analysis of its marketing mix. In your analysis you should consider the following:

- The core product and the actual product
- The target market
- The market in which it exists and the competition it faces
- Which stage of the product life cycle the product is at
- The packaging and branding of the product
- The price of the product and any pricing strategies used to help sell the product
- The advertising and promotion of the product
- Where the product can be purchased

Chapter 10: MARKET PLANNING AND STRATEGY

10

BUSINESS PLANNING

Business planning is the process through which organisations attempt to anticipate the future and devise courses of action that will help them achieve their corporate objectives.

An effective business plan is an essential component of any successful business, since it helps firms focus on the important tasks and provides a mechanism for assessing progress towards meeting key objectives.

As illustrated on the diagram below, an effective business plan will be made up of a range of smaller plans for each of the functional areas of the business.

While each of these individual plans will have their own specific objectives and strategies they will all interact to produce a coherent plan for the overall business.

Business planning

MARKETING PLAN

The marketing plan is one of the most important components of the overall business plan and is simply a written document which details the actions which are required to ensure the business meets its marketing objectives.

To create an effective marketing plan the business will typically follow seven key steps.

1. CONDUCT A SITUATION ANALYSIS

The first formal step in the marketing planning process is that of conducting situation analysis. To conduct a situation analysis a firm must carry out an audit of all the internal and external factors that are likely to influence the buying behaviour of consumers.

Information which should be collected in this audit includes:

- What is the product that is to be offered for sale and what are its key features?
- Who are the customers and what are their key characteristics?
- Who are the main competitors and what are their strengths and weaknesses?
- What is the current economic climate and how does it impact on the market?

There are a number of analytical tools available to help businesses carry out an audit of this type. The two most commonly used tools are a PESTLE analysis and a SWOT analysis.

A **PESTLE** analysis is a business tool which allows the firm to analyse its external environment in terms of political, economic, social, technological, legal and environmental factors. You will learn more about PESTLE analysis when you study business strategy and planning in more detail as part of the business decision-making unit of the A2 course.

A **SWOT** analysis is a tool for auditing both the organisation and its external environment. SWOT stands for **strengths, weaknesses, opportunities and threats.**

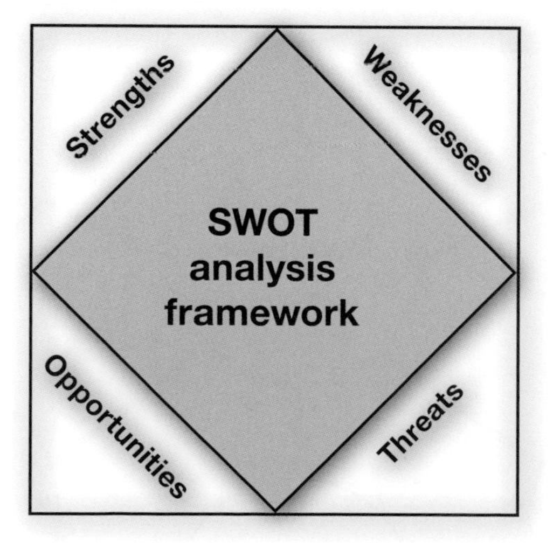

In a SWOT analysis, the strengths and weaknesses of a firm are considered to be **internal** factors.

A firm's strengths are their resources or capabilities that can be used to create a competitive advantage. For example, the strength of the business could be:

- a new, innovative product or service
- the location of the business
- the quality processes and procedures adopted by the business
- any other aspect of the business that adds value to the product or service

A weakness could be:

- a lack of marketing expertise
- an undifferentiated product
- a reputation for poor quality goods or services
- a poor corporate image

Opportunities and threats are considered to be external factors.

An opportunity for a business could be:

- a developing market such as the Internet
- the possibility of a merger or joint venture
- a new international market such as China or India
- a market opening created by an ineffective competitor leaving the industry

A threat could be:

- a new competitor in your home market
- the possibility of a price war starting with competitors
- a competitor producing a new innovative product or service
- a competitor gaining access to a superior channel of distribution

ACTIVITY 10.1

SWOT ANALYSIS FOR DG DIVING

DG Diving is a Northern Ireland based scuba diving company which operates from a shop in Portaferry. Its main business includes commercial work for local fishermen and training recreational divers.

Perform a SWOT analysis on DG Diving based on the following issues:

1. The centre is located in Portaferry town centre and has limited space for parking.
2. Portaferry has a growing reputation for some of the finest dive sites in the UK.
3. DG Diving has its own boat and indoor swimming pool in which to train divers.

ACTIVITY 10.1

4. It is widely acknowledged that DG diving has the best-trained and most respected staff of all of the dive centres in Northern Ireland.
5. Due to an increase in disposable income over the last ten years, local residents have more money to spend on leisure activities.
6. After a heated argument with the manager of the local leisure centre, the leader of a respected local scuba club is looking for a new venue to train divers.
7. A private joke between staff states that if you want a day off from work, you should order food from the centre's canteen.
8. A fish farm has started operating in the area and will require divers to maintain the fish farm.
9. A former employee of DG diving has just started a similar business in the same area.
10. DG diving has just received the prestigious PADI 5 star dive centre award. The company is currently the only one in Northern Ireland to hold such an award.

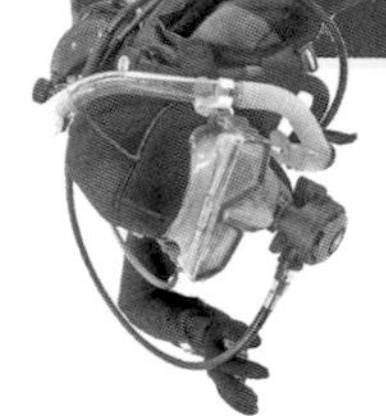

Once an organisation has completed its situation analysis it is ready to move on to the next stage in marketing planning – objective setting – which is seen by some as the most important in the whole marketing process.

2. SET MARKETING OBJECTIVES

Setting objectives is the key to the whole marketing plan because it is the objectives which provide the direction for all the other phases of the plan, while also acting as the standards against which firms can evaluate their performance.

There are a number of different marketing goals or objectives which a firm might have. The precise marketing objective adopted by a firm will depend on the range of factors that the firm considered in its situation analysis. However, the most common objectives include increasing sales or increasing market share.

When setting its marketing objectives, firms must ensure that the objectives are **SMART**. **SMART** objectives are objectives which are:

1. **SPECIFIC** – the objectives should specify exactly what it is the firm wants to achieve.
2. **MEASURABLE** – there should be some method of measuring whether the objective has been achieved.
3. **ATTAINABLE** – the firm should be able to achieve the objectives within the available resources.

4. **REALISTIC** – the objectives should be challenging but they must also be realistic.
5. **TIME BOUND** – there should be a defined timescale setting out when the objective should be achieved.

An example of a smart objective that might be adopted by a firm such as Cadbury, would be to increase the market share held by dairy milk by 5% over the next 12 months.

This is regarded as a **SMART** objective because it is specific, measurable, attainable, realistic and time bound.

3. FORMULATION OF THE MARKETING STRATEGY

Once the firm has decided on its marketing objectives it can then set about formulating its specific marketing strategy to ensure that its marketing objectives can be achieved. The marketing strategy simply refers to the explicit tactics the firm intends to use to meet its marketing objectives.

Before a marketing strategy can be formulated or implemented the firm must first identify and select that section of the market that they intend to target with their good or service.

To select an appropriate target market, the firm must carry out a careful analysis of just what type of consumer it is they want to reach. When they have done this they can then tailor the marketing mix to suit the needs and wants of the target market.

To accurately identify their target market, the firm needs to identify the different market segments and analyse their specific needs.

MARKET SEGMENTATION

A market segment is a sub-group of consumers who share one, or a number of characteristics, which result in them having similar wants and needs.

Market segmentation, therefore, is the process of dividing a market into distinct groups or segments that share common characteristics. Good market segmentation will result in segment members that are homogeneous or as alike as possible and in this way they are likely to respond similarly to a given marketing strategy.

While market segmentation is a useful strategy it cannot be used in all cases. To be effective, market segmentation must meet the following requirements.

- The market segment must be measurable both in terms of the number of potential customers and the value of potential sales.
- The market segments must be large enough to be potentially profitable.
- The firm must be capable of marketing effectively to one or more of the market segments.

There are a number of different factors upon which firms can base their market segmentation. Examples include:

GEOGRAPHIC SEGMENTATION

Geographic segmentation is based on regional characteristics such as climate, terrain, language and population density.

Geographic segmentation is particularly relevant to multi-national or global businesses, which will typically have regional or national marketing strategies and these in turn will be altered to meet the specific needs of the different geographic regions. The most obvious example of this is the use of different languages in the labelling of goods in different countries.

Within countries or regions where there is a common language, geographic segmentation can be based on factors such as city size or population density. For example, major petrol retailers such as Shell and BP use traffic density data as a basis for deciding on the location of their forecourts. If the traffic density in a certain area falls below a particular threshold, that area will not be considered to be a viable market segment.

DEMOGRAPHIC SEGMENTATION

Demographic segmentation is the most commonly used approach to market segmentation, probably because the segments are easy to identify and measure and there is a wealth of data available to marketers to use.

Demographic segmentation attempts to divide consumer groups into segments based upon characteristics such as age, gender, ethnicity, income and family status.

(a) Segmenting by age

Many firms identify market segments on the basis of age as they consider the consumer's age to be a key factor in determining the type of good or service they will require.

The holiday industry is a classic example of an industry which segments its market by age. To illustrate this, consider the differing age profiles of the customers of Club 18–30 and Saga holidays (who market their holidays exclusively at the over 50s).

CASE STUDY

SAGA PLANS LONDON SHARE LISTING

Holidays-to-insurance Company Saga is planning to list its shares on the London Stock Exchange.

The family-run firm, which targets the over-50s, had also been considering a sale to private investors.

Kent-based Saga is being sold after chairman Roger De Haan announced his retirement. The company was founded in 1951 as a single hotel in Folkestone.

Today, it specialises in a wealth of services for the over-50s and has almost eight million people on its books.

CASE STUDY...

Saga also has a best-selling magazine which offers health advice, and in addition runs a number of radio stations.

"We are very pleased with the level of interest shown by customers and other members of the public in registering their interest in participating in the possible IPO," said Andrew Goodsell, Saga's chief executive officer.

"Looking forward, I believe that Saga is well positioned to benefit from a demographic shift, which expects to see its target market increase by five million people over the next 20 years."

(Adapted from BBC News, 15 September 2004)

(b) Segmenting by gender

Gender is a common variable for segmenting certain markets since many products, most notably, clothes, toiletries and, to a lesser extent, magazines are gender specific.

In recent years some businesses, which have traditionally only produced products for one gender group, have begun to develop products that are targeted at the other gender in an attempt to increase their overall level of sales.

(c) Segmenting by ethnicity

In recent years companies have become increasingly aware of the varying wants and needs of different ethnic groups and have begun to respond by producing products to satisfy the specific requirements of these different ethnic groups. For example, L'Oreal has begun to produce different hair products for Black and Asian hair types.

CASE STUDY

ADVERTISERS MISSING OUT ON THE BROWN POUND

Advertisers are missing out on a huge potential market by failing to communicate properly with black and Asian people, according to a new report.

The combined disposable income of ethnic minorities in the UK is £32bn, according to trade body, the Institute of Practitioners in Advertising (IPA). However, it said that businesses are often guilty of ignoring specialist ethnic media and failing to reflect minority cultures in mainstream advertising.

Anjna Raheja, of PR agency Media Moguls, which specialises in targeting South Asian consumers, said "in the same way that we have recognized a grey pound, and a pink pound, then actually there is a brown pound," she told BBC Radio Five's Wake Up to Money.

"And there are characteristics of that brown pound and the communities that make it up, that need to be understood and then targeted."

(Adapted from BBC News, 22 September 2003)

(d) Segmenting by income

Another common way of segmenting a market is by income or social class. For example, many companies produce a range of products, some of which are specifically targeted at either high income earners, middle income groups or lower income groups. Consider the range of own brand products produced by Tesco which has three distinct ranges: the Tesco finest range which is aimed at those on higher incomes; the regular Tesco brand which is aimed at those on middle incomes; and the Tesco value brand which is aimed at those on lower incomes.

(e) Segmentation by family status

Many firms segment markets based on the concept of the family life cycle. The family life cycle is the term used to describe the process of family formation and dissolution.

The family life cycle has five key stages and each stage has a number of distinct sub groups.

The five key stages of the family life cycle are:

- Young singles
- Young married or unmarried couples
- Parents: babies through to adolescents
- Launching adult children
- Retirement or senior years

The buying behaviour of people in each of these stages is likely to be significantly different. For example, young singles tend to be much more likely to purchase new fashion items and spend more on recreation, whereas parents are likely to spend more on baby products.

GEO-DEMOGRAPHIC SEGMENTATION

Geo-demographic segmentation is an attempt by marketers to segment the market using not one criteria, but rather a number of different geographic, demographic and economic factors. Geo-demographic segmentation will include factors such as, where the customer lives, the size of their family, their job type, their yearly income and so on.

The most commonly used geo-demographic categorisation is the ACORN or A Classification of Residential Neighbourhoods to give it its full title.

ACORN is a geo-demographic tool which categorises all of the **1.9 million postcodes in the UK,** using over **125 demographic statistics** and **287 lifestyle variables.** ACORN is used widely by businesses such as banks and other financial institutions when making decisions on how to market their products.

MARKET TARGETING

Once a firm has segmented its market it must then choose which segment or segments to which it will focus its marketing strategy. The market segment to which the firm has chosen to market its products is known as the **target market.**

Selecting a target market segment for a product can result in a much more efficient use of resources than attempting to sell a generic product to the entire market. It is often the case that a greater market share can be achieved by capturing most or all of a segment, via a carefully directed marketing plan that reaches precisely the right people with the right message, than by trying to capture the whole market with a generic approach.

After the firm has selected its target market from the different market segments, the next stage is to decide how it wants to **position** itself within that chosen market segment.

Market positioning is the process by which firms try to create an image for their product in the minds of potential consumers. Essentially, positioning refers to how organisations want consumers to view their products in comparison to competitors' products. For example, car manufactures such as Hyundai and Daewoo have positioned themselves as value or economy brands, whereas Mercedes and BMW have positioned themselves as luxury or premium brands which represent high quality. This is illustrated in the diagram below.

When deciding how to position their products, marketers often find it useful to use a positioning map. A **positioning map**, which is also known as a perceptual map since it is based on consumer perceptions of a product, takes two key aspects of a product and compares them to other products in the industry.

When plotting a positioning map, the two most common dimensions used are price and quality but other criteria such as style, reliability, and safety, can also be factored.

A quality/price positioning map

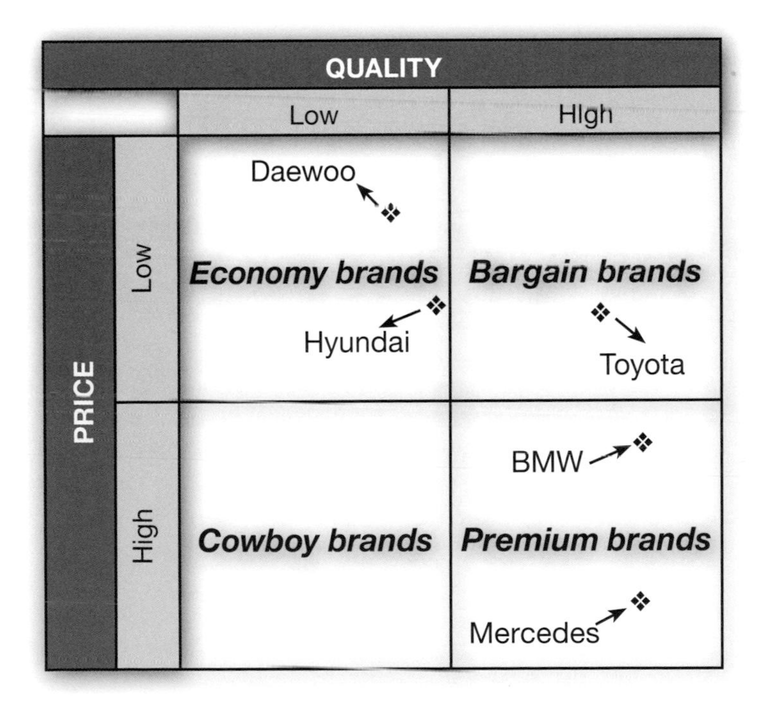

CASE STUDY

THE REPOSITIONING OF SKODA

Why does a Skoda have a heated rear windscreen? To keep your hands warm when you push it!

This joke, which is typical of the type of jokes told about Skoda in the 1980s, represents the view that many people had of Skoda cars, ie low priced, low quality products.

However, this perception has changed significantly over the last ten years as a result of the repositioning strategy adopted by the owners of the Skoda brand, Volkswagen.

Volkswagen used the previous poor image of Skoda in its advertising and promotions campaign with the slogan "It's so good you won't believe it's a Skoda".

The campaign was a huge success and Skoda is now one of the fastest growing UK brands, with the Skoda Octavia Superb being the preferred choice of the nation's taxi drivers – always a very good indicator.

Most UK consumers no longer see Skoda as representing poor quality; many of them now see it as representing a lower priced Volkswagen.

ACTIVITY 10.2

THE UK CONFECTIONERY MARKET

Draw a price/quality positioning map for the UK confectionery market and place the following brands on the map based on the perception you feel most consumers would have about the brand.

1. Galaxy
2. Mars bar
3. Twix
4. Milk Tray
5. Ferrero Rocher
6. Curly Wurly
7. Green and Blacks organic fair trade chocolate

4. CREATE DETAILED PLANS FOR EACH ELEMENT OF THE MARKETING MIX

The process of market segmentation, targeting and positioning, is used by the firm to help inform the decisions that need to be taken with regard to each element of the marketing mix.

At this stage detailed plans will be developed for each of the 4 Ps (and for service organisations – each of the 7 Ps).

Organisations need to ensure that they produce a product which satisfies the wants and needs of their chosen market segment. They also need to ensure that they offer their product for sale at a price which suits the target market's expectations and budget.

All of the advertising and promotion must communicate the correct message to the target consumer and the distribution channel chosen must ensure that the product is available in those places where consumers would wish to buy it.

At this stage of the marketing plan the aim is to devise all of the individual plans that will work in unison to ensure that the company can meet its marketing objectives, ie fully satisfying the expectations and needs of its customers.

The marketing plan and its constituent plans:

5. DETERMINE THE MARKETING BUDGET

A marketing plan will only be successful if sufficient resources are available to implement the plan fully.

At this stage of the planning process the company must set out clearly all of the resources that will be required to execute the plan in its entirety. This section of the plan should not only set out the financial resources required to implement the plan but also the human resources and the time budget required.

If the firm fails to adequately cost the marketing plan in terms of time and finance, it will be confronted with an unrealistic plan, which it will struggle to execute effectively.

6. DESIGN A MONITORING AND REVIEW PROCESS

Every plan needs to be carefully monitored and reviewed to ensure that the planned outcomes are being achieved. The purpose at this stage is to create a system whereby the plan can be examined and evaluated at set intervals so that if it is not functioning as originally predicted, then the plan can be amended.

The marketing plan should set out clearly the targets or standards that are to be achieved, the mechanism for monitoring these targets and the key dates at which it will be reviewed.

7. IMPLEMENT THE PLAN

The final stage of the planning process is the implementation of the marketing plan. This is the stage where all of the individual plans are put into action. If all the other stages of the planning process have been carried out effectively then the firm should realise that they are on target to meet their marketing objectives. If, on the other hand, the plan has not been well thought through it is at the implementation stage that the firm's errors will be revealed.

Writing a marketing plan

There is a commonly used phrase in business which says 'that a failure to plan means that you are planning to fail'.

When firms decide to market a product it is essential that they plan effectively by creating a formal written marketing plan so that they will have a clear and unambiguous statement of the activities they intend to carry out as part of the marketing process.

While there is no set format for this document, experience has suggested that it should contain the following:

- *An executive summary* which outlines the purpose of the marketing plan, its key points and the objectives to be achieved.
- *A situation analysis* which describes the internal and external factors which are likely to affect the business.
- A clear description of the *objectives* to be achieved.
- A clear explanation of the *marketing strategy* to be followed with reference to the market segment to be targeted and the position within that target market that the company hopes to achieve.
- Detailed *practical plans* for each of the elements of the marketing mix.
- A *budget* which pulls together all of the costs (and in some cases the revenues) involved in implementing the marketing plan.
- A section which outlines clearly how the marketing plan is going to be *monitored and reviewed.*

KNOWLEDGE REVIEW

- **THE MARKETING PLAN** is a written document which details the actions which are required to ensure that the business meets its marketing objectives.
- **A SWOT** analysis is a tool for auditing both the organisation and its external environment and involves analysing strengths, weaknesses, opportunities and threats.
- **MARKET SEGMENTATION** is the process of dividing a market into distinct groups or segments that share common characteristics such as age, gender, income or family type.
- **MARKET POSITIONING** refers to the process of determining a product's position in a market relative to competing products.
- **POSITIONING MAPS** show how a product compares with competitors' products against two key features.

ACTIVITY 10.3

DISCO BISCO LIMITED

Disco Bisco are a Northern Ireland based confectionery manufacturer who make and sell cereal and energy bars to UK based retailers.

They have recently designed a new product that is aimed specifically at the teenage market but which has the potential to cross over to other market segments.

Disco Bisco have recently updated their website, which now has the capacity to function as an e-commerce site. The company hope that the site will raise brand awareness and help it market its products in foreign markets such as the USA.

1. Explain what is meant by the following terms:
   (a) Market segment
   (b) Brand awareness
   (c) E-commerce
2. Analyse how a firm like Disco Bisco might segment its market.
3. Analyse what is meant by market positioning.
4. Explain the key elements that should be included in the marketing plan for Disco Bisco's new product.
5. Explain how their website will help them market their products in the USA.
6. Discuss the pros and cons of Disco Bisco marketing their products on an international basis.

products for individual consumers. Due to the fact that the product or service is customised to meet the specific requirements of a customer, the firm is able to charge a premium price for its output.

Job production also allows for greater flexibility and this means that plans can be changed or adapted at the buyer's request, even after production has begun.

The difficulty with job production though, is that it increases the average cost of production since it requires the use of specialist labour, which can slow down the production process.

CASE STUDY

JOB PRODUCTION IN ALWOOD KITCHENS

Alwood Kitchens is one of the oldest fitted kitchen companies in Northern Ireland and produces handcrafted quality kitchens and bedrooms using the finest materials from around the world.

The family-owned business began producing furniture in 1933 and today produces a range of kitchen and bedroom furniture in its Lurgan factory.

Every kitchen is individually designed to suit the specific needs and tastes of its customers, with each kitchen being an original piece. The company provides a complete tailor made service which includes an initial site survey, an individual design to meet the needs of its customers, quality manufacture and final installation.

(Source: www.alwoodkitchens.com)

BATCH PRODUCTION

Batch production occurs when a number of identical (or in some cases similar) products are produced in a batch. In batch production the products are not necessarily produced for a particular customer but are made at regular intervals and then sold to a number of customers. Batch production is often used in bakeries where a batch of one product, for example brown bread, is made before moving on to the production of some other good, for example white bread.

The main advantage of batch production, as opposed to job production, is that it reduces the need for a skilled and flexible workforce and allows the firm to avail of economies of scale in production and purchasing.

The problem, however, with batch production is that all equipment must be stopped, cleaned and reset in between jobs. This **down time** clearly impacts on the cost of production.

In addition, because batch production involves the production of a consignment of identical goods, products cannot be customised to meet the specific needs of individual consumers.

ACTIVITY 11.1

DREAMBEDS

Dreambeds is a very successful family-run business which specialises in the production of hand-made beds and mattresses. Each bed is uniquely designed and built to meet the needs of each customer and all production is completed by hand.

The company employs 30 production staff who work in teams of three to produce an individual bed to the specific requirements of their customers.

Demand for their beds has increased dramatically in recent years, despite the fact that prices range from £1,000 to £8,000. They have also recently secured a contract to supply 100 beds to a chain of up-market hotels.

The company is struggling to meet the increase in demand and is considering an expansion programme which involves the purchase of modern bed-making equipment and a shift to batch production.

1. Which type of production best describes the method presently used by Dreambeds?
2. Explain what is meant by the term 'batch production'.
3. Evaluate the view that a planned expansion strategy is the best way for the business to meet the increasing demand for its product.

FLOW PRODUCTION

Flow production, which is often referred to as mass production, occurs when production takes place as a continuous process. The product is produced along an assembly line with components and parts being added at each subsequent stage. In firms that produce multipart or complex products, a number of sub-assembly lines can be used in addition to the main assembly line.

Flow production is normally used in the production of a standardised product such as a can of peas or a bar of chocolate, although with advances in technology and modern robotic production techniques it is possible to produce small variations in the products as they are passed through the production process.

The main advantage of flow production is that it is capital intensive and therefore allows the firm to benefit from technical economies of scale. Furthermore, using capital rather than labour allows for 24/7 production and shift work, which lowers average costs.

The main drawback with flow production, however, is that it leads to a loss of flexibility as it can be very difficult to alter a product once production has started. Moreover, flow production means that all products have to be standardised and cannot be tailored to meet the specific needs of individual consumers.

ACTIVITY 11.3

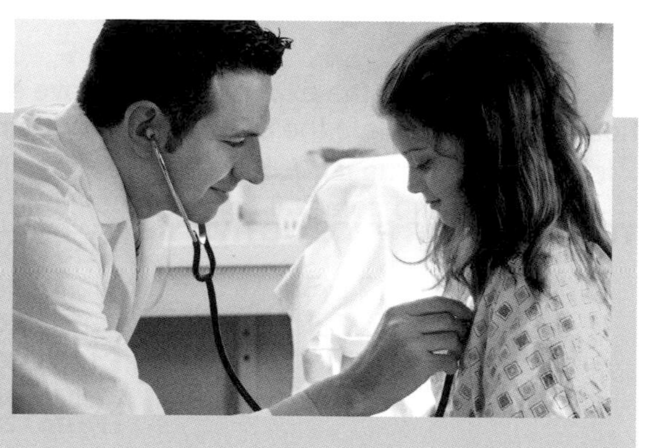

NHS PRODUCTIVITY RATE FALLING

NHS productivity is stagnant or falling by most measures, according to a report published today.

Using the standard comparison of NHS outputs to inputs, productivity has been falling by between 0.6% and 1.3% a year from 1995 to 2004.

This comes after record levels of money have been pumped into the NHS.

But the Office for National Statistics said a debate was needed about how NHS productivity was calculated as the results differed when other factors were included.

Comparing outputs (hospital activity) to inputs (labour and capital) has to date been widely accepted as the best method of measuring productivity and is used by the Treasury and Bank of England to inform policy.

But attempts are now being made to take into account the quality of treatment by using patient experience and survival rates.

When quality of treatment is included, productivity rates improve significantly.

National Statistician Karen Dunnell said the latest results showed that there needed to be a discussion over how productivity was going to be measured.

Measuring value for money in the public services is of major importance to everyone. Nigel Edwards, director of policy at the NHS Confederation, which represents health service managers, agreed that measuring productivity was "complex".

"Previous measures of productivity in health have measured health inputs versus outputs and miss a large amount of what the NHS actually does."

And Alan Maynard, Professor of Health Economics at York University, said: "The problem is that we are not very good at measuring the physical and mental outcomes of treatment and therefore, while the results are interesting they are somewhat limited.

"We have to improve the way we measure outcomes, in particular, in regards to primary care, where there is very little data."

(Source: BBC News, 27 February 2006)

1. Explain what is meant by the term 'productivity'.
2. Analyse two separate measures upon which estimates of NHS productivity could be based.
3. Evaluate the view that it is so difficult to measure productivity accurately in the health service that all estimates are essentially useless.

FACTORS INFLUENCING PRODUCTIVITY

As stated earlier in this chapter, the key to improving productivity lies in either increasing output while keeping inputs constant, or, reducing the quantity of inputs used while keeping output constant.

When attempting to increase productivity rates, firms will generally focus on two main areas:

1. **Improving labour productivity**
2. **Improving capital productivity**

IMPROVING LABOUR PRODUCTIVITY

Basic management and behavioural theory suggests that labour productivity is a function of the skills or ability of workers and the level of motivation they possess.

They often write this relationship as the expression:

PRODUCTIVITY = (SKILLS + ABILITY) × MOTIVATION

Clearly then, there are two main ways through which a firm could increase its labour productivity. Firstly, they could try and improve the skills and abilities of workers or secondly they could attempt to motivate their workers to work harder and better.

IMPROVING THE SKILLS OF WORKERS

UK firms often complain that workers do not have the skills necessary to complete their job roles effectively. Indeed, in the UK some 23% of firms report that they have workers who are less than fully proficient in their jobs. It seems that the most obvious way for a firm to increase productivity is to improve the skills of their workforce. This is because better skills make better workers.

Research by the ONS suggests that human capital is one of the major drivers in explaining differences in productivity. It is important to note that the problem of a skills deficit applies not only to production workers and those workers at the bottom of the chain of command but also to those at the top.

The same research by the ONS found that many managers lack formal qualifications and undertake only limited training. The result being that they are often less efficient than they should be. In fact, poor management and leadership are often cited as the main reason behind the closure of small businesses in the UK.

It has also been suggested that poor management skills are one of the main factors behind the lower productivity levels in the UK. Research by Oulton in 1998 found that there are sizeable differences in productivity between UK firms under UK ownership, and UK firms under US ownership. The research found that US ownership increased productivity rates by as much as 30%.

If firms are able to secure effective training, and if they are prepared to spend the time and money required to train their workers effectively, they will find that labour productivity rates will increase dramatically.

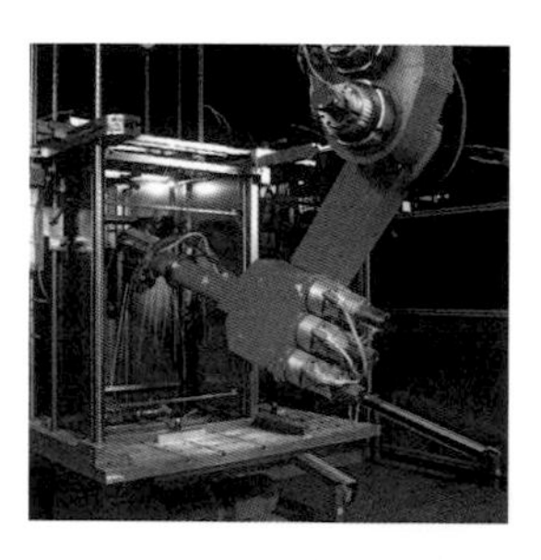

MAINTENANCE OF MACHINERY

If a firm makes a financial commitment to purchase new, expensive machinery it must also factor in the extra maintenance costs that this new piece of machinery will bring with it.

It is clear that spending huge sums of money on new equipment and then failing to maintain that equipment properly will lead to lower levels of productivity and may result in the firm losing money as a result of the initial investment.

If a firm does not maintain its equipment properly it may find that it breaks down in the middle of a production run, which can lead to the firm failing to fulfil orders and in the process place future orders in doubt.

Moreover, failing to maintain equipment properly may mean that it may become run down or obsolete more quickly than would normally be the case, which obviously increases the firm's costs.

ACTIVITY 11.4

GRIBBEN LYNCH

Gribben Lynch plc is a large manufacturing company that uses flow production to make metal shelves for sale to industry. The product is standardised and cannot be adapted to meet individual needs. It employs 240 workers at its factory in Toome and a further 20 in its main office in Antrim.

The company has recently found that there is a significant demand for made-to-measure shelves and is considering switching to job production to meet this demand.

The company has had a policy over the last few years of operating at almost full capacity, but without reaching 100% capacity.

The worry for the company is that if they switch to job production it will reduce their ability to work at such high capacity.

1. Explain what is meant by flow production.
2. Explain why a company such as Gribben Lynch would not want to work at full capacity but would like to work close to full capacity.
3. Explain the importance to Gribben Lynch of proper maintenance of their equipment and machinery.
4. Evaluate the likely impact on Gribben Lynch if the decision to implement job production is taken.

ECONOMIES OF SCALE

Economies of scale are defined as those advantages of increased size which lead to falling average costs. In essence, economies of scale are the cost advantages that a firm receives from operating on a larger scale.

Economies of scale are one of the main reasons why firms wish to grow. The larger the firm becomes, the greater the economies it can take advantage of and the lower its average costs will be. Clearly, if a firm can lower its average cost of production then it will automatically increase total productivity.

The diagram below illustrates the impact that economies of scale can have on a firm's average cost.

The impact of economies of scale on average costs

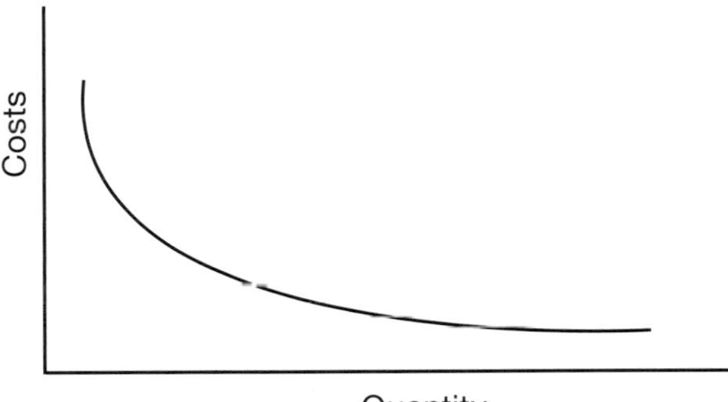

If a firm can take advantage of these economies of scale then it will be able to reduce price, and in turn increase the demand for its product at the expense of its competitors. On the other hand, if the firm only has a few competitors then it will be able to keep price constant and increase its profit margins.

Either way, the firm is better off if it can avail of economies of scale.

There are many sources of economies of scale which include:

1. Technical economies

Large firms are able to take advantage of increased capacity machinery, or use their existing machinery more efficiently, both of which allow for faster, more efficient production. Similarly, large firms are able to use mass production techniques which allows for the use of specialisation and the division of labour, which in turn enables the firm to increase production at very little extra cost.

2. Marketing economies

All forms of marketing involve a cost and most costs associated with marketing a product, for example advertising, are fixed. As a result, large firms are able to spread their marketing costs over a much larger level of output, thereby reducing the average cost of the marketing campaign.

3. Financial economies

As we saw in chapter 2, many small firms find it difficult to obtain the finance they require to operate efficiently, and when they do obtain this finance they often have to pay higher rates of interest as banks consider them to be high risk.

Large firms, on the other hand, can get loans more easily – and at lower rates of interest – because they are considered more credit-worthy. In this way their average costs are lower.

4. Commercial economies

Just as large firms are likely to get cheaper finance due to their size, they are also likely to get a better deal when it comes to buying raw materials, stock or other inputs. Large firms, such as Tesco, are able to buy in bulk and negotiate prices with suppliers, gaining discounts on most items purchased.

CASE STUDY

M&S SEEKS £100M SUPPLIER SAVINGS

Marks & Spencer has said it is renegotiating deals with suppliers in a bid to save at least £100m a year.

The retailer has held meetings with food and general merchandise suppliers in a move instigated by new chief executive Stuart Rose.

M&S management are understood to be focusing on cutting supply-chain costs – the money paid to firms for goods and the means to get them into the shops. However, they are not looking to reduce the number of suppliers and say they will pass on some of the savings to customers.

The negotiations involve around 70 firms in total. M&S works with 15 main suppliers in the UK, as well as a number of smaller companies.

Richard Ratner, analyst at Seymour Pierce, said: "We're not surprised by M&S's move, as we have always said that for a firm of its size and buying power, M&S has been overpaying for its non-food merchandise by well over 5%, and in some cases much more."

(Source: BBC News, 1 July 2004)

5. Managerial economies

Large firms can employ specialist managers, accountants and sales people, whereas in small firms one person may have to fill many roles. These specialist workers are more likely to be efficient because they will possess the qualifications and training needed to fulfil the role effectively, and in turn boost the productivity of the firm.

6. Risk bearing economies

Risk bearing economies refer to the ability of large firms to diversify their output into other market segments or into foreign markets and spread the risk of a reduction in demand in one market. As a result, large firms are better able to cope with the ups and downs of the business cycle than small firms. For example, in the UK there are thousands of bankruptcies every year, the vast majority of which occur in SMEs (small and medium-sized enterprises). This suggests that large firms are more resilient and can enjoy certain advantages over smaller firms.

DISECONOMIES OF SCALE

When firms become too large they may actually find that their average costs increase rather than decrease. When this happens the firm is experiencing **diseconomies of scale.** Diseconomies of scale are those disadvantages of increased size which lead to rising average costs.

The diagram below illustrates the impact that diseconomies can have on the average costs of a firm.

The impact of diseconomies of scale on average costs

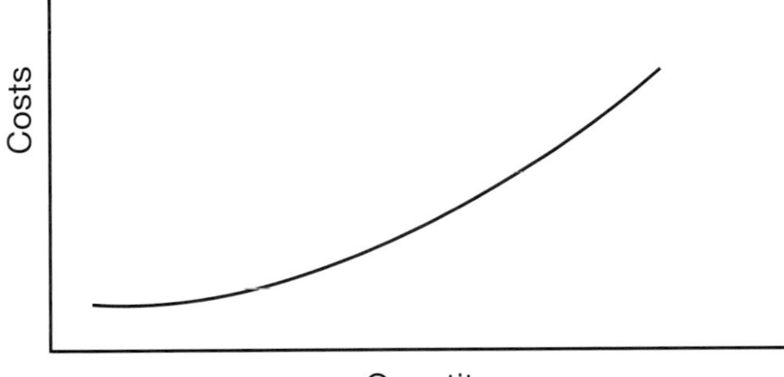

Diseconomies of scale can occur for a number of reasons, although normally as a result of management problems.

1. COORDINATION

Large firms often find it difficult to co-ordinate the work of a whole range of different sections. Therefore, firms may find that at certain times some workers are not working as hard as they could be because they are waiting for other people to finish their work before they can start. This obviously increases the firm's costs since these workers still have to be paid.

2. CONTROL

Keeping an eye on every worker in a large organisation is often very difficult, and workers may take advantage of this situation and use the time to engage in activities which add nothing to the firm's output. This slack, or what economists term X-inefficiency, can lead to significant increases in average costs.

CASE STUDY

THE COST OF WEB AND EMAIL ABUSE

Research from the Cranfield School of Management revealed that UK businesses are picking up the bill for a workforce of cyber-loafers.

The research found that small businesses in the UK are losing £1.5bn per year as a result of their employees' email and web abuse.

The research also found that SMEs (small-to-medium-sized enterprises) are paying staff for around 343 million wasted hours which are spent surfing the net or sending personal emails.

CASE STUDY...

The report suggests that this represents a 15% dent in their potential profits.

Other research published recently suggested that the problem is much more widespread and that the average worker spends 21 days per year reading, sending and replying to personal emails.

Yet despite the finding the Cranfield research also revealed a lack of concern among management about the problem. Of those companies surveyed, only 20 per cent said they were worried about email misuse within their offices – putting it below issues such as marketing, overheads, recruitment, insurance and cash flow in their list of priorities.

(Source: www.silicon.com)

3. CO-OPERATION

Large firms often find that worker morale is quite low because workers feel a sense of detachment from the overall business. This is due to the fact that it is more difficult for managers in large organisations to build good team environments where every worker feels loyal to the company. As a result, large firms often find that workers become de-motivated and consequently productivity falls and unit labour costs increase.

4. COMMUNICATION

As businesses grow, they often find that communication channels between departments, and along the chain of command, become less efficient. This results in confused or unclear messages passing through the organisation, which can in turn lead to lower levels of productivity.

ECONOMIES OF SCALE AND AVERAGE COSTS

Economic theory suggests that as a result of a combination of economies of scale and diseconomies of scale a firm's long term average cost curve is likely to be U shaped.

This is because as a firm increases the level of production from Q1 to Q2, it will initially find that its average cost of production falls, as the firm is able to avail of economies of scale. However, at some point, further increases in production will cause average costs to increase as the firm begins to experience diseconomies of scale. In this way, the long run average cost curve for the firm will be U shaped as shown below.

The average cost curve

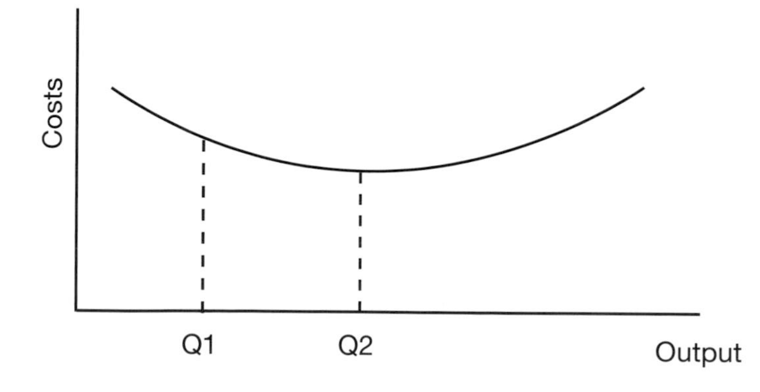

Nonetheless, empirical evidence suggests that in certain industries the average cost curve is more likely to be downward sloping or L shaped. For example, in high-tech industries like aerospace and car manufacturing the average cost curve is often L shaped.
The reason for this L shaped average cost curve in these industries is that continuous advancements in technology allow a steady reduction in average costs, which outweigh any diseconomies of scale which may be experienced by the firm.

In other industries a possible reason for the L shaped average cost curve is that firms are becoming more adept at organising and managing the production process and their workforce, which helps to ensure that the managerial problems, which cause the diseconomies, do not set in.

For example, in recent years managers have become more aware of the need to motivate staff to reduce the problems associated with a lack of co-operation. As stated earlier, they do this through bonus systems, more flexible working arrangements and reward schemes like 'employee of the month'.

If the firm is able to prevent diseconomies of scale from setting in, then it will be able to continue to increase production without experiencing increases in average costs and thus its average cost curve will be L shaped, as shown below.

L shaped average cost curve

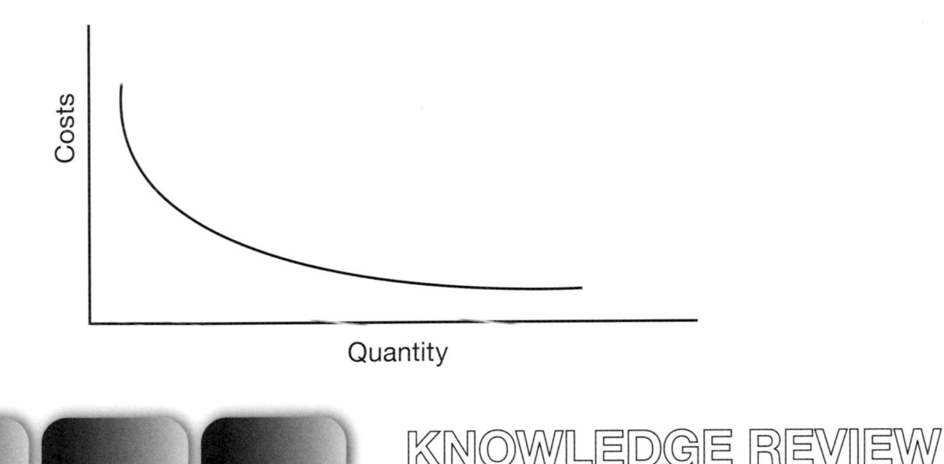

KNOWLEDGE REVIEW

- **PRODUCTIVITY** measures the efficiency with which a business converts its resources (inputs) into goods or services (output). Common measures include labour productivity and capital productivity.

- **ECONOMIES OF SCALE** are the cost advantages that a firm receives from operating on a larger scale. Examples include commercial economies and financial economies.

- **DISECONOMIES OF SCALE** are those disadvantages of increased size which lead to rising average costs. Diseconomies of scale normally result from management problems and include poor communication and a lack of control.

ACTIVITY 11.5

UISCE LTD

Uisce Ltd is a small family-owned company which is based just outside Belfast, which bottles natural spring water. The company uses batch production and currently employs 20 people, each of who fulfil a number of roles. Demand has increased so much over the last ten years that the company has out-grown its current premises.

Management are considering moving to much larger premises where they will be able to use new machinery and different production techniques.

The expansion plan will also require them to adopt flow production techniques and employ more staff. Nonetheless, they are confident that the changes will allow them to avail of economies of scale and in turn develop higher levels of productivity.

1) Explain what is meant by the term 'batch production'.
2) Explain the benefits to Uisce Ltd of investing in new machinery.
3) Analyse two methods Uisce Ltd could use to increase labour productivity.
4) Evaluate the view that continual increases in the scale of operations will always result in productivity improvements.

Chapter 12: QUALITY MANAGEMENT

12

QUALITY

Quality is a difficult concept to define as it means different things to different people.

In its broadest sense, quality is a measure of excellence or the extent to which something is fit for its purpose. In its narrowest sense, quality is simply a measure of how free a product is from defects or fault.

Because the term 'quality' means different things to different people there is no single definition which sums up perfectly what quality means. However, a commonly used definition is **the degree to which a good or service fulfils its requirements.**

This definition is used by the ISO (international standards organisation) and measures the degree to which a good or service is fit for the purpose intended.

The judgement of whether a product or service is of high quality requires a comparison between what is necessary and what was provided and is judged not by the producer but by the consumer.

For most people the term 'quality' will include aspects such as reliability, safety, durability, usability, after sales service and customer care. Therefore, we can say that a quality product or service is one which delights customers by fully meeting all of their needs and expectations.

WHY IS QUALITY IMPORTANT?

As stated in chapter 2, the aim of most businesses, although not all, is to carry out production in a way which maximises the return or profit for the owners of the business. Yet, a business will only be able to maximise profits if it can attract and retain customers. The key to attracting and retaining customers is to provide them with quality goods and services, and quality is vital to the survival of almost every enterprise.

Quality will impact on a firm's success in a number of ways:

Quality adds value to the firm's products

In recent years the real disposable income of consumers has increased and as a result they have become increasingly more concerned with the quality of the goods and services they purchase rather than with the price.

This means that if a firm can build a reputation based on quality it will be able to charge premium prices for its goods and services.

Quality reduces cost

Many people assume that attempts to improve quality will lead to higher costs of production but if a firm can improve the quality of its output, it should lead to fewer returns and replacements, and this in turn will lead to lower, rather than higher costs.

CASE STUDY

MATTEL RECALL TOYS

Mattel, the world's biggest toymaker, has announced its third major recall of Chinese-made products in a month.

About three quarters of a million toys are being recalled because they are decorated with paint containing too much lead, the US company says.

Mattel apologised for the new incident but the Chinese government insisted that people could still have "confidence" in Chinese-made products.

"I want to tell everyone that they can have confidence in the quality of Chinese products and food safety."

In the past month Mattel has recalled 18 million Chinese-made toys because their paint was found to contain lead. Market analysts are predicting a sharp fall in sales for Mattel toys as consumers react to this further safety scare.

(Adapted from BBC News, 5 September 2007)

Quality leads to customer loyalty

High quality products lead to higher levels of customer loyalty. If customers are happy with the product or service they purchase, they will return and make repeat purchases, so increasing the firm's sales. Furthermore, happy customers will recommend the product or service to others and in this way too, the firm will attract more customers.

Quality improves the brand image

Having a strong brand reputation for quality means that when a firm introduces new products onto the market, consumers will automatically assume that the new product is of high quality and be more inclined to purchase it.

Quality attracts good staff

Firms which have a strong brand reputation as the providers of high quality goods and services generally find it much easier to attract and retain high quality workers. If a firm can attract these high quality workers productivity levels should increase, thereby benefiting the firm.

The table on the next page illustrates the impact quality can have on a firm's profits, ie on its income and costs.

If a firm provides high quality products it should experience higher levels of income as it attracts more customers. At the same time, high quality should lead to lower production and inspection costs. If, on the other hand, a firm produces low quality products it will lose business to its rivals and face the higher costs associated with dealing with rejected or returned products.

Impact of quality

	Income	Expense
'Good' quality	• More customers • Repeat business • Competitive advantages	• Lower production cost • Lower inspection cost • Lower working capital through reduced inventory
'Poor' quality	• Loss of business • Penalties for late delivery or service • Partial or late payments due to customer dissatisfaction	• Scrap and rework cost • Warranty costs • Sorting cost • Express shipping cost

HOW IS QUALITY MEASURED?

As we stated earlier, quality is a very difficult concept to define and as such it is an extremely difficult concept to measure accurately. If there are a number of different definitions of quality there must also be a number of different ways of measuring quality.

The method a firm uses to measure quality will depend on how the firm views quality. For example, some firms measure the quality of their goods and services through measurements such as failure or rejection rates or through the level of product returns.

For other firms quality might be measured through the number of customer complaints or through a customer satisfaction survey.

CASE STUDY

MEASURING QUALITY AT RLC LANGFORD LODGE

RLC Langford Lodge is a precision engineering company which supplies components to the aerospace industry. The plant is based in County Antrim and was formed in 1959 to supply the Martin Baker Aircraft Company, which is the world leader in aircraft ejection systems. The company currently employs 301 staff and has an annual turnover of £22m (2005).

RLC Langford Lodge has a world wide reputation which is based on its ability to supply products which lead the sector in terms of quality, cost and delivery.

RLC Langford Lodge has a detailed quality system in place which includes a number of different quality measures. Typical quality measures include:

1. Measuring the quantity of internal rejections
2. Measuring the total number of customer complaints
3. Measuring the quantity of parts returned from the customer

CASE STUDY...

Every section of the company has very strict targets with regard to these measures and each month an analysis is conducted to assess performance against these targets.

An example of a monthly quality analysis is shown below.

Form Table, December 2006					
Ranking (relative to target)	Cell	Qty parts returned from customer	Target parts returned (less than)	Qty parts supplied to customer	% against target
1	Treatments	0	42	27770	0%
2	Goodrich Wingset	0	2	7026	0%
3	MBA Direct Machining	0	16	5312	0%
4	MBA Fabrics	0	5	5202	0%
5	MBA Spares	0	10	1315	0%
6	MBA GSE Assembly	0	4	997	0%
7	MBA Cartridge Case	3	25	27341	12%
8	MBA SR Hardware	1	3	1105	35%
9	Goodrich new contracts	9	4	1557	231%
Season Table, June 2006 – present					

SYSTEMS FOR MAINTAINING QUALITY

We learned earlier in this chapter how the process of production involves taking a range of inputs, such as labour and raw materials, and processing them in a manner which produces an output that can be sold to consumers.

If a firm wishes to produce a high quality output it must first analyse its production process in detail to ensure every part of the process is consistent with the production of a quality output.

The firm must examine all of its inputs including its raw materials, its staff, its equipment and indeed the skills and abilities of its management to ensure that they have the capacity to produce high quality output.

The firm must also examine all of the processes and procedures which are used in the organisation to ensure that they are sufficient and that they add value to the firm's output.

Finally, the firm must also analyse all of their outputs to ensure that they too are of high quality. When firms analyse their output it is important that they do not limit themselves to simply analysing the product they hope to sell. To ensure high quality, the firm needs to analyse not only the actual product but also the other outputs which make up the augmented product, such as the paperwork and the after sales service.

The production process of a high quality output can be illustrated on the diagram opposite. This diagram is similar to the one we saw earlier but it has been expanded to cover all of the tangible and intangible inputs, processes and outputs which are involved in the production of a high quality product.

Quality production process

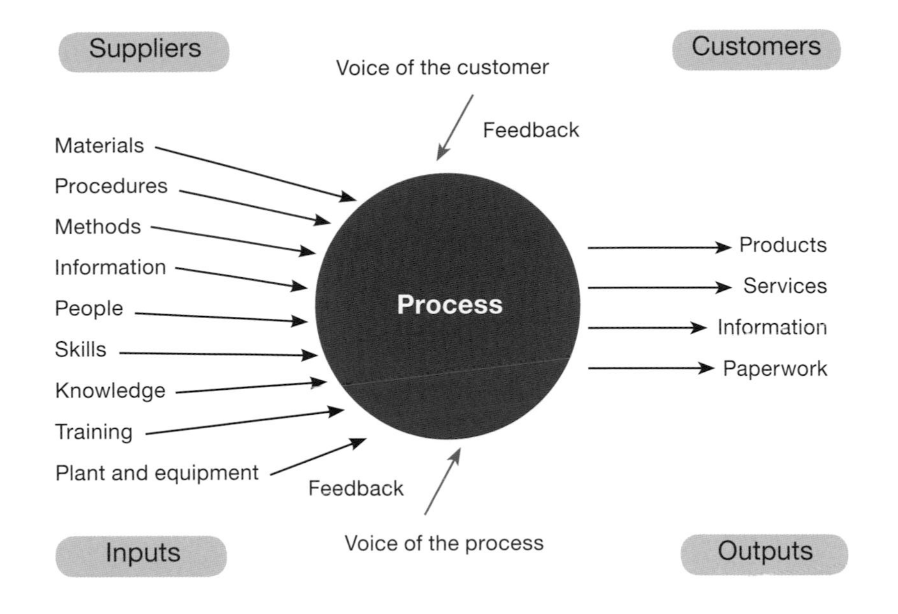

There are a large number of different quality systems that a firm can use to ensure its output is of the highest quality: quality control, best practice benchmarking, quality standards and balanced scorecards. We will look at each of these systems in more detail in the remainder of this chapter. Regardless of whichever system a company chooses to adopt, it is vitally important that it is understood and accepted by all members of staff and is implemented fully throughout the organisation.

QUALITY SYSTEMS

QUALITY CONTROL

Quality Control is a process or set of processes which are designed to detect and remove components or products which fall below predetermined targets.

Quality Control is normally carried out by specially trained staff who inspect and test products before they are despatched to the customer. These quality inspectors may test every product produced, or alternatively, only test a sample of products. How the products are sampled depends on the type of production being employed by the firm. For example, if the firm employ a batch production system, a random sample will normally be taken from each batch. In job production, on the other hand, each individual product will normally be tested before it is shipped to the customer.

Traditionally, the inspection and testing associated with quality control took place at the end of the productive process, but in more modern quality control systems, inspection and testing can take place at any point along the production process. Typical points for inspection include:

- When the raw materials and components are delivered to the company
- At various stages throughout the production process
- When the product is finished but before they are sold to customers

The main advantage of quality control is that it should, if implemented correctly, reduce the chance of faulty products reaching the final consumer. Moreover, since quality is the responsibility of specially trained inspectors it should be relatively easy for the firm to identify aspects of production which do not meet the required standard.

The primary disadvantage, however, is that individual workers become detached from the quality process because they are not responsible for assessing their own work. This can lead to problems with staff motivation and productivity.

In addition, rejecting products at the end of a production cycle can be very costly for the firm, particularly if the product cannot be reworked or improved.

CASE STUDY

CAR COMPANY TO TACKLE QUALITY CONTROL

One of the world's leading car manufacturers may have to delay the roll-out of some new models while it resolves quality control issues that have seen more than a million cars recalled.

The president of the company said the firm was looking at all aspects of car development, from manufacturing and design to dealing with customer gripes.

A report in the Wall Street Journal said the changes could delay some new models by up to six months.

The company has recalled some 1.5 million cars in Japan and the US this year.

On Friday, authorities in China announced that the company would recall 20,000 cars due to a faulty rubber seal used to fix the windscreen.

Car manufacturers are increasingly trying to cut costs by using the same components across a range of models, but this has led to a rise in the number of recalls.

This company had built up a reputation for reliability in many world markets, a key contributor to its success as it looks to become the world's biggest car maker.

(Adapted from BBC News, 25 August 2005)

QUALITY ASSURANCE

Quality assurance is different from quality control in that quality control is concerned with ensuring that faulty products are identified and removed, while quality assurance is concerned with trying to stop faults happening in the first place.

Quality assurance aims to achieve quality by analysing and planning every process to ensure that the product is produced **right first time** so that the product will have **zero defects.** Under quality assurance the responsibility lies with the workforce, who often work in teams or cells to self-check the product, rather than with quality inspectors.

One benefit of quality assurance is that it leads to a reduction in the number of faulty parts or products produced and reduces the costs associated with wastage or the reworking of products which fall below accepted standards.

Furthermore, workers who have greater responsibility and feel part of the quality process are more likely to have higher levels of motivation and productivity.

CASE STUDY

QUALITY CONTROL AND QUALITY ASSURANCE AT CCBU

The quality assurance department at CCBU works very closely with the production department to ensure that each bottle or can of Coca-Cola is perfect. CCBU have to meet both the requirements of the Coca Cola Company itself and the official agencies, such as the National Standards Authority. CCBU also holds the quality standard ISO 9002.

Each of these organisations regularly audit the quality performance and systems of CCBU to ensure it continues to meet their standards.

To maintain quality, CCBU carry out a number of tests in their own labs. These include checking the standard of all raw materials as they arrive and again after they are mixed and ready for bottling. Samples of the finished product are sampled every half hour as they come off the production line, and every month a company representative will purchase around 60 CCBU products from retailers to check quality at the point of sale.

CCBU also analyse all of their production stages to ensure quality is maintained and all equipment and machinery is checked at regular intervals to ensure that they are clean and working properly.

Additional checks are carried out after each production batch to ensure that there is no cross-contamination of flavours.

The quality assurance department also works closely with the customer services department to ensure that any customer queries about quality are dealt with promptly and effectively.

(Source: CCBU)

QUALITY BODIES BS 5750 / ISO 9000

BS5750 is a British standard for quality assurance. It originated in World War II munitions factories when the UK government became concerned about the quality and safety of their munitions.

To ensure that the munitions were of high quality the government began to demand that the munitions factories had clear procedures for all their business processes and that they kept detailed records to ensure that these procedures were being followed. The principles set down by the government were outlined in a management standard which became known as BS5750.

This standard proved very popular and spread very quickly to a wide range of different industries. In 1987 the standard was adopted by the International Organisation for Standards and became known as ISO 9000.

In order to achieve the ISO standard a company must have a clear quality policy which is implemented at all levels of the organisation. This quality policy must cover a range of issues from the production of a quality manual and the methods of measuring quality against set targets to the company's policy with regard to quality improvements.

If the company meets the required standard and is certified by the ISO then it can state publicly that it is ISO 9000 certified or registered. This will indicate to potential customers that the quality procedures of the company are reliable and that they can expect the company to provide high quality goods and service.

Nevertheless, the fact that a company is ISO 9000 certified does not guarantee that the product will be of high quality or of superior quality to the product of an uncertified firm. It simply indicates that consistent quality procedures are being implemented.

ISO certification brings many benefits, not least that it focuses the firm's attention on its quality processes and provides a comprehensive model on which to build a quality system. Similarly, if a company can declare itself as ISO certified, it can gain a competitive advantage as potential customers will be attracted to the firm's quality status. Indeed, a survey by Deloitte and Touche suggests that gaining ISO certification leads to higher profits in most cases.

However, critics of the ISO 9000 model argue that the system is costly in terms of management time and money because it requires a great deal of paperwork. Meanwhile, it is suggested that some companies become overly concerned with gaining certification at the expense of real improvements in quality.

CASE STUDY

BELFAST COMPANY ACHIEVES ISO 27001 STANDARD

Belfast company Wilson Waste Management has become the first firm in its field in the UK to achieve the globally recognized ISO 27001 standard for information security.

ISO 27001 is part of a family of international information security standards which features a strict security policy, disaster recovery and regular audits ensuring physical security of premises and information, ongoing security training and employee vetting.

Wilson Waste Management, which has been providing a confidential shredding service for over 15 years, said achieving the ISO showed that it was rigorously adhering to data security industry best practice.

The company has also recently introduced a new information security management system, thus adding to its growing expertise in handling sensitive and confidential information.

"We already had established policies and security measures in place covering the confidential shredding service. With the help of our management solutions company, Quadra, we have been able to easily adapt these to provide compliance with the standard.

"We are confident that certification will demonstrate our commitment to providing our customers with a quality service they can trust," explained Andrea Bailie, Wilson Waste Management's HR and quality manager.

(Adapted from the Belfast Telegraph, 7 August 2007)

BENCHMARKING

Benchmarking or best practice benchmarking is a quality process which attempts to identify best practice in the industry. Benchmarking can be conducted internally by assessing the processes of each department, or externally by analysing how other firms in the industry operate.

When the firm has identified the best practice it can then develop a plan to adopt this best practice technique into its own production processes, as well as set its quality targets at the level of the best practice organisation.

For example, an engineering firm might identify RLC Langford Lodge as being the benchmark for the industry. They would then analyse the quality processes at RLC Langford Lodge and adapt their own processes to match them. Once they have adopted these quality procedures they would then set quality targets in line with those set at RLC Langford Lodge.

The main advantage of benchmarking is that it can open an organisation up to a whole new set of methods, ideas and processes which may be vastly different from their current procedures. Likewise, if the processes are taken from a company which is widely regarded to be the most successful firm in the industry, then they are more likely to be accepted by staff because the processes can be shown to work elsewhere.

The main problem with benchmarking is that while it may be possible to identify the best performing firm in the industry it may be more difficult to identify the processes which enable it to perform so well. This is especially true if the firm is not willing to allow competitors access to its operations for fear of revealing information which may harm its competitive advantage.

The second problem with benchmarking is the time and cost involved in trying to discover the key to the best practice techniques adopted by the benchmark firm.

ACTIVITY 12.1

BENCHMARKING TO BE USED TO IMPROVE FAILING SCHOOLS

A new task force is to be created to tackle alarmingly poor reading, writing and maths skills within the Northern Ireland education system.

The move has been revealed by the Government in its official response to severe criticism from MPs. The Government reply to MPs also stated: "The Department of Education (DE) notes the committee's comments and shares its concerns regarding the gap in performance between Protestant pupils in socially deprived areas of Belfast and their Roman Catholic counterparts."

The official response to the committee said: "DE is committed to undertake significant benchmarking exercises both in the near future and on an ongoing basis. Contact is being made with local authorities in Glasgow and Liverpool and meetings have been arranged to discuss the various strategies in operation in those cities.

"Further, a research project has been initiated to inform DE about what is working successfully in delivering better literacy and numeracy outcomes in comparator cities elsewhere in the United Kingdom; this project is due to be completed in June 2007."

The Department is also reviewing existing research on the under-achievement of boys in schools. "DE accepts fully the importance of taking action to address the underperformance of boys, especially in the Belfast area," the Government reply said.

The Commons report highlighted a number of disturbing statistics from the Northern Ireland schooling system. These included a finding that 41% of 11 to 14-year-olds in secondary schools had failed to reach the standards expected for their age.

(Adapted from the Belfast Telegraph, 22 February 2007)

Write a detailed report explaining how benchmarking could be used to improve the performance of Northern Ireland pupils in English and Maths.

THE EFQM EXCELLENCE MODEL

The EFQM Excellence Model was introduced at the beginning of 1992 by the European Foundation for Quality Management as the framework for assessing organisations for the European Quality Award. It is now the most widely used organisational framework in Europe and it has become the basis for the majority of national and regional Quality Awards.

The EFQM Excellence Model is a practical tool that can be used in a number of different ways:

- as a tool for Self-Assessment
- as a way to Benchmark with other organisations
- as a guide to identify areas for Improvement
- as the basis for a common Vocabulary and a way of thinking
- as a Structure for the organisation's management system

The EFQM Excellence Model is a non-prescriptive framework based on nine criteria. Five of these criteria are known as 'Enablers' and four are known as 'Results'. The 'Enabler' criteria cover what an organisation does, whereas the 'Results' criteria cover what an organisation achieves.

'Results' are caused by 'Enablers' and 'Enablers' are improved using feedback from 'Results'. The EFQM model and the nine criteria are shown on the diagram below:

EFQM Framework

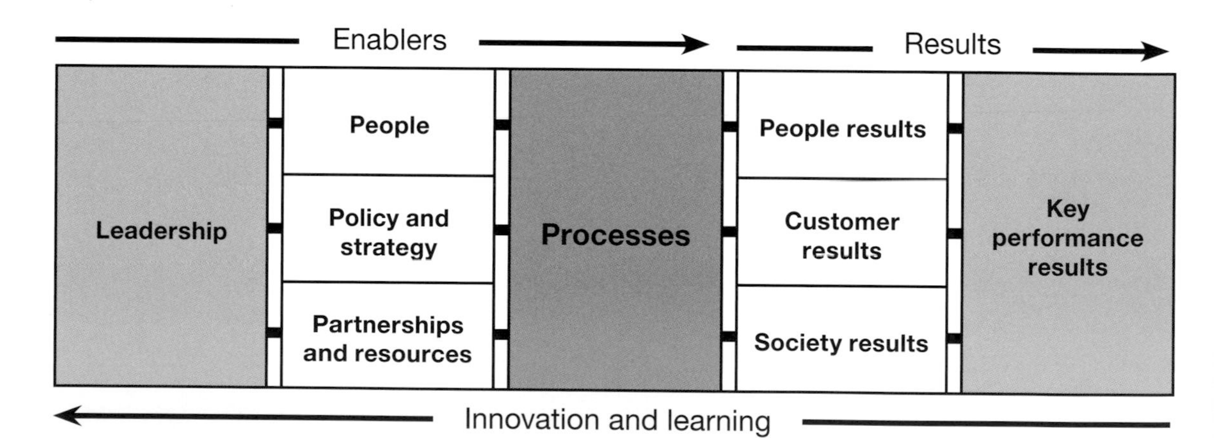

Many people believe that the EFQM quality model is a European standard much like the BS5750 or the ISO family of standards but EFQM is not a standard; it is simply a framework for quality that can also be used as a diagnostic tool.

There are various recognition schemes based on the Excellence Model. These recognition schemes, which are known as Levels of Excellence, are standards designed to allow an organisation to highlight to its customers that it has achieved a particular standard and to allow it to benchmark its performance against the best in Europe.

A key feature of the EFQM Model is its use as a diagnostic tool for self-assessment, where organisations grade themselves against a set of detailed criteria under each of the nine headings. The overall score from this diagnostic test acts as a European benchmark and helps organisations identify areas for improvement.

The EFQM Excellence Model is an over-arching quality framework that can be used alongside other tools and standards such as Investors in People, Charter Mark, ISO and the Balanced Scorecard.

The diagram below highlights how the EFQM model fits in with these other quality models.

EFQM and other quality models

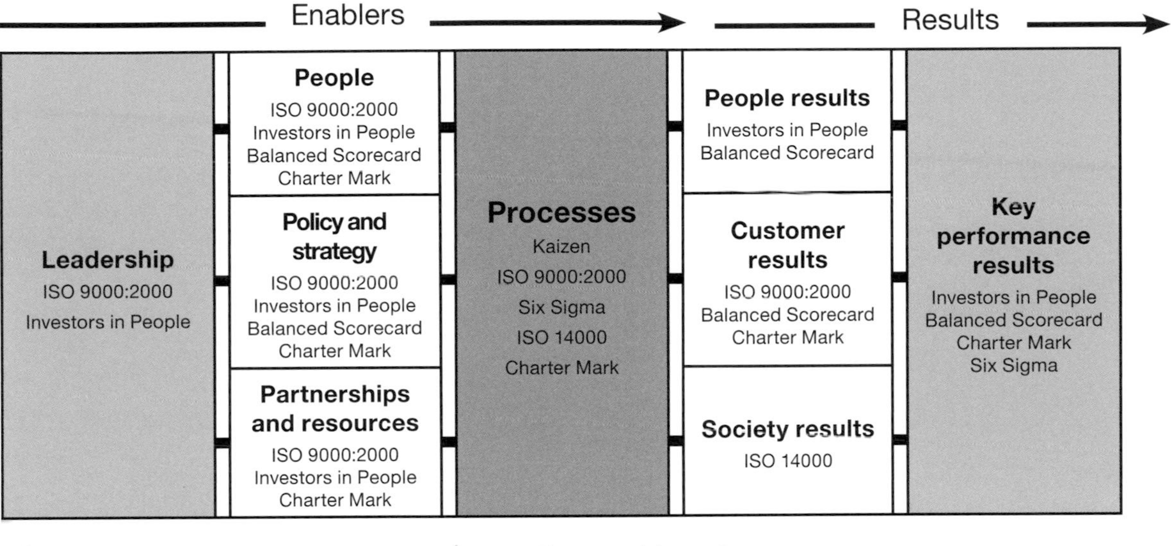

The main advantage of the EFQM model is that it focuses the firm's attention on its quality processes and provides a comprehensive framework on which to judge its current performance and improve its quality system.

In addition, being able to declare that it has achieved a particular level of excellence can give a firm a competitive advantage as it will indicate to potential customers that the quality procedures of the company are reliable and that they can expect the company to provide high quality goods and services.

Indeed, independent studies have concluded that successful implementation of the EFQM model results in improved performance in terms of quality and, most importantly, sales.

However, critics of the EFQM model argue that the system is costly in terms of management time and money and that it offers very little in the way of actual solutions to the problems or areas of concern, which the self-assessment exercise might highlight.

Others argue that there is nothing new in the EFQM model and that it simply highlights other quality management systems that the firm should already be aware of.

BALANCED SCORECARDS

The concept of a balanced scorecard was introduced in 1992 as a result of research by Robert Kaplan and David Norton of the Harvard Business School. The research was sponsored by a number of major US corporations who had become increasingly dissatisfied with traditional financial measures as a means of assessing the performance of their corporations.

To overcome the perceived weaknesses of tradition performance measures Kaplan and Norton devised the balanced scorecard system, which is a quality management scheme that involves creating a detailed set of measurements for four key strategic perspectives.

These four perspectives of the balanced scorecard are:

- Financial
- Customer
- Internal business processes
- Learning and growth

The balanced scorecard system suggests that for each of these four perspectives the company should develop between four and seven distinct measurements which can be either quantitative or qualitative in nature. The company will then be able to analyse its performance in light of all of these measurements.

Having this large number of measurements should provide the business with a detailed set of data which addresses all of the relevant areas of performance and give the management team a more comprehensive view of the overall success of the company.

The structure of the balanced scorecard is shown on the diagram below.

Balanced scorecard framework

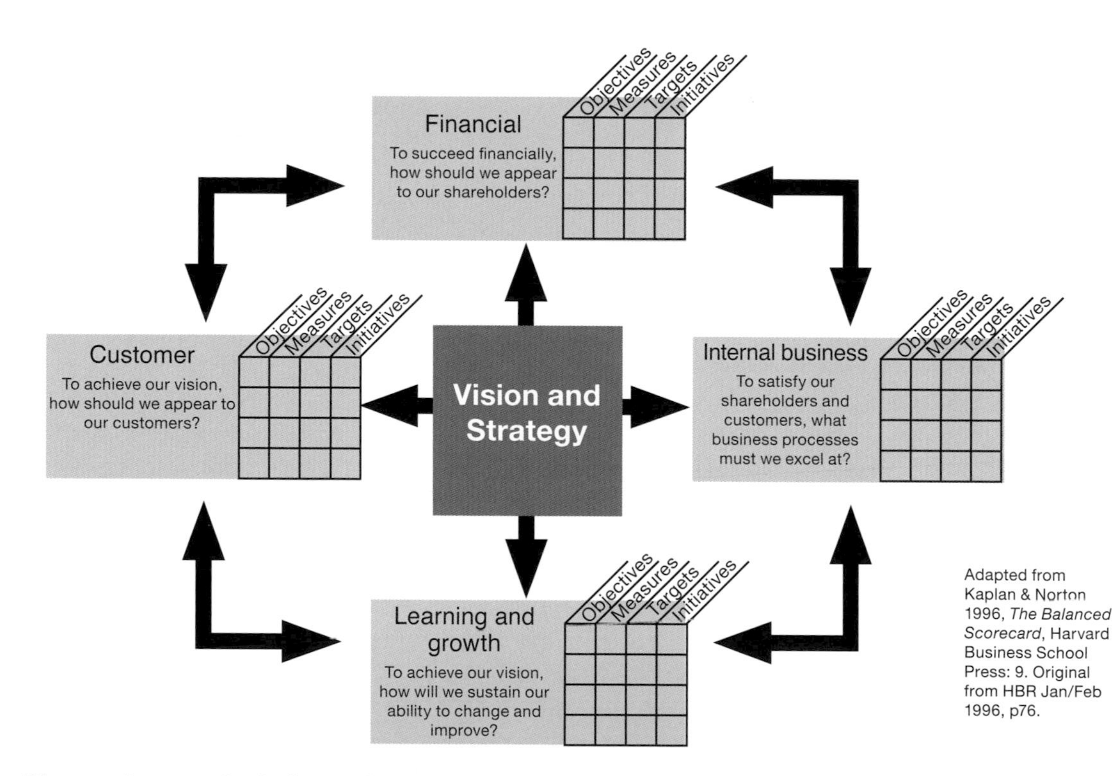

Adapted from Kaplan & Norton 1996, *The Balanced Scorecard*, Harvard Business School Press: 9. Original from HBR Jan/Feb 1996, p76.

Those who use the balanced scorecard argue that its main benefit lies in the fact that it provides a much wider basis for judging the performance of an organisation than the other quality management systems because it is based on four distinct areas rather than just one.

They also argue that it is extremely useful in breaking down strategic quality measures into easy to understand targets so that all employees can see what is required at their level. As a result, it is argued that the balanced scorecard is more likely to lead to success than a system which sets targets at a strategic or management level.

Those opposed to the balanced scorecard argue that it is too reliant on quality targets and measures and that it may lead to workers in the organisation striving to meet the targets rather than trying to improve quality. As with any target, the targets in the balanced scorecard are affected by Goodhart's law, which argues that whenever a measure becomes a target then it ceases to be a good measure.

CASE STUDY

THE BALANCED SCORECARD

The balanced scorecard, below, is taken from a private non-profit organisation that provides care homes for the elderly and those at risk. We can see that for each of the four perspectives the company has set two aims and for each of these aims the company has set itself clear objectives, measures and targets upon which to assess its performance.

For example, under the financial perspective the company are aiming to increase the efficiency of direct care. To achieve this aim the company's management team have set an objective of reducing overtime. The target is to get overtime hours down to less than 6% of the payroll and success will be measured by looking at payroll data to ensure that overtime falls below this target.

Under the learning and growth perspective one objective is to retain highly qualified staff. To achieve this objective the company has set a target for staff turnover of less than 24%.

VINFENS' FY 2006 CORPORATE BALANCED SCORECARD DASHBOARD

Area	Objectives	Measurement	Target
Financial Perspective			
F2: Increase direct care cost efficiency	1. Reduce overtime (OT)	1. % of direct care payroll, FTE of OT hours.	1. OT hours less than 6.5% of payroll
F4: Achieve financial sustainability	1. Meet budget growth targets	1. Revenue growth v budget targets	1. Budget targets for growth
Learning & Growth Perspective			
L3: Recruit and retain a highly skilled workforce	1. Retain best qualified staff	1. Turnover rate	1. Will not exceed 24% (annualised rate)
		2. Promotion rate	2. Will not fall below 4%
L4: Ensure organisational learning based on data, outcomes and experience	Increase organisational learning	1. Track all external trainings and conferences for divisions and departments. (Reports from VPs and Dep Heads)	1. Baseline
		2. Number of hits to the Intranet	2. Baseline
Internal Perspective			
P2: Improve business practices and efficiencies	1. Maintain the physical quality and appearance of Vinfen's group homes	1. Average response time to complete a work request	1. Improvement from FY05
P4: Manage increased clinical and business risk	1. Manage the activity level of clients through increased clinical consults and assessments	1. Number of clinical consults (Reports from VPs)	1. Baseline
Customer Perspective			
C1: Deliver services consistent in service and value	1. Increase management retention	1. Management retention/ management vacancies for Site Managers and up	1. Baseline
C2: Increase public awareness and visibility	1. Increase positive media placement	1. Positive media placements	1. Increase positive media placements from FY05 totals

- **QUALITY** is a measure of excellence or the extent to which something is fit for its purpose and includes aspects such as reliability, safety, durability, usability, after sales service and customer care.
- **QUALITY CONTROL** is a process or set of processes which are designed to detect and remove components or products which fall below predetermined targets.
- **QUALITY ASSURANCE** is different from quality control in that quality control is concerned with ensuring that faulty products are identified and removed, while quality assurance is concerned with trying to stop faults happening in the first place.
- **BENCHMARKING** is a process through which firms attempt to identify best practice in the industry and apply those best practice techniques to its organisation.
- **THE BALANCED SCORECARD** is a quality management scheme that involves creating a detailed set of measurements for four key strategic perspectives upon which the success of a business can be assessed.

ACTIVITY 12.2

IMPROVING QUALITY AT TECHNO LTD

Techno Ltd is a manufacturer of electronic components for use in household products such as vacuum cleaners, microwaves ovens and washing machines.

The company has been relatively successful in recent years and has grown quite rapidly, doubling in size over the last five years.

In recent months a number of the firm's customers have complained about the declining quality of the products that Techno supply and have warned that unless quality improves they will begin sourcing components elsewhere.

Techno Ltd have tried to find the source of their quality problems but have been unable to identify the problem areas.

To overcome the problem the company has recently employed a new quality manager who has suggested a number of possible solutions. These include achieving a recognized quality standard, using best practice benchmarking and implementing a balanced scorecard quality management system.

1. Explain why it is important for Techno to achieve quality in production.
2. Explain how Techno Ltd might use best practice benchmarking.
3. Examine how gaining a recognized quality standard might benefit Techno Ltd.
4. Critically evaluate the suggestion that implementing a balanced scorecard is the best way to improve the quality of Techno Ltd's products.

The following tradenames and trademarks are owned by their respective copyright holders:

OTHER TITLES

GCE Applied Business Series

Also available

ISBN: 978 1 904242 74 1
Price: £10.99
Author: Ian Bickerstaff

ISBN: 978 1 904242 73 4
Price: £10.99
Author: Eddie McKee

ISBN: 978 1 906578 02 2
Price: £12
Author: Ian Bickerstaff

Contact Colourpoint Educational at:

Tel: 028 9182 6339 Fax: 028 9182 1900

E-mail: sales@colourpoint.co.uk

Web: www.colourpoint.co.uk

Colourpoint Books, Colourpoint House, Jubilee Business Park,
21 Jubilee Road, Newtownards, Co Down, BT23 4YH